The Interpretation of
St. Paul's Epistle to the Galatians

R. C. H. LENSKI

Augsburg Fortress
Minneapolis

THE INTERPRETATION OF ST. PAUL'S EPISTLE
TO THE GALATIANS
Commentary on the New Testament series

First paperback edition 2008

Copyright ©1946, 2008 Augsburg Fortress. All rights reserved. Except for brief quotations in critical articles or reviews, no part of this book may be reproduced in any manner without prior written permission from the publisher. Visit http://www.augsburgfortress.org/copyrights/contact.asp or write to Permissions, Augsburg Fortress, Box 1209, Minneapolis, MN 55440.

Richard C. H. Lenski's commentaries on the New Testament were published in the 1940s after the author's death. This volume was copyrighted in 1937 by the Lutheran Book Concern, published in 1946 by the Wartburg Press, and assigned in 1961 to the Augsburg Publishing House.

ISBN 978-0-8066-8081-1

The paper used in this publication meets the minimum requirements of American National Standard for Information Sciences—Permanence of Paper for Printed Library Materials, ANSI Z329.48-1984.

Manufactured in the U.S.A.

DEDICATED TO
LUTHER THEOLOGICAL SEMINARY
ST. PAUL, MINNESOTA

ABBREVIATIONS

R. = A Grammar of the Greek New Testament in the Light of Historical Research, by A. T. Robertson, fourth edition.

B.-D. = Friedrich Blass' Grammatik des neutestamentlichen Griechisch, vierte, voellig neu-gearbeitete Auflage besorgt von Albert Debrunner.

C.-K. = Biblisch-theologisches Woerterbuch der Neutestamentlichen Graezitaet von D. Dr. Hermann Cremer, zehnte, etc., Auflage, herausgegeben von D. Dr. Julius Koegel.

B.-P. = Griechisch-Deutsches Woerterbuch zu den Schriften des Neuen Testaments, etc., von D. Walter Bauer, zweite, etc., Auflage zu Erwin Preuschens Vollstaendigem Griechisch-Deutschem Handwoerterbuch, etc.

M.-M. = The Vocabulary of the Greek Testament, Illustrated from the Papyri and other Non-Literary Sources, by James Hope Moulton and George Milligan.

R., W. P. = Word Pictures in the New Testament by Archibald Thomas Robertson.

INTRODUCTION

Saint Paul's Epistle to the Galatians has always been famous; Luther's use of it, together with his commentary on it, have increased this fame. The Reformer prized its doctrinal contents, its mighty defense of justification by faith alone, and its glorious vindication of liberty from the law. Galatians is the impregnable citadel, a very Gibraltar, against any attack on the heart of the gospel. This epistle is the grand arsenal which is stocked with the weapons that assure victory in the ceaseless battle for the central truths of the gospel.

Romans, too, has its militant side. Romans 2 is the annihilation of the greatest foe of justification by faith alone, of the moralism, pagan (Rom. 2:1-17) as well as Jewish (Rom. 2:18-29), which proposes to save the sinner by means of law and moral reform, by which every moralist condemns himself and his following the more by his reliance on moralism. See the writer's interpretation of this great chapter. Aside from that chapter Romans is thetical and not polemical. Galatians is polemical and militant throughout. Luther loved this short letter because he had to fight Paul's battle over again. He fought with the same joy and the same assurance of victory. We range ourselves behind Paul as Luther once did. Galatians is our love as it was his.

Only a letter of six short chapters, written almost 2,000 years ago, but a document of such power as has never been duplicated! Immortal victory is set upon its brow. It is not Paul whom we admire; he, indeed, penned these lines, but the Holy Spirit speaks in them, speaks to this day. The supreme proof of Inspiration is its product. Galatians, read in this light, leaves nothing to be desired.

More recent scholarship has busied itself with the historical side of the letter, a task that was neglected until these latter times but is now accomplished with thoroughness. The epistle itself contains most valuable historical data. Failure to apprehend what they convey, as well as any misunderstanding of their content and their bearing would mean great loss. Dispute is, of course, still rife. Whatever ardor may be developed in this part of exegetical polemics must not be allowed to supersede our ardor for the supreme contents of this epistle, the blessed, saving, glorious doctrines which it defends. All the historical data only support the main thesis: their great value lies in this fact.

Many introductions compile all the available information about Paul and his two great missionary journeys and often include what lies beyond. In addition to this fact, in their introductions many writers discuss the bulk of the details found in the epistle itself and thus duplicate the exegesis they offer. This fills many pages and creates bulk. Is it necessary? We confine ourselves to the essentials. In the interpretation of Acts Paul's missionary journeys are fully treated in a manner which is impossible in an introduction to Galatians. The careful student must necessarily delve into Acts. This is true also with regard to the historical material embedded in Galatians. Any adequate study of the material offered can best be made on the basis of the epistle itself by treating each item fully in the context where it occurs. This is the really satisfactory method.

* * *

Every present-day student is compelled to face the question: "Who were the Galatians?" Is the word Γαλάται used in the original ethnographic sense as denoting nationality, or is it to be understood in the geographic sense as designating the inhabitants of the Roman province that was called Γαλατία in Paul's time? If the latter is correct, then we must ask further: "Were the churches addressed by Paul located in the great stretch of northern Galatia, in the widely separated cities Pessinus, Ancyra, and Tavium, or in the smaller area of southern Galatia, in the cities that were more closely contiguous, which we know so well from Acts: Antioch, Iconium, Lystra, and Derbe?" We note two answers: 1) congregations in Upper Galatia; 2) congregations in Lower Galatia. Please examine the map.

The name Γαλάται is only a later modification of the original name Κέλτοι or Κέλται, who were Celtic tribes of ancient Gaul, in particular the Τρόκμοι and Τολιστοβόγοι, combined with the Germanic Tectosages (from Toulouse). These tribes invaded Greece and pillaged Delphi in 280 B. C., established a kingdom in Thrace which was called Thyle, and then appeared on the shores of the Hellespont. They crossed into Asia on the invitation of Nikomedes I, king of Bithynia, to aid him in a civil war. Once established in Asia Minor, these warlike tribes extended their ravages far and wide. During the following years they were repressed and finally conquered, and in the final wars, which established the power of the Romans in their territory, they were subdued by Manlius, the Roman consul, in 189 B. C., and appear as a subject kingdom, at first under a tetrarch and then under a king of their own. The boundaries of the territory they inhabited varied from time to time. They retained their language and their customs for many years.

After the death of Amyntus, the last king of the Galatian tribes, in 25 B. C., the Roman province of Galatia was formed by adding to the northern territory, over which these Celts had spread, certain southern sections, the greater part of the Pisidian region, Isauria, Lycaonia, and portions of eastern Phrygia, the whole province as thus formed being called Galatia.

A valuable observation is this, when Luke speaks of Asia Minor and of other districts he employs the old ethnographic names without regard to the boundaries of the Roman provinces; Paul, however, employs the names of the Roman provinces regardless of the nationalities inhabiting them. Part of the confusion of the commentators is due to failure to note this fact. We need not again compile the proof from Luke and from Paul. Suffice it to say that the province of Galatia is not identical with the old kingdom ruled over by the descendants of the Celtic tribes. The province included the added southern sections which incorporated the descendants of other ethnographic stocks. In Lystra, for instance, the natives were Lycaonians who still clung to their ancient language. Acts 14:11. The southern parts of the province were not made up of a Celtic population.

All this, however, does not yet locate within the province the churches addressed by Paul as "Galatians." They might still be located in either Upper or Lower Galatia, possibly even in both parts of the province. Yet so much is already assured that "Galatians" does not necessarily mean Celts; it may refer to any of the inhabitants of the Roman province irrespective of their extraction, including even Jews, certainly also Greeks and Latins, living anywhere in the province.

* * *

Luke describes Paul's missionary journeys very accurately by taking us from place to place without leaving a gap. In the whole of Acts there is not a word about a visit of Paul's to Upper Galatia. The only time, according to Luke's account, when Paul might have entered Upper Galatia, his mind was set on Bithynia, but the Spirit directed him away from that province to the city of Troas and after he reached that place led him to cross into Europe to the province of Macedonia. Acts 16:6-10. After visiting the churches already founded in Southern Galatia, no work was done on this second missionary journey until Paul reached Philippi in Macedonia. Now the epistle not only presupposes that Paul founded the congregations to which it is addressed but that, after founding them, he had visited them and had spent some time in their midst on this second visit. If these were churches in Upper Galatia, time and occasion must be found when Paul could have founded and afterward visited churches in this locality. Attempts to find these are unsatisfactory.

On the other hand, we know all about the churches in Southern Galatia. We have the full story of their founding, also the account of Paul's visit to them on his second missionary journey when he brought them the letter from the convention held at Jerusalem and thereby confirmed these churches and increased their membership. Acts 15:23-29; 16:4, 5. All this agrees with the epistle. Also the fact that all was well with these churches when Paul visited them as Luke reports. No Judaizers had appeared in their midst. The invasion came later, after Paul had left, possibly some weeks later.

This, then, is the situation: Paul's letter fits exactly all that we know about the churches in Southern Galatia, not a single point can be urged to the contrary; on the other hand, the very existence of churches in Northern Galatia is hypothetical, we do not have the name of one city and, of course, not a word about number, size, or character of the members. If we accept the view that our epistle is addressed to cities in Upper Galatia, all we are able to do is to transfer to them whatever we may gather from the epistle and ignore the southern churches. We ought, then, also to reconstruct Luke's record of Paul's journey so as to make room for two periods of gospel work in Upper Galatia on the part of Paul. We therefore conclude that the epistle was addressed to churches in Lower Galatia.

Yet the commentators of an early date and also most of the moderns, Lightfoot being prominent among the latter, advocate what is called the northern theory. Smith's *Bible Dictionary*, for instance, under "Galatians" merely quotes Lightfoot at length and does not even mention another view. Those of the ancients who touch upon this subject wrote after 350 A. D., and were probably misled by the fact that since 297 A. D. Galatia had again been reduced to the old territory that was once dominated by the Celtic tribes.

* * *

The following may be added. If Paul had worked in Upper Galatia, he would have encountered language difficulties since Greek culture and Greek speech were not dominant in these regions. Again, if Paul desired to name the churches of Phrygia, Pamphylia, and Lycaonia in Lower Galatia with *one* name, that name could have been only "Galatians." In the same way he speaks of "Macedonians" although different nationalities were represented in these European churches. Even in Upper Galatia the churches would have been of a mixed population, could not have been Celtic alone or even predominantly Celtic.

A good deal is usually made of Paul's remark in 1:6 that the Galatians so quickly gave up their faith. It is supposed that the bulk of these congregations were made up of Celts, and that therefore Cæsar's estimate of the Gallic Celts is reflected in Paul's remark: "The infirmity of the Gauls is, that they are fickle in their resolves, fond of change, and not to be trusted." Thierry: "Frank, impetuous, impressible, eminently intelligent, fond of show, but extremely inconstant, the fruit of excessive vanity." This invites to pertinent homiletical application, which few resist. But it is evident that these characterizations apply to Paul's words only if the bulk of the churches were made up of actual Celts. Any congregation even in Upper Galatia would include a mixed population and probably have but few real Celts. Paul's words are such as fit any church in which heresies had secured a hold in a comparatively brief time. Moreover, the epistle itself shows that the conclusion is unwarranted that these churches had turned away from Paul's teaching in fickleness of mind; they had not as yet turned away. Paul also expects to keep them true to his teaching. This connects with the following points.

* * *

Throughout the entire epistle Paul proves himself fully informed as to the situation in the Galatian churches. He knows even the details of the arguments used by the Judaizers. Yet nowhere does he mention the sources of his information — not as though he were concealing the sources, but quite the contrary, he takes it for granted that his readers know these sources. We get the impression that Paul's information has not come from a letter that was sent to him by the churches. Private letters and news through private persons are also excluded; First Corinthians shows us that when Paul uses information of this kind he says so in all frankness. Only one assumption satisfies us regarding Paul's complete information and the lack of necessity for stating its source: a delegation must have been sent to Paul by the Galatian churches, a committee that was duly commissioned by the Galatian churches, a committee that was duly commissioned by the Galatians themselves and was thus known to all. This also explains why Paul does not need to refer to this commission in the epistle since these men will receive this epistle and will bear it to Galatia.

Paul offers no excuse as to why he does not repair to the Galatians in person. In some of his other letters he tells what detains him or what prevents his personal coming at that time. He does not plan to come to Galatia in the near future in order to follow up any good effect his epistle may produce. His whole reliance is placed on the curative effect of the epistle itself. To this we add 1:2: "all the brethren with me," which undoubtedly includes the brethren of the Galatian commission. Paul had completely convinced them of the mistake the Galatians were making by having anything whatever to do with the Judaizers who had invaded their churches. Their conviction would support Paul's epistle.

All this has its bearing on determining the place where Paul wrote the epistle. The older assumption that this place was Ephesus, and that the time of writing was Paul's stay of two years in Ephesus, becomes improbable. This assumption is based on the idea that the churches were located in Upper Galatia. If they were, Paul could have made a quick trip from Ephesus to Upper Galatia and attended in person to the danger that was threatening. He could have made such a trip to Lower Galatia even more easily. The fact that he contemplates nothing of the kind implies that he was much farther away and in the midst of work that could not be interrupted by a journey to Galatia.

Other points must be added. We know that Paul usually dictated his letters to an amanuensis. This epistle he writes with his own hand. He must, then, have been alone. He sends no greetings from Timothy or from Silas or from any of his assistants. This again makes the impression that he was alone. He names as being associated with him in writing "all the brethren with him." This includes those of the committee from Galatia plus a number of other believers. He sends no greetings from a church.

Taking all these points together, where do they place Paul, and at what time do they place him after his second tour through Galatia? Certainly not in Ephesus nor at so late a time. The time and the place that match these data is Corinth a short time after Paul first began to work there, probably before Silas and Timothy joined him (Acts 18:5). Then Paul was alone, far from Galatia, in southern Europe where the Lord had given him specific orders to work, in Corinth where the Lord directed him to stay on, at the time when a church had not yet been formed, when only the first converts had been won.

This is the most likely time and the most likely place. Then, however, Galatians is the *first* Pauline epistle we have. Then First Thessalonians must have been written a little later. These conclusions are not absolute, but they do agree with *all* the data available. The only uncertainty is whether Corinth is the place. Might it, perhaps, have been Athens? It was written at some place near this time, and Corinth is by all odds the likeliest locality.

Corinth appeals to others, who, however, think of the much later stay of Paul in this city, of his stay of three months during the winter just before he accompanied the delegation that bore the great collection to Jerusalem. This is entirely too late, to say nothing more. It would project the journey of the Galatian delegation into the winter. Then shipping ceased. Then the delegation would have traveled by land. This supposition places the date of Galatians close to that of Romans. But Romans in no way hints that it was composed near the date of the epistle to the Galatians. When Paul wrote Romans he was not alone and was in a congregation that had been established for some years, whose greetings he would send when writing to other churches. The collection was about to be sent to Jerusalem at this time. Romans speaks of it. The Galatians were participating in it. Not a word of this appears in Paul's epistle to them. This epistle must be dated at a far earlier time. The old subscription: "Sent to the Galatians from Rome," (A. V.) is spurious.

* * *

The Judaizers who had invaded the Galatian churches were of the kind that at one time came to Antioch in Syria and then received their answer at the great convention held at Jerusalem (Acts 15). We hear nothing further about Judaizers until this time. What they were must be gathered from Acts 15 and from our epistle, to which we may add II Cor. 12. In brief, they were Jews who accepted the gospel but combined it with Jewish legalism. What they had of Christ and the gospel was thus no more than a sham. Their claim that they had the real, original, full gospel was a fiction but appealed to many when they represented Paul's gospel as an emasculation, a false liberalization. Did Christ not observe the whole Jewish law? Did the Twelve whom the Judaizers represented as the only true apostles, not continue to live in the Jewish fashion like all the members of the mother church in Jerusalem? We do not know all the details regarding the activity of these Judaizers, especially how they came to invade the Galatian churches, and how they afterward appeared in Corinth. They started no churches of their own but appear as fanatic proselyters in Paul's churches.

In order to gain adherents they attacked the apostleship of Paul and made the highest claims for themselves. In Galatia they came out openly with their false gospel. Those who afterward appeared in Corinth kept their real teaching under cover and assailed not only the apostleship of Paul but also his personal character and the mode of his work. That explains Paul's defense and his attack in II Cor. 10-13, which does not center on their false gospel as does our epistle.

After the convention at Jerusalem, where the Judaizers lost out completely, Paul returned to the Galatian churches and then went on into Europe. It seems that a few of the rabid Judaizers, who had only been silenced at Jerusalem, followed Paul and broke into his Galatian churches after he had gone on to Europe. They found the coast clear and set to work by energetically sowing their evil seed. Paul's epistle shows that this invasion greatly disturbed the Galatian churches and was making headway. Yet, while the danger was great, these churches had not fallen away. If the conjecture of a commission is correct, they did not intend to change without first communicating directly with Paul and hearing him. This was a hopeful sign. The commission returned to Galatia thoroughly enlightened and convinced and also brought Paul's great epistle. This settled the matter. Later references to Galatia show no further trace of disturbance, nor do we again hear of Judaizers until the interval between First and Second Corinthians. Their effort in Corinth again ended in complete defeat although the struggle lasted a little longer.

The most acceptable date to which we are able to assign Galatians is near April in the year 53 while Paul was at Corinth. The whole subject is involved in much controversy, in which both German and English commentators are divided. The data here presented have produced conviction in the writer. We may add, for the sake of completeness, that some have altered the Upper Galatian theory from a reference to the northern cities Pessinus, Ancyra, and Tavium to towns that are just a little north of Iconium, north enough to be able to say they were in Upper Galatia.

* * *

Attacks on the genuineness and integrity of our epistle may be dated from the year 1888. Since then assaults have been made on Galatians which involve also Acts, Romans, and other epistles. The very center of the so-called *Corpus Paulinum* has been attacked. But on the base of hypotheses. The historical facts offered by the New Testament are first denied. After these have been removed, theories are substituted which place these epistles in the second century. We are left with no genuine letters of Paul to study or to interpret. Of late, however, critical scholarship is returning to more conservative views.

CHAPTER I

THE GREETING, 1:1-5

"Paul — to the churches of Galatia — grace and peace!" The writer's name in the nominative, the recipients of the letter in the dative, the words of greeting exclamatory nominatives. It is the ancient form for beginning a letter but has two impressive Christian nouns instead of the secular χαίρειν. While it is so common when we compare Paul's other letters, this greeting arrests attention because of the modifiers that are added to the first and to the third member and because of the lack of these in the case of the second member. The thoughts and the feelings of the writer reveal themselves with clearness in this greeting. It foreshadows the contents as well as the character and the tone of all that the epistle contains. The greeting is made of the same steel as the entire epistle. It is admirable in the highest degree.

Paul, an apostle not from men nor by means of man but by means of Jesus Christ and God the Father who raised him from the dead, and all the brethren with me:

To the churches of Galatia:

Grace to you and peace from God the Father and our Lord Jesus Christ, who gave himself for our sins that thus he might deliver **us for himself from the present eon** (which is) **wicked according to the will of our God and Father: to whom** (belongs) **the glory for the eon of the eons. Amen.**

Printed thus, the unmodified character of the second member of the greeting strikes the eye with full force. Place no comma after "apostle" and make no parenthesis of the following phrases, for these phrases modify "apostle" most closely and directly. The force of the apposition is not that Paul is an apostle but that he is *this kind* of an apostle. The whole impact lies in the phrases. They meet a challenge, meet it head on. They are not an incidental, parenthetical appendix.

Paul's father, strict Pharisee that he was, named his boy "Saul" after the one king that his tribe of Benjamin produced for Israel. This name was used in the old Jewish circles. As a Roman citizen of Tarsus the father gave the boy who was born into this citizenship a second, a Roman name, such as every Roman citizen bore: Παῦλος, "Paul." The idea that at a later time Paul took this name, took it from Sergius Paulus mentioned in Acts 13:9, is probably incorrect. When as a lad Paul played in the streets of Tarsus, his father, when calling him home, shouted: "Saul, Saul!" but the Greek boys on the streets called him "Paul." When Paul's mission work among the Gentiles began in earnest, when in his travels far and wide his Roman citizenship became a valuable asset for him, the sensible thing for him to do was to confine himself to the use of his Roman name, which he also did.

When Paul calls himself "an apostle of Jesus Christ" in a letter heading, perhaps adds, "by the will of God," he would indicate only that he writes officially, that he specifies his office as being ambassadorial and by direct divine appointment. Ἀπόστολος = one commissioned and sent. Paul says more here. Two unexpected negative phrases meet us at the very first glance, against which a double positive phrase is set in strongest contrast. To find this opposition and negation in a letter heading in connection with the writer's own title is startling. There must be a reason for its use. There is. The Judaizers had attacked Paul's apostleship, had denied its direct origin from Christ. Their method was shrewd. In regard to one who is commissioned everything depends on *who* commissioned him. The value of what he brings is no greater than the power of him in whose name he is entitled to speak.

Paul is probably quoting the phrases of the Judaizers who maintained that, whatever his apostleship was, it was either altogether only "from men" or at best had come to him only "through man." Whatever office he claimed he had was either altogether human or divine only in a secondary and thus more or less doubtful sense. Paul might claim what he pleased, the Judaizers pretended to have the facts in Paul's case, and these facts, they maintained, proved that Paul's gospel was not the genuine, original gospel, but one that had been highly modified, not indeed by Paul, but already at the source from which Paul had drawn it. They, the Judaizers, were bringing the genuine article to the Galatians.

Paul's first drop of ink is a decisive, challenging contradiction: "Paul, an apostle *not* from men *nor* by means of man." Men did not send and commission him. He is not the ambassador or representative of men. What he utters is not the word and the wisdom of men. The authority back of him and his message is not human.

We at once see that the Judaizers referred to the church at Antioch in Syria which sent forth Paul and Barnabas on that first missionary journey, in the course of which these two reached Galatia (Acts 13:1-4). At the end of the tour Paul and Barnabas also returned to Antioch and made report to the church that had sent them out (Acts 14:26-28). How easy it was to suppress the fact that the church at Antioch had acted only on direct orders from the Holy Ghost; to suppress also the direct call of Jesus at the time of the very conversion of Paul (Acts 26:16-18). How easy it was to make it appear that only one of the churches had sent Paul, that he was ἀπό only from a church, and that that was not even the old mother church at Jerusalem but an inferior Gentile church which had altered the genuine gospel by removing the ancient legal requirements just in order to attract the Gentiles. Paul, they said, was an emissary of this erring church at Antioch — men had sent him and not Christ.

"By means of man" is only a variation. The ἀπό phrase refers to the ἀπό in ἀπόστολος: sent *from* men, from a body of men, having only a human commission and message. Διά expresses medium. Paul might have obtained his commission from Christ through some human intermediary. In passing to Paul through that human medium the genuine gospel, the Judaizers claimed, was altered, adulterated, falsified. Paul had not gone to the source, he had dipped from the stream lower down where it was already contaminated and impure. He thought he had the pure article and the real office but he was sadly mistaken.

The unarticulated singular does not mean: "through some man," i. e., an individual man. Some think of Barnabas who twice did much for Paul (Acts 9:27; 11:25). But even if this phrase could be referred to an individual, Barnabas could not be considered because he and Paul had worked together in Galatia, where Paul was the leader. It is unwarranted to think that the Judaizers even knew what Acts 9:27 and 11:25 contain; and if they did they could not claim that Paul was made an apostle "through Barnabas."

The noun is generic; "by means of man" = "by means of human agency." It is properly singular after the plural "men." Paul regularly uses plurals and singulars in this way. One could be sent "from men" (some body of men) or "through man" (human agency of some kind). Οὐδέ does not make the phrases exclusive of each other. The stress is on the prepositions as alternatives and not on the nouns and their number, plural and singular. One could look at a human commission in two ways; as emanating "from men" (whoever they might be) or as mediated "through man" (whatever the human medium might be). Both phrases refer to Acts 13:3. They include both ways of looking at Paul's commission when trying to make it human. The two phrases in Paul's denial are used to indicate completeness.

In flat contradiction Paul asserts that he is an apostle *in toto* only "by means of Jesus Christ and God the Father who raised him from the dead." Although it is only one phrase that has two objects, this phrase is of the highest possible importance. Paul uses only the second, διά, of the two previously employed prepositions. "Yes," Paul says, "I did receive my apostolate through a certain mediation." But he names the two divine persons themselves as the one medium. He purposely uses διά and not ἀπό nor ὑπό. For there is no one who is higher than these two persons who could use these persons as his medium. He could have said, "an apostle *from* or *by* Christ and the Father." This would have left a loophole, namely the question: "by what means," on which there might then have been quibbling. This is excluded by the use of διά, the lower preposition "through," "by means of."

"By means of Jesus Christ" refers to Acts 26:16-18, Paul's original commissioning. He uses the ordinary designation for the person and his office. And lest someone think that another used Christ as a medium, he names "God the Father" as the joint medium with Christ. Both are thus placed on the same absolutely supreme level with no higher one remaining "by" (ὑπό) or "from" (ἀπό) whom Paul was commissioned; and at the same time with no lower one "through" (διά) whom Paul was or could have been commissioned. Masterly is this διά! Subordinationists claim that Paul really means: *through* Christ and *from* the Father. They invent the meaning they want and then substitute it for the plain meaning Paul himself sets down.

Θεὸς Πατήρ, "God Father," is a unit name exactly like "Jesus Christ"; neither term needs an article in the Greek. In the holy Trinity the first person is distinguished by the term "Father." But was not Paul commissioned at Antioch by the Spirit (Acts 13:2, 4)? Undoubtedly. All the *opera ad extra sunt indivisa aut communa*. For Paul's purpose, to contradict any and all allegations that his apostleship was merely a human and faulty thing, it was enough to name Christ and the Father as proof that his office was wholly divine.

The participial modifier attached to "God the Father" is highly significant: "he who raised him from the dead" (apposition). This connects the two. More than this: it is the risen and glorified Christ who commissioned Paul, the same risen Christ who commissioned all the other apostles. He appeared to Paul even more gloriously than he appeared to the other apostles during the forty days. He made Paul a witness of his resurrection and his glory equal to that of the others. It was, indeed, only Christ who appeared to Paul on the road outside of Damascus, changed his whole life, and appointed him an apostle, but the Father had raised Christ from the dead, and thus in Christ the Father was active in Paul's call. Regarding ἐκ νεκρῶν, regarding the absence of the article, and regarding the misuse which is made of this absence, see Matt. 17:10; Mark 9:9; Luke 9:7; John 2:22; Acts 3:16.

2) In other epistles one or more of Paul's assistants are named as joint writers with Paul; only in this epistle we have "Paul . . . and all the brethren

with me," not μετά, "in my company," but σύν "with," in the sense of supporting me. The idea is not that these brethren are joint writers who help to compose this epistle. We see that Paul alone writes; "I" runs through the letter. All these brethren are at Paul's side, all of them know about the situation in Galatia, all of them know what Paul is writing, all of them agree with him and support him in all that he is writing. The Galatians are not to suppose that Paul is alone and writing by himself in a sort of private way. Nay, all the brethren with him, down to the last one, and "all" implies a goodly number, are backing Paul. It is usually supposed that this refers to Paul's assistants. Then "all" is too strong. If any assistants are included, those known to the Galatians (Silas, Timothy) are excluded, for Paul would have inserted their names.

"All the brethren with me" denotes Christian believers. If the deduction is correct that the Galatians had sent a delegation to Paul, Zahn is right, this delegation itself is included (see the introduction). Paul had fully and completely satisfied this delegation. These Galatians themselves subscribed to all Paul says in this epistle. When they go back with it they will support it and will tell that all the others who are with Paul give it the same support. Paul is happy to point the Galatians to this unanimity of all those with him.

May we not conclude one thing more? Paul's assistants, at least those known to the Galatians, were not with Paul at the moment but were busy with their work. Paul says, "all the brethren with me," and does not name a church at the place where he is writing; he also sends no greetings from a church. Does this not make the impression that he was in the early stages of his work at the place of writing? He had made converts, but a fully established church had not as yet been formed. If Corinth is the place of writing, the time must have been during the first weeks of his work there. Ephesus and Paul's second stay at Corinth are excluded already for the reason that at least greetings would have been sent from the church at either place.

In sharp contrast with the first member of the letter heading is the second, the unmodified dative: "To the churches of Galatia." Not one word more. No predicate of honor or esteem. No other epistle of Paul's shows a phenomenon similar to this. Paul is not a hypocrite. He does not lower himself by pretending. The words of praise and esteem found in other epistles are not cheapened and made hollow by bestowal where none is deserved. Paul's was not a case of personal feeling in a private matter; nor was what we might call his official pride wounded. Paul's concern is Christ and his gospel. His displeasure is due to the treatment the Galatians had begun to bestow upon the Lord who had commissioned him and upon the gospel which formed the burden of his commission. Paul would have been recreant to both if he had not used sternness.

See the introduction regarding "the churches of Galatia." "Of Galatia" was the only term available to designate the churches in Lower Galatia.

3) Luther is right regarding the third member of the heading: "See how he here turns all his words against the own righteousness (of man). Are they not all nothing but thunder crashes down from heaven against all men's own righteousness and piety of all kinds?" Here there is no stinting. Paul wishes the churches of Galatia all that they so greatly need in order to be freed from the errors of the Judaizers who had gained a hold among them. "Grace to you and peace from God the Father and our Lord Jesus Christ" is the same greeting that is found in other epistles, but in this instance it conveys the thought to the Galatians that grace and peace come to them from the two persons from whom Paul's apostleship came. As an apos-

tle of Christ and the Father he prays grace and peace from the Father and Christ for them. Paul is the apostle of this grace and this peace; all the brethren with him are recipients of this grace and this peace. The Father and Christ dispense these two fundamental gifts through the apostles they have called and not through the Judaizers who are false apostles.

"Grace" is fundamental, "peace" is its result. This order is never reversed. The grammars supply εἴη, the optative of wish: "May grace and peace be with you." We prefer to supply nothing and regard the statement as an exclamation: "Grace to you and peace!" Χάρις is the undeserved *favor Dei* by which alone sinners are received and cleansed from sin and guilt. Its connotation is free, gratuitous pardon. When it is again and again bestowed upon those who already have this grace (John 1:16), it is still the undeserved pardoning favor which constantly frees us from sin but includes all the gifts of this favor which we need in order to build up our spiritual life. "Grace to you!" = "All the abundant spiritual gifts of grace to you in one ceaseless stream!"

Εἰρήνη is the Hebrew *shalom* in the sense of the German *Heil*, the condition of well-being when God is our friend and all is well with us. The condition of peace is objective, the peace established by God through Christ, but it produces also the corresponding subjective realization of peace, the rest, satisfaction, and happiness that flow from the possession of peace.

"From" conveys the idea that grace and peace flow down upon us. Here the names of the divine givers are chiastically reversed, the Father is named first, Christ, second, both are again equal, both together are the joint source. As the natural order in the calling of Paul was Christ and the Father, so now in the bestowal of grace and peace it is from the Father and Christ. The slight variants in the reading do not affect the meaning. We note only that the soteriological title "our Lord" is added to the name "Jesus Christ" used in v. 1. This is the full designation, which is full of solemnity, that is so frequently used. "Our Lord" is a confession: we belong to him, are wholly dependent on him. He has purchased and won us and made us his own (I Cor. 7:23); he directs us in all things.

4) The apposition: "he who gave himself for our sins," etc., refers to the expiatory self-sacrifice of him who is now our Lord Jesus Christ. The substantivized aorist participle denotes the historical fact as such. "He gave" means by a voluntary act; "himself" is his own person and no less, and that means his life. The readings vary between ὑπέρ and περί, "in behalf of" and "concerning"; the difference is small, and the variation in reading appears in other similar statements. In what way our sins required this giving of himself is not stated, but it is perfectly clear from all Paul's teaching. In the LXX περὶ ἁμαρτίας regularly denotes the expiation and removal of sins; and this is what the phrase means here. The reason that Paul attaches this apposition is plain. Nothing removes sin save the self-sacrifice of Christ on the cross; through that sacrifice alone grace and peace are ours. The Galatians were listening to a different doctrine. The Judaizers could not make Christ's expiation the sole fountain of grace and peace.

The addition of the purpose clause emphasizes the point still more: "that thus he might deliver us for himself from the present eon (which is) wicked," etc. Ἵνα expresses simple purpose; ὅπως, purpose and manner combined, the manner being indicated in the governing clause. Christ's purpose is that in the manner just mentioned, namely by giving himself for our sins, he might deliver us, etc. Note the middle voice of the aorist subjunctive (ἐξαιρέω): "take us out for himself," i. e., to be his own. We should not think of the future deliverance at the end of the world or at the moment of our death. When the Scriptures speak of this they refer to the resurrection of Christ or to his exaltation. The deliverance connected with Christ's expiation is the one effected now, in this life. The aorist is effective, it is an actual deliverance.

A greeting is not the place to expand and to teach in detail how Christ's death accomplishes this purpose for us. This purpose was not accomplished already in the instant when Christ died. Paul writes of himself as an apostle, as one who preaches the gospel in order that men may be brought to faith and justification. All this is included in the accomplishment of the purpose of Christ's death. The reconciling death involves the Word of this reconciliation, its proclamation, and the personal reconciliation of all those who are delivered by Christ (II Cor. 5:18-21). "Might deliver us for himself," is an effective aorist and at the same time constative. Each person is individually delivered, and with "us" Paul takes them all together and thus speaks of the act as being one. That is sufficient; we need not think of "us" as including all the saved of all the ages until the last day.

The great point that the Galatians are to note is the fact that grace and peace are ours through the merits of Christ's self-sacrifice alone. All is due to his death for our sins. We are able to add nothing by any work of ours. We are not delivered by any observance of law. The whole epistle is aimed at this error; the foundation is laid already in the greeting.

Paul writes: might deliver us "from the present eon (which is) evil." The idea of time in αἰών remains but is advancced to include what transpires during this eon of time, what thus marks and distinguishes the great era. Thus a modifier is added, here the predicative adjective: "(which is) wicked," πονηρός, actively and viciously evil. We may use "world" in place of "eon" but only in the sense indicated. Instead of "the present eon" we sometimes have "this eon"; both are in contrast with ὁ αἰὼν μέλλων, "the eon about to come," i. e., that of the blessed eternity. Ἐνεστώς is the perfect participle which is always used in the present sense. The "present" eon is the one which began with Christ's death and is thus now present; it is the final eon of the world which is to be followed by eternity. Satan rules it so that it is "wicked" through and through.

Our one hope is that Christ take us out of it for himself, and this he does by means of his death for our sins. These sins tie us to this world age. Being wicked, all of them, they hold us to this wicked world. Freed from them, we are delivered "out of" this eon. For the time being we, indeed, live in this world, but we are no longer of this world. Christ has made us his own. Our life in Christ separates us from this eon or world, in particular from all that is "wicked" in it. The Galatians were in danger of being drawn back into this present wicked eon by losing the deliverance of Christ, by trusting in the law and in works of their own.

The κατά phrase modifies the entire apposition "he who gave," etc., plus the purpose clause. All this is "according to the will of our God and Father." Θέλημα does not mean the act of willing but what God willed. When Christ gave himself he did what God wanted; when he delivered us he again did what God wanted. This is God's good and gracious will (Luther). One article combines the two names "our God and Father" and designates one person. But in this combination "God" brings out all his greatness and his majesty, "Father" all his love and his tenderness to us who are delivered by Christ. "Our" modifies both nouns: he who in all his majesty and in all his love is ours in order to bless us for evermore. In v. 1 and v. 3 "Father" indicates the trinitarian relation which as such is already soteriological; for God revealed himself as triune only in order to show us how all three persons work out our salvation. Here in v. 4 "Father" with the possessive "our" is likewise soteriological but at the same time confessional as in the Lord's Prayer.

5) The fact that Paul adds a doxology at the end of a greeting is exceptional in the highest degree and thus significant. The greeting is usually followed by a word of thanks to God for the good accomplished in the readers. But what can Paul say about the Galatians who had begun to forsake the gospel? Instead of adding a word of acknowledgment and appreciation regarding their faith and their faithfulness Paul looks up to God and praises him for his gracious purpose and will as much as to say to the Galatians: "Praise him with me by allowing that will and purpose to have full sway among you also!"

The copula is usually omitted in these doxologies, when it is written it is ἐστίν and not εἴη. Moreover, δόξα is often combined with other terms that denote actual possessions of God and not merely something that we bestow on him. So we do not translate *Ehre* but use the objective *Herrlichkeit*. Paul is not thinking of men's bestowing glory and honor upon God but of God in his own eternal glory, the manifestation of his infinite attributes, especially as they shine forth in Christ's death and the saving purpose connected therewith. Ἐστίν with the dative is one of the common ways of indicating possession; the relative used in doxologies is demonstrative: "he, he alone, to whom (belongs) the glory," the sum of the divine attributes in their manifestation.

"For the eon of the eons" is a Hebraistic circumscription for eternity, the grandest of all found in the Greek, which multiplies the idea of "eon" indefinitely. How anyone can think of earthly eras is difficult to understand. In human language terms that denote time must necessarily be used to express what is in reality the opposite of time. "Eternity" is itself a term that designates time. We have no others. The Scriptures condescend to use such terms. Our minds are so tied to time and to space that even the philosophers cannot rise beyond them, cannot even form the concepts timelessness and spacelessnes except in a vague, negative approach.

'Αμήν is only the Hebrew noun for "truth" or "verity" written with Greek letters; call it an adverbial accusative. It has been taken over into other languages unchanged. At the end of a statement, a doxology, or a prayer it solemnly confirms; it is like the affixing of a sacred seal. Jesus alone doubled it and used it as an introduction to his statements as is evident in John's Gospel.

INTRODUCTION

The Denunciation, 1:6-10

6) Instead of saying that he is delighted with this or that in the Galatians when he begins the body of his letter, Paul declares that he is shocked at what the Galatians are on the point of doing. The very first paragraph is stunning. Soft Melanchthonian methods are not in place; heroic measures are demanded. Here there is no error in life; the heart of Christendom is assailed. The foe is deadly. A cancer threatens the vitals; palliatives would be a fatal mistake, the remedy must destroy the ailment to the very roots.

The apostle not from men or by means of man but from Christ and God speaks, speaks in the power of Christ and of God. His words have a conquering ring. He speaks to the churches of Galatia who as churches are bound to hear and to heed every word unless they intend to cease being churches. The voice they hear is fearless and scorns to please men. This is the voice of the slave of Christ, the slave who knows only one obedience, that to his heavenly Master alone. This voice rings with divine authority and power.

The tone of this section is tense and dramatic. Paul is not swept away by passion. He writes with perfect self-control. He knows the weight of every sentence. Every statement is deliberate and straight to the point. The very first sentence reveals the fact that he is completely informed; all hesitation of uncertainty is absent. We have only one explanation for this decisiveness: not a mere report that has at last reached Paul, not a letter from Galatia that brought a certain amount of information, but a delegation from the churches, men whom Paul had questioned on all points and who had told him all the facts as they actually were. These facts the apostle meets with incisiveness.

The issue is nothing less than the gospel itself. That issue Paul states at once. **I marvel that so quickly you are making a change away from him who called you in grace, (namely) Christ, to a different gospel which is not (even) another except in the sense that there are certain ones who are disturbing you and want to pervert the gospel of Christ.**

"So quickly." That is the fact that causes Paul astonishment; he would not have believed it possible if it were not for the complete information that he has. The two adverbs are heavily reproving for the Galatians. The statement contains no point from which to reckon; hence we cannot translate "so soon" (A. V.) but must translate "so quickly" (R. V.). Paul had given the Galatians credit for more solidity and more fidelity. He is deeply pained and hurt. His confidence has been misplaced. A conclusion is involved, namely the fact that when Paul last visited the Galatians, all was well with them. Then came the Judaizers, and instead of being promptly escorted to the door, all these churches began to listen to them and to find something attractive in their false gospel. This is what happened "so quickly."

The middle μετατίθεσθαι is regularly used to express what the Germans call *uebertreten*, to change from one political party or from one philosophic school to another and thus from one religious conviction to another. There is nothing in the context that points to this being the passive voice, hence we regard it as the middle; to make a change of this kind is a voluntary act. Here we have a case in which the tense is vital. An aorist would mean that the change had been actually made; the present tense states only that the change had begun, is in progress but not yet completed. The cause is not yet lost although there is no time to lose. Paul is stepping in strenuously.

The defection in progress is "away from him who called you in grace." Paul makes the charge personal by naming the person who had called the Galatians and not merely the gospel by which they had been called. At the same time he brings out the full aggravation of this unfaithfulness: the Galatians had been called "in grace." The phrase has no article and is thus to be understood in the sense of "graciously," i. e., without deserving it, yea, deserving the very opposite. "Into the grace" (A. V.) is incorrect. The aorist participle states the past fact.

In the epistles καλεῖν is always used with regard to the successful call and never only with reference to the *invitatio* which one has rejected. Whether the genitive Χριστοῦ is textually genuine or not, he who called the Galatians is Christ. The statement that it is always ὁ Θεός who calls is unwarranted. Paul himself was called by Christ; Rom. 1:6 names the Christians as "called of Jesus Christ." Here the gospel by which the Galatians were called is designated as "the gospel of

Christ." Χριστοῦ is in apposition to the substantivized participle; it does not modify χάριτι.

Nothing in the world should ever make the Galatians change away from him who had called them in grace and at the price of his death delivered them from this present world which was wicked and doomed (v. 4). They should have resisted the most powerful and the most persistent efforts to the last breath. Yet they are quickly beginning their apostasy! Paul might have used a stronger word than "I marvel." He names the deadly thing the Galatians had begun to do: change away from Christ. The Galatians themselves would disavow this. They intended to stay with Christ; the Judaizers themselves taught Christ, yea, came as the genuine apostles of Christ (II Cor. 11:13, 14). Why, the Galatians were now getting Christ better than they ever got him! Any plea of that kind is silenced by the next phrase: "to a different gospel which is not (even) another" but so different as to be no gospel at all.

The point to be noted is that Paul does not say: away from *Christ* — to a different *Savior*. No other person exists who could be placed beside Christ. He says: away from *Christ* — to a *gospel* that is no gospel at all. By forsaking the true gospel and by accepting a substituted fake gospel the Galatians are losing the one Savior there is. That is the dreadful danger toward which they are verging.

The emphasis is placed on this fake gospel, on the adjectives which declare it a fake: "different — not another." The A. V. confuses this: "another — not another." The words ἕτερος and ἄλλος at times amount to the same thing; but here ἕτερον = οὐκ ἄλλο. This gospel is "different" because it is *"not* another." A gospel might be "different" only because it is "another," is couched only in "other" words but leaves the substance the same. But when it is "different" because it is *"not* another," the very substance is changed; such a gospel is a fake, a mere pretense or sham. Its proponents call it a gospel only to gain its acceptance as brass is sold for gold; those who buy are cheated. This is the charge Paul launches. See R. 747. The genuineness of the gospel is so vital because the true gospel is the one and only means by which Christ calls us, transmits his grace to us, in a word, delivers us from this wicked world (v. 4). The substitution of a fake gospel loses us this call, grace, deliverance, does so whether we are aware of the fact or not.

The deception practiced on the Galatians has been repeated to this very day. A "different" gospel is offered which is *"not* another." It is even the same adulteration that is offered. Yes, the name "gospel" is retained, the "Christ" or at least "Jesus" are preached, but for pure grace in his atoning death there is substituted the law, the requirement of works as the means of salvation. The multitude applauds and, like the Galatians, is so quickly and easily deceived.

7) The relative ὅ refers to ἕτερον εὐαγγέλιον, and the relative clause states that this "different" gospel is not another gospel in any sense. Ὅ does not refer to the whole previous statement: "which" in the sense of "your changing to another gospel" is nothing but that some are troubling you. This thought would require ἄλλο τι or οὐδὲν ἄλλο ἐστίν. With εἰ μή, "except," Paul qualifies the clause "which is not another." One might understand this clause to mean that what the Galatians were changing to is totally unrelated to the true gospel and in that sense "not another." Then the matter would be easy, indeed; then the Galatians would scarcely have been deceived. There is an exception to the broad "not another." Paul states what the exception is. This "different gospel" does bear a relation to Christ's true gospel. Right there is where the terrible danger lies; not another "except in the sense that (εἰ

μή) there are certain ones who are disturbing you and want to pervert the gospel of Christ," not another except that its advocates pretend that it is "another," in fact, the genuine article itself.

It is not another except in the sense of a most dangerous perversion. Paul scornfully calls its advocates "certain ones." Substantivized participles must have the article even when they are used as predicates; here, moreover, subject and predicate are identical and interchangeable (R. 768). "Who are disturbing you" is the preliminary, minor description of these perverters. They have come to the Galatians and have made this their business. The present participle says only that they have begun their disturbing work. The main statement is found in the second participle: "and want to pervert the gospel of Christ." Note that Paul does not use the participle μεταστρέφοντες, much less the aorist participle. He does not say that they *are* perverting Christ's gospel or that they have already succeeded in doing so. He says only that they "are wanting" to succeed in this nefarious work. They have only the vicious will.

When Paul writes, "to pervert (aorist, actually to pervert) the gospel of Christ," he is not thinking of what these perverters actually teach. That is an actual and a complete perversion and not merely a willingness to pervert. Paul is thinking of the gospel of Christ which the Galatians had received from him. This gospel these perverters wanted to upset in the hearts of the Galatians so that the Galatians should no longer believe it. Yet thus far they only wanted to do this damnable thing, they had not yet succeeded. Paul is writing in order to prevent their success.

It is well to note that in "the gospel of Christ" the genitive denotes the author. It is the gospel which emanates from Christ, which he has entrusted to his apostle. This is not the objective genitive: the gospel "about" Christ. The Judaizers, too, had much to say about Christ when they converted him into another Moses. But theirs was not Christ's own gospel which he himself had preached, which he then commissioned his apostles to preach, which also the Galatians had received from Paul. This genitive of source and authorship shows the correctness of the interpretation that Christ is the one referred to when it is said that he called the Galatians (v. 6).

8) After thus in the most direct way stating the vital point at issue with the perversion of Christ's gospel to which the Galatians had begun to give ear, Paul utters a solemn malediction on anyone who would dare to pervert this gospel. **But even if we or an angel from heaven shall preach gospel to you contrary to what we preached to you, let him be accursed! As we have said before, also now again say I: If anyone preaches gospel to you contrary to the one you received, let him be accursed!**

'Ἀλλά is adversative, it takes direct issue with τινές: there are people of this kind, "but" whoever they may be, they are accursed. Note the difference in the conditional clauses: καὶ ἐάν vividly supposes a case; εἰ in v. 9 takes up the real case that is now occurring in Galatia. What is said of the supposed case lends greater justification and strength to what is equally said about the real case. This is augmented by making the supposed case deal with the highest persons, with even an angel, and the real case with lower persons, thus securing the argumentative weight of a *conclusio a majori ad minus*.

"Even if" is concessive: suppose that such a thing should occur, that we ourselves or, still worse, an angel from heaven should so preach. The more improbable, yea impossible the supposition, the more justified the verdict of damnation. Paul intends to state a rhetorical extreme (R. 1026). How could those who had preached the real gospel turn around and preach its contrary? Or how could an angel from heaven do such a thing? The fact that ἡμεῖς and the "we" in the verbs "we preached" and "we have said" cannot be literary plurals and refer to Paul alone and not to Paul and his assistants, is plain from the latter, for there occur together, *"we* have said," and, *"I* now again say." No writer uses "we" and "I" with reference to himself in the same breath; to assume that Paul does this here is untenable.

Paul puts "we" first because he would in no way spare himself and his own best friends and assistants if they should ever falsify the gospel; he also gains a climax by adding "or an angel from heaven." He must add "from heaven," for Satan is able to masquerade as an angel of light (II Cor. 11:14). The reading ὑμῖν (a few texts have ὑμᾶς as in v. 9) is textually well attested. If it is omitted, the proposition is more general; but if it is retained, the sentence is a more personal reference to the Galatians. The Greek idiom for the English "contrary to" is παρά, literally "beside" (R. 313); so here and again in v. 9: "contrary to what we preached to you" — "contrary to what you received (from us)," v. 9. These two relative clauses (both are object clauses) define what Paul means by "a different gospel which is not another," namely a gospel "contrary to" the true one which Paul and his assistants preached and the Galatians received.

The verb εὐαγγελίζομαι means to proclaim good news and is generally used in the New Testament to indicate the preaching of the gospel. We use it in the missionary sense of "to evangelize." Here it is first used with the dative and then with the accusative of the persons to whom the gospel is preached; the sense is the same. Note the tenses: two aorists in v. 8: "if . . . shall actually preach as gospel" — "contrary to what we actually did preach to you"; then the present in v. 9: "if anyone ever preaches as gospel." One might use the absolute "gospelize." In the present connection the verb is used with reference to both false and true gospelizing as the context makes plain. The correlative idea is always faith in what is proclaimed as good news; in v. 9 it is expressed by the verb λαμβάνω, "to receive." Such faith and reception are wrought by the gospel itself. The enormity of refusing the glad tidings of salvation in unbelief is at once apparent; it brands this news as a lie.

The most damnable thing, however, is to proclaim as the true gospel something that is contrary to that gospel; yea, to induce people who have received the true gospel to cast this aside and to accept something contrary in its stead as though this contrary were the genuine, true gospel. Bad enough for his own soul for anyone to make this exchange but infinitely worse to make it one's business to delude others into making this exchange. The divine gospel is branded as a lie, the lying gospel is offered as the truth; the double falsehood leads souls to destruction. Whoever is guilty of this crime, "let him be accursed!" even if it be one of us, Paul says, *yea,* an angel out of heaven itself.

The Hebrew *cherem* = something that is removed from the possession or use of men and set aside for God, either as an object upon which God's wrath rests or as an object that is dedicated to God as a gift. Hellenic Greek used ἀνάθεμα for the former in the sense of "accursed," ἀνάθημα for the latter. The later ecclesiastical "anathema" found in the Decrees of the Council of Trent is the continuation of "accursed." It is not known whether anathema was used in excommunication from the synagogue. Any late ecclesiastical use of this word sheds no light on our passage. Paul is not acting as a human court nor is he calling on the Galatian churches to act as a court by pronouncing an anathema. An angel would not be subject to a human court. The view that Paul is exercising the right of excommunication is not substantiated but answered by I Cor. 5:3-5. Paul had no such right, did not pretend to have it.

As the apostle and representative of Christ and the Father Paul pronounces the verdict: "Let him be anathema!" He repeats the verdict which Jesus himself uttered against the Pharisees in Matt. 23:13-39 (note v. 15 and 33). Anyone who promulgates a different and contrary gospel is *eo ipso* "accursed," not because we say so, but because Christ has said so, and we only repeat his judgment. This includes the devil himself. (I Cor. 6:3; II Cor. 11:14). The *damnamus* found in the Confessions is fully justified. In a ministerial conference a Lutheran was challenged: "You certainly would not damn a Jew?" He replied: "Christ has already done that!" R. 939 states that the imperative crowded out the classical optative of wish; the untenableness of that view is the fact that Paul is here not expressing a wish but a verdict.

9) This is not a new verdict nor one that is pronounced by Paul alone. The Galatians have heard it from him and from his associates before: "As we have said before." Paul is now merely repeating it: "also now again say I." Whether this is a reference to the first missionary journey when Barnabas was Paul's associate and these uttered an advance warning against any falsification of the gospel, or to the second visit in Galatia when Judaizers had already appeared in Syrian Antioch and then in Jerusalem, no one can say. The latter seems more probable. Of course, what was then said to the Galatians does not need to agree verbatim with the denunciation as it is now worded with the repeated anathema. Then the Galatians were told about what might occur, now Paul speaks of what has occurred: "If anyone preaches gospel to you con-

trary to the one you received (from us), let him be anathema!" Παρ' ὅ has the same force in both verses; in both cases the relative is not indefinite: "contrary to what," but refers to the εὐαγγέλιον embedded in the verb. But note the advance: "contrary to the one we preached to you" (v. 8) points to the bringing of the gospel to the Galatians; "contrary to the one you received" completes the bringing by noting the reception in true faith. This also fits the condition of reality now employed; the Galatians had in fact received the true gospel.

As certainly as what the Galatians "did receive" was the divine gospel and that alone, so certainly it was most damnable to seek to subvert that gospel and to supplant it by a sham gospel. But were the Judaizers not sincere? The devil is even more sincere in promulgating the false gospel in order to crowd out the true. Vicious sincerity never escapes the anathema.

Perhaps they were unconscious of their sin, acted ignorantly and not intelligently? The answer to this then as now is the one Jesus gave to the Pharisees in John 9:41: "If ye were blind, ye should have no sin: but now ye say: 'We see!' therefore your sin remaineth." The truth is not that the Judaizers never knew the true gospel. It is not even only the fact that, when the true gospel came to them, they did not believe it (Mark 16:16b). The fact is that the Judaizers had the true gospel before them and determined to destroy it, and that not by open opposition and persecution but by the insidious substitution of a fake gospel, than which no more devilish means exists. They were worse than the Pharisees who claimed: "We see!" and thus refused the truth; they were like those mentioned in Matt. 23:15, who made their proselytes twofold more the children of hell than themselves; yea, even worse than these, for these operated with proselytes from paganism to Judaism while the Judaizers proselyted true believers.

10) Two startling questions close the double denunciation: they are followed by Paul's own decisive answer. **Indeed, am I now trying to get the approval of men or of God? or am I seeking to curry favor with men? If I were yet currying favor with men I would not be a slave of Christ!**

In this instance γάρ cannot mean "for" (our versions) as either stating a reason or offering an explanation. The insertion of "now," which repeats the "now" of v. 9, restricts us to the thought of what Paul is doing with these startling verdicts. It is as plain as day that he is neither seeking the approval of men nor trying to curry favor with men. Γάρ is but the confirmatory adverb which is here used in a question in order to point to what the previous statements make decidedly plain and thus make the question more urgent and the desired answer more inevitable (Zahn).

Like a flash the questions reveal the charges the Judaizers had launched against Paul in order to discredit him and his gospel. They alleged that Paul toned down the rigorous legal requirements of the original gospel in order to gain the approval of Gentiles, to make the gospel palatable to them, to curry favor with them. In his ambition to build churches and to gain a great following he had emasculated the gospel and stripped it of essential parts. The Judaizers came to Galatia in order to restore the gospel to its true content. Paul's gospel of liberty was a piece of conscienceless accommodation to Gentile reluctance in accepting the Jewish law. O yes, the Judaizers also preached Christ, but in the full legal setting without which the Galatians could not be saved!

Paul meets all this with sudden, smashing questions. Indeed, does anybody who is trying to please men approach them with anathemas? The present tense is conative: "Am I now trying to get the approval of men — seeking to curry favor with men?" If at any time before I have spoken softly, is this now soft language? And have we not before, when we were with you Galatians, spoken in the same uncompromising way (v. 9)?

The force of both πείθω and ἀρέσκειν lies in the personal objects. The former does not mean "persuade," for God cannot be persuaded. It means trying to secure the approval of someone. The second verb is used only regarding men and not regarding God and thus means "to please" in the sense of "to curry favor." The second question thus makes the first clearer; "or" is not adversative and exclusive but conjunctive. Paul puts the questions in such a way that the Galatians will have to answer *no* if they are still honest. Only a man whose sole aim it is to have the divine approval will write as Paul now writes even as he and his assistants have in the same way spoken face to face with the Galatians.

This refutation of the slander spread among the Galatians may well open their eyes to the character of the Judaizers and to the base means with which they work. What the Galatians have found Paul to be before, they will also find him now, a man without fear or favor, with his eye on God and on Christ alone. He is an apostle, not from men or by man, but through Christ and God alone (v. 1). The interpretation that "now" refers to Paul's whole Christian life in contrast with his former Judaism disregards the context and the close connection with the preceding "now" (v. 9); both refer to the present moment.

Paul answers his own question with a conditional sentence that expresses present unreality (εἰ with the imperfect — the imperfect with ἄν): "If I were yet currying favor with men I would not be Christ's slave." This is the verdict under which Paul would then rest.

Not a slave of Christ = a mere slave of men (I Cor. 7:23). The point of δοῦλος or "slave" is not hard labor done for a master; it is absolute obedience which knows no will but that of the master. Ἔτι, "yet." If at this late time in his apostleship Paul did not yet serve Christ as his supreme Master, then the Galatians might, indeed, turn away from him. Paul would rather alienate all the Galatian churches from himself than reduce in a single point the gospel committed unto him by Christ to please them or anybody else.

PART 1

The Apostle of Christian Liberty Received His Gospel by Revelation Alone.
1:11-2:21

In the body of this letter Paul first thoroughly silences the plea of his Judaizing opponents that, because he was not one of the Twelve who had been in the school of Jesus, his gospel was therefore unreliable since he had obtained it from men, who themselves, perhaps, understood it wrongly, or whose doctrine Paul modified to suit himself. This plea, which Paul overthrows, includes the claim that the leaders in Jerusalem taught a different doctrine, one in which the old law was still made binding. In fact, it was claimed that Paul himself occasionally observed the old legal requirements. By discrediting him the Judaizers hoped to discredit his gospel so as to substitute their own.

These false claims Paul overthrows by means of three replies, all of which are historical in substance. The first is the fact that he received his gospel directly from Christ by revelation alone and not at secondhand from the other apostles (1:11-24). The second, that the other apostles fully acknowledged Paul's gospel (2:1-10). The third, that on one occasion Paul was obliged to correct Peter himself regarding this very point of complete liberty from the law, and that Peter accepted the correction (2:11-21). This reply, consisting of clear facts, is at once complete and convincing in every respect.

I. *How Paul Obtained His Gospel, 1:11-24*

11) With perfect calmness Paul presents the detailed facts regarding the manner in which he received his gospel. Only one question is to be answered: "What

are the facts?" They and they alone are decisive. Paul presents them to the Galatians whom he clearly distinguishes from the Judaistic teachers. On these latter he has pronounced his anathema, but the Galatians he addressed as his brethren throughout. Paul writes as one who is confident that the truth will prevail; the note of defeat is foreign to him.

For I inform you, brethren, in regard to the gospel preached as gospel by me, that it is not in human style (at all). **For also, as far as I am concerned, I did not receive it from man and was not taught; on the contrary,** (I received it) **through Jesus Christ's revelation.**

These opening statements present the whole matter in a nutshell. No human agency of any kind was employed in transmitting the gospel to Paul, to equip him for preaching it as an apostle who was on a par with the Twelve. The means employed was direct, immediate revelation by no less a person than Jesus Christ himself, the same Jesus Christ who equipped the Twelve in the same way.

"For" at the beginning of the whole paragraph is explanatory in a broad way: "so that you may understand this whole matter aright." "For" does not intend to prove that Paul is "Christ's slave," for it does much more. Of course, it elucidates all that precedes in v. 1-10, but even this is not enough. The elucidation focuses on the great point as to how Paul got his gospel; after this is clear, all will see that this is Christ's very own gospel, and that any "different" gospel cannot come from Christ and must, therefore, be false, a human invention, a vicious substitute. Further elaboration takes care of the details and furnishes the strongest support for the proposition laid down at the start.

The address "brethren" conveys a good deal. The Galatians had been disturbed (v. 7) by the Judaizers, their certainty was not as strong as it had been before, they were in great danger, but they were still "brethren," to whose rescue Paul comes. The Galatians are "brethren," not so the Judaizers whom Paul repudiates utterly. These "brethren" are to listen to Paul who writes to them as their true "brother"; and as "brethren" they will be certain and even glad to do so.

"Brother" has been cheapened by many. Some unionists call anybody "brother," would have called the Judaizers by this name. In the New Testament "brother" and "brethren" are terms that are applied to those only who believe and confess the true gospel and never to those who have become guilty of a repudiation of any part of that gospel. Such "brethren" may need help to maintain the gospel; they then get that help in fullest measure.

"I inform you, brethren," sounds formal and impressive, and for that very reason is tinged with irony. To "brethren" one would expect a brother to say: "You know, brethren," not, "I inform you," unless he were telling something new. The fact "that the gospel gospelized by Paul" is not κατὰ ἄνθρωπον, "in human style," was certainly not news to the Galatians; for if it were news, why had it not been told them at the start? And if Paul withheld this information until this time when he is challenged, how could he suppose that this late telling would make any impression on the Galatians? The effectiveness of Paul's "I inform you" lies in the very fact that Paul has to tell the Galatians, as though it were a piece of entirely new information, what he had told them when he first gave them the gospel. He might have exclaimed because of their forgetfulness or have stirred them to remembrance in some other way; he chose a way that was telling, indeed.

The aorist passive participle indicates the past fact: "gospeled by me." The entire stress rests on the last phrase: κατὰ ἄνθρωπον, "according to or after man," *menschengemaess*, normated in a human way. We are able to give only the general sense: it is not a gospel "in human style." The phrase is broad and does not specify. The points about which Paul is here concerned follow with an explanatory "for." These, however, do not exhaust the phrase, for it covers just about everything in the gospel. In all respects it shows its non-human, its divine nature, quality, power, effect, etc. How strange that this must again be told to the Galatians as though it were news — shame on them!

12) The readings vary. The easier ones are οὔτε — οὔτε and οὐδέ — οὐδέ. We might adopt the latter: "neither — nor." We then get a contrast. The trouble with this reading is the fact that to receive the gospel from man (a human being) and to be taught is not a contrast that fits "neither — nor." For how can one receive the gospel from man except by being taught? If "nor was I taught" means that Paul was not taught even by Christ, the phrase "by Christ" should be in the text. The more one studies the statement, the more the difficult and unusual reading: οὐδέ — οὔτε seems correct, the former specifying, the latter merely adding a point of the one specification: "For also (B.-D. 462, 3 on Rom. 8:7; B.-P. 949: *denn auch nicht*), as far as I am concerned, I (emphatic ἐγώ, subject of both verbs) did not receive it from man and was not taught." This is the one decisive point here at issue. If Paul had received his gospel from man he, of course, was taught by man. In this vital point his gospel would then be "according to man." He would be on the same level with true Christians in general and with the Galatians in particular and not on a level with the Twelve.

"On the contrary (ἀλλά after negations), (I received it) through or by means of Jesus Christ's revelation" exactly like the Twelve. We cannot supply both verbs: "I received and was taught by means of revelation," for, to say the least, it would be peculiar to state that revelation conducts a course of instruction. Revelation reveals instanter, to be taught is a different process. This, too, indicates that οὔτε is correct, and that the two negatives describe the ordinary human reception of the gospel.

What seems to confuse some is the fact that the Twelve were taught by Jesus. But that teaching never enabled them to act as apostles. Much of it they failed to understand; after three years they deserted Jesus and fled. Jesus promised them the Spirit (John 14:26; 16:13, 14). That means revelation, exactly the same thing that Paul received. Before his call to the apostleship Paul knew many things about Jesus, not, indeed, nearly as much as the Twelve; but they as well as Paul needed direct, divine revelation. It and it alone supplied every lack. The least lack was intellectual grasp, the supreme need was power (Acts 1:8). The revelation which supplied the greater need certainly did not fail in the smaller.

"Of Jesus Christ" is the subjective genitive; he is the revealer. The fact that Christ revealed by the Spirit in no way discounts this act as being his. No one is able to say whether the revelation was one act or a succession of acts, nor is this point vital in any way. The veil was withdrawn from Paul's soul, and by a miraculous intervention of the Christ who called him the entire gospel was put into his possession for his office as an apostle. When did this occur? We do now know. The main point is that it did occur.

We meet a peculiar reluctance to admit that Paul received the entire gospel exactly as he here says he received it. Some hold the view that Paul had after all to learn the story of Jesus from Christians who knew it and could teach him. The decisive answer to this is the fact that the revelation which gave Paul the main substance of the gospel would certainly not stop short in regard to the minor things. If Christ had in a way made Paul dependent upon men, he would have placed Paul below the apostolic plane. The fact that Christ did nothing of the kind is the very point here settled once for all.

We cannot accept the view which has the Judaizers claim only that Paul's gospel was one κατὰ ἄνθρωπον, of human type, a perversion that was due to Paul who ambitiously wanted to get a great following among the Gentiles, but excepts from the Judaizers' claims the thought that Paul got his gospel from man and allows that he obtained it from Christ. Their claim included what v. 1 intimates, that he was an apostle from men, by means of man, not from Christ and God; thus certainly also that his gospel was according, received from man or man's teaching and not by means of Christ's revelation. The correspondence between v. 1 and v. 11, 12 is too great to admit of any other view. The Judaizers did not need to specify the man or the men from whom Paul derived either his alleged apostleship or his alleged gospel.

It is incorrect to say that Paul was made the first man who taught Christian liberty for the church. Syrian Antioch stands out in this respect. Paul's missionary journeys had started from there. While one must be careful when he extracts the charges against Paul from his defense, there is no reason for striking out the items that he had his gospel, not from Christ, but from men. The fact that Paul himself then further altered his gospel in order to make it still freer for the Gentiles may be admitted as an additional charge against him on the part of the Judaizers.

13) With "for" Paul explains still further. **For you have heard of my own mode of life at one time**

in Judaism, that beyond measure I continued persecuting the church of God and ravaging it. And I kept advancing in Judaism beyond many as old as I in my race, being more exceedingly a zealot for my ancestral traditions.

"You heard," aorist, is sufficient to the Greek who cares to mark only the past time; our "have heard" marks the relation of the action to the present. It is an old story, long known to the Galatians. For this very reason Paul refers to it now in order to remind the Galatians how rather impossible it was for one who had been what he had been even to be converted by the agency of man, to say nothing of being made an apostle. The longer the Galatians have known what a frightful Jew Paul once was, the more effect Paul's recalling it will have upon them in the present connection. He needs to touch only the worst points.

We note ἐμήν which is stronger than the enclitic "my," for Paul's conduct in life was an exception. "In Judaism" has the article, like the German *in dem Judaismus*, whereas we do without it; the term itself does not refer to the Jewish religion (our versions) except as this is the main thing in Judaism. Paul at once states the worst: "that I continued persecuting the church of God and kept ravaging it." He was the supreme Jewish fanatic of his time. The two verbs used do not exaggerate in the least. As imperfects they describe the persecuting and the ravaging. Πορθεῖν is used with reference to devastating a city with fire and sword; it is the word found in Acts 9:21. The enormity of Paul's criminal course is expressed by the adverbial "beyond measure" and by the formulation of the object "the church of God." Is there a greater crime in all the world than to *devastate* — and that *beyond* all measure — *God's* own church? "God's" is the proper possessive, for the word itself denotes deity; "Christ's" would do that to a lesser degree.

14) In v. 13 Paul lets his former acts speak, now he adds the animus that drove him to these and to other fanatic acts. He says that he cut ahead (προκόπτω) in Judaism beyond many of his own age, left many young men as old as he was far behind. As is so often the case in the Greek, the participial clause presents the main point: being more excessively than the other young Jews of his age "a zealot for my paternal traditions." The word used means that he literally burned with zeal that demanded action against anything that was opposed to the Jewish traditions; it recalls the name that was applied to the Jewish sect of the Zealots who preached the sacred duty of revolt against Rome.

Paul was of the same fanatical type, but his zeal was "for my ancestral traditions" (objective genitive). Πατρικός is the adjective formed from the genitive τοῦ πατρός and refers to one's father, grandfather, etc., and not, like πατρῷος or πάτριος, to national ancestry. Paul's father was a strict Pharisee and had trained his son to be even stricter. The adjective makes the impression that this Pharisaism was a trait of long standing in the family. Its proudest and most militant member was Saul.

By "my ancestral traditions" Paul refers to the traditions of the Pharisees, that whole hedge of 613 human commandments which the rabbis had built around the law, and which the Pharisees made it the business of their party to maintain at all costs. Here we should recall all the virulent clashes of Jesus with the Pharisees, for instance, the climax in Matt. 23:13, etc. Paul's violence against the Christians was so excessive because the church meant the death of Pharisaism. A converted Jew and Pharisee might live in the old Jewish way and freely choose to observe parts of the Mosaic law; but he would certainly give up the traditions of the elders as being mere useless and dangerous "commandments of men." These very traditions were the apple of Paul's eye; for them he wished to tear the church of God to pieces.

What Paul conveys is the idea that he was more than a defender of the Mosaic law, more than a Pharisee who saw the glory of Judaism in that law. He saw the crown of Judaism in the traditions. The church had to be crushed so that these traditions, built to support the Mosaic law, might be maintained. The point in all this is not that Paul could not be converted as many other Pharisees were converted. Although they believed, some of these still thought that parts of the Mosaic law were binding (Acts 15:5), but not, of course, the rabbinical traditions.

Paul was utterly extreme. On the one hand, he raged for the traditions and went far beyond the Mosaic law; on the other hand, he now stood for complete liberty even from the Mosaic law and was the very apostle of this liberty. Once the supreme protagonist of the traditions, now the very apostle of Christian liberty! Let the Galatians visualize the gulf that lay between these extremes. How was it possible that such a fanatic traditionalist should now be the apostle of perfect Christian liberty? If he was converted at all *he* should have been a Judaizer like those referred to in Acts 15:5. But we already have the full answer: "Jesus Christ's revelation," v. 12.

15) This concise answer is now amplified. **But when is pleased God, who separated me from my mother's womb and called me by means of his grace, to reveal his Son in me in order that I may preach the good news of him among the Gentiles, immediately I conferred not with flesh and blood, nor did I go to Jerusalem to those** (who were) **apostles before me but I went off into Arabia and again I returned to Damascus.**

This is the full account of the revelation which converted the zealot for the rabbinical traditions into the apostle of Christ and of gospel liberty. God did this by an act of revelation, did it completely without the aid of any man, without in any way employing any man as a means in his hand.

It was due to God's pleasure, his εὐδοκία, which is here expressed by the verb εὐδόκησεν. God "had the good pleasure." The word conveys the idea that God was moved only by what is in himself and not by any merit or worthiness in Paul. It also contains the thought of grace and kindness so that all arbitrariness and determinism are excluded. The "good pleasure" of God is the free will whose content is something good (C.-K. 354). This term is used in connection with the bestowal of salvation, cf., Eph. 1:5. It is one of the lovely terms applied to God in the Scriptures. What God did in his good pleasure is stated by the infinitive: "to reveal his Son in me." Distinct from this act are two others which are not connected with the infinitive but made descriptions of the subject: "God who separated and called" (note the article which makes the participles attributive).

"Who separated me from my mother's womb" means more than that God ushered Paul into this life as he does every child that is safely born. Not only does "it pleased God" precede, but a second participle, "called," follows. We are reminded of Jer. 1:5 and may think of Luke 1:15. The intentions of God's good pleasure are not conceived at the time of their execution but long before, so long in advance that he shapes and directs all things toward the good end he has in view. How the divine and the human factors are combined in attaining the good outcome is beyond mortal insight. Speculations are generally unsatisfactory. The point which we should note is the full stress Paul lays on the divine agency which made him the apostle that he was. No one would have believed that the babe born away off in heathen Tarsus, the child of the strictest Pharisees, would come to be the apostle who fought this Pharisaism so mightily.

The Hebrew *pharush*, Aramaic *pherisha'*, "Pharisee," is the Greek ἀφωρισμένος, one separated. Because Paul here uses the aorist participle of this verb, the supposition is advanced that Paul means that God in his good pleasure made him "a separated one," i. e., a *pharush* or Pharisee in a higher (Christian) sense. Even in Rom. 1:1, where we do have the perfect participle, this idea is too superficial to be entertained. It is more so here because of its modifier: "who separated me from my mother's womb."

"Called me by means of his grace" takes us to Damascus. The purpose God had already at the time of his birth came to its fulfillment in the call of grace. While all that intervened between the birth and the call seemed so contradictory to God's good pleasure regarding Paul, it in reality served the divine purpose. What a triumph of grace! What an effect upon the Jews themselves! The Pharisaic career of Paul, once it crashed before grace, made pure grace stand out in its supreme effectiveness in Paul's own experience. When Paul writes, "called me by means of his grace," all the wonders of grace rise before our minds. Yes, this is grace with its connotation of utter guilt in the recipient who ought to be damned, with its implication of absolutely unmerited favor. In the epistles "to call" always denotes the successful call (see v. 6). Here, as in v. 6, Paul has in mind the call that made him a Christian. It is true enough that the same grace called him to be an apostle, and even that both calls were united in one grand act; yet here Paul distinguishes and lets the infinitive say how he was made an apostle.

16) The main statement, which is vital for Paul's object, is that God pleased "to reveal his Son in

me." What is meant is at once shown by the addition of the purpose of this revelation: "in order that I may preach him as good news among the Gentiles." This revelation was to make Paul the apostle to the Gentiles. The infinitive is an aorist, it denotes a complete and an effective revelation. Paul does not say, "to reveal Jesus Christ," but "his Son," Jesus Christ in his deity, in all that his deity means for the contents of gospel preaching. Subtract the deity, and all that remains is hollow sound.

The claim is made that Paul never calls Jesus "God's Son." Here we have one of the numerous places where he does so. The fact that "his Son" makes Christ equal with the Father, makes Christ the second person of the Trinity, we have seen in v. 1 and 3, where this equality is beyond question. "In me" is stronger than the mere dative "to me." R. 587 and *W. P.* translates "in my case" — a strange idea: "to reveal in my case." "In me" is even more than "in my experience." This revelation was not intended for the senses of Paul but was vastly more. It filled his very heart, soul, and spirit so as to abide with him forever.

In v. 12 Jesus Christ is the revelator, here the revelator is God. This fact may be stated either way. God ever reveals his Son, the Son ever reveals God. Whatever this revelation did for Paul's personal faith as a believer — here it is regarded as making him the apostle to the Gentiles. This revelation made Paul the equal of the Twelve as we have already brought out. One hesitates to say whether it included more than took place on the road to Damascus. Its absolute sufficiency for Paul's apostleship is beyond question. Paul was made an apostle to the Gentiles from the start. The strange fact that years passed before he actually worked among the Gentiles does not change God's appointment. Like Moses, Paul had to await God's own time.

Paul did not confer with flesh and blood. This verb is regularly used in this sense (M.-M. 546) : to consult with someone in order to obtain advice, to get someone's judgment so as to arrive at a decision. "Flesh and blood" is often thought to refer to Paul himself, i. e., to his own natural inclinations, with the idea that he did not let these speak in the matter. It is claimed that the analogy of Scripture supports this view. Yet in Eph. 6:12 "flesh and blood" denotes earthly opponents, and in general σὰρξ καὶ αἷμα, *basar w^edam*, derives its meaning from the context. Here Paul has in mind fallible men in general; he uses the highly descriptive abstract expression in place of a concrete term. "Flesh and blood" is in contrast to "God who separated me," etc. Paul in no way referred God's revelation and appointment to the apostleship among the Gentiles to earthly judges before accepting it.

We might think that Paul's emphatic "immediately" refers back to his bloodthirsty ravaging of the church and thus stresses the suddenness of the change in him: one moment tearing the church to pieces, the next going forth with the commission to gospelize even the heathen. But "immediately" is to be construed with two peculiar negative statements. These read like refutations of lying reports; as though Paul had learned from the Galatian delegation that the Judaizers claimed that he did at first listen to others and seek their guidance and then afterward broke away and adopted the wrong course of discarding all the Jewish legal requirements. That was a cunning way of winning the Galatians away from Paul's present teaching, his opponents pretending that theirs was the original doctrine that was held by Paul himself when he at first listened to others. Paul never consulted any man. To have done so would have discredited God himself, the all-sufficiency of God's own revelation.

17) "Nor did I go up to Jerusalem to those (who were) apostles before me" singles out the Twelve as the ones who were worthy of being consulted more than any others. The higher the Twelve stood, the more one must remember that they, too, were only "flesh and blood" as compared with God. "Immediately" is to be construed also with this clause. Paul did not hurry to Jerusalem to get anything, whether information and instruction or corroboration and approval, from any of the Twelve. Paul's action was not a reflection on the Twelve as though he cared nothing about a judgment of theirs. Quite the contrary. He acknowledges them as "the apostles" exactly as God had made him such a one. He also acknowledges the one point in which they outranked him: they were the apostles "before me." God had appointed Paul as the last apostle.

It would have been wrong for Paul to have consulted the Twelve or any number of them whom he might have found in Jerusalem. It will not do to say that they would undoubtedly have approved. They would have rebuked Paul for trying to consult them regarding God's own revelation. Not one of them would have ventured a word where God himself had spoken. Were they higher than God? By his revelation God had not only made Paul an apostle but had equipped him in every respect exactly as he had equipped them, the Twelve, on Pentecost.

Over against the double negation and in order the more to down the false reports the Judaizers were spreading Paul states the facts regarding what he did do in the early days: "on the contrary (ἀλλά after negatives), I went off into Arabia and again I returned to Damascus." We at once see that Paul is writing to people who know where he was called and received God's revelation. Whether they also knew about his trip to Arabia must remain an open question; they did know that he eventually left Damascus never to return there. The point of importance is that there was no apostle in Damascus either at the time of Paul's conversion or when he returned; and in Arabia there certainly was no one with whom it was possible to confer.

But for this mention of Arabia we should not know that Paul had ever been there. Luke says nothing about it although we have no difficulty in fitting Paul's visit to Arabia into Acts 9:20-27. How long Paul remained in Arabia, how long a second time in Damascus, no one knows. Why did he choose Arabia, and what did he do there? Our curiosity is keen, various guesses are ventured, but no one knows more than this brief statement contains.

18) Now we learn when Paul first came to Jerusalem, what his purpose was in coming, and whom he found there. **Thereupon, after three years, I went up to Jerusalem to become acquainted with Cephas and remained with him for fifteen days. But another of the apostles I did not see save James, the brother of the Lord.**

We regard "thereupon," ἔπειτα, as meaning after the return from Arabia, and "after three years" as being in contrast with "immediately" (v. 16), hence three years after Paul's conversion and not three years after his return to Damascus from Arabia. The latter would hang in the air, since the length of time between Paul's call and his return from Arabia is not mentioned. Nor is any reason apparent why the return from Arabia and three years from that indefinite date are of importance. But the fact that Paul waited three years after his conversion before going to Jerusalem is exact and to the point; also that during these three years he had taken a long journey, but *not* to Jerusalem; also that he returned to the place of his call, namely Damascus. So three years went by since Paul was called.

And since so long a time had elapsed, any idea of consulting the apostles about his revelation was rather late. Paul now tells the Galatians why he went to Jerusalem: "to become acquainted with Cephas." Why only Cephas? Paul could scarcely expect to find all of the Twelve in Jerusalem. We must conjecture that he had learned from traveling Christians that Cephas was making a stay in Jerusalem and hastened to make the acquaintance of this leader among the Twelve.

Here Paul writes "Cephas," the old Aramaic name of Peter; in 2:7, 8, where Jewish opponents are not so prominently in mind, "Peter" is used. Paul remained πρὸς αὐτόν, in reciprocal contact with Cephas, only fifteen days, a trifle over two weeks. This is the extent of Paul's first contact with any apostle. Ἱστορέω = "to visit" for the purpose of learning to know, to become acquainted with, B.-P. 596, not "to inquire of," to get information from.

19) During these brief days Paul did not even see another of the apostles. They were evidently absent from Jerusalem and in other cities. When he adds: "save James, the brother of the Lord," we should at once see that, having just denied seeing a single other apostle, his meaning cannot be that he after all saw another apostle, namely this James, but that Paul feels that he must name the one other person of special importance whom he saw although without really getting acquainted with him. This was not one of the Twelve as Paul makes plain, but one whom he must name since the Judaizers might claim him in support of their teaching. There is not a conflict with Acts 9:27, where Luke says that Barnabas brought Paul "to the apostles" (plural); for Luke calls Barnabas, too, an apostle (Acts 14:14) and could well consider James an apostle in this wider sense of the term.

At this time the church at Jerusalem was no longer under the direct management of the Twelve but had its own elders, chief among whom was James. We know him as a man of great importance; Acts 15 is enough to establish this fact. He is called "the brother of the Lord" in order to distinguish him from James, the brother of John, and probably from James, the son of Alphæus. He came to faith after the resurrection of Jesus. We have shown in connection with Acts 1:14 that the "brothers of Jesus" were not sons of Mary (see that passage); whether they were stepbrothers or cousins is an open question. The writer does not accept the more recent claims which rest their contention on ἀδελφοί as if this settled the question that sons who were born to Joseph of Mary after Jesus are referred to. Acts 1:14 is an impediment in their way, and there are other obstructions that are not removed by this word.

20) This is the whole of that visit of fifteen days three years after Paul's call as an apostle: acquaintance with Peter, seeing James, no conference on Paul's revelation, no passing of his call through any man's hands, nothing to lower Paul's apostleship in any way. **Now as regards what I am writing to you, lo, before God, I am not lying!**

This solemn assurance is called forth by the insinuations and falsifications of the Judaizers who used all that they had heard about Paul in order to discredit him. Some of the Galatians might ask: "Is that really all there was to that visit in Jerusalem?" Paul gives the most solemn answer as if he were before God's own judgment seat. He is writing them the facts, the entire truth without a falsehood. Paul's gospel had its own convincing and faith-working power. Outward proofs add nothing whatever to that; but they do remove barriers which would otherwise block acceptance of the truth such as plausible and cunningly twisted allegations about the apostle himself.

"What I am writing to you" may be regarded as a pendent nominative. Ἰδού is an interjection as the accent shows and has no object; but the formula of solemn assurance: "lo, before God," has adverbial force and thus has the ὅτι clause as its subject, "that I am not lying."

21) What about the time after those fifteen days? That, too, is highly significant. **Thereupon I went into the regions of Syria and Cilicia.** Acts 9:27-30 briefly tells the story of the fifteen days and how the threat of persecution drove Paul from Jerusalem. Paul touches upon only his contact with Peter and with James because the Judaistic falsifications tried to make capital of that. Brought from Jerusalem to Caesarea, Paul went to Tarsus. What made him leave Jerusalem was really a communication from the Lord himself (Acts 22:17-21). He could go by either sea or land. If he went by land, he would go first to Syria and then to Cilicia. It is sometimes supposed that he went by sea and that he here reverses the names and writes Syria first because it adjoins Palestine and then Cilicia because it adjoins Syria. The fact is that after years spent in Tarsus, Barnabas brought him back to Antioch in Syria where they worked together. Paul may mention Syria first because he did not work in Cilicia but finally did considerable work in Antioch.

The remarkable thing is that Paul spent eight years in Tarsus, his native city. They are a blank for us. It is only a guess when one reads of missionary work done during these years in Tarsus and Cilicia. This is impossible. Luke has many silences due to his plan of Acts; but he could not have been silent regarding any work done in Cilicia, for this would have been Paul's *first* great work among the Gentiles, the very work Luke records in Acts. No; Paul was inactive, in retirement. Christ did not as yet deem him ready; like Moses, Paul had to wait. But all this belongs to a consideration of Acts; the point to be noted here is the fact that after fifteen brief days Paul for so many years went far away from any contact with the Twelve. This fact speaks volumes against the Judaistic falsifications.

22) **Moreover, I was not known by sight to the churches in Judea which are in Christ.** Because of the lack of an adjective such as "Christian" we have the phrase "in Christ" added attributively. The Judean churches had never even seen Paul, and he had now been absent from them for years. This does not, of course, include Jerusalem where during those fifteen days Paul went in and out among the brethren and even disputed with the Hellenistic Jews who then tried to kill him (Acts 9:28, 29).

23) **Only they continued to hear: He who was once persecuting us is now preaching the faith which he was once ravaging; and they went on glorifying God in me.**

Note the periphrastic imperfects in v. 22, 23, both stress continuation: "continuing unknown — continuing only to hear." It is easy to see how the Judean churches again and again heard about the man they had never seen. They heard when they came to Jerusalem, or when someone from Jerusalem came to them. Many, no doubt, wondered what had become of Paul. He was certainly not forgotten.

What was said about him in all these churches? Anything derogatory? Any criticism of his gospel, of his apostleship, of his relation to the other apostles? Not a word. On the contrary, everybody got to hear this astounding news that their one-time persecutor is now preaching the very faith he at one time tried to wreck. Note the direct discourse, the sharp contrast "once — now," and again "once" and the significant final clause. All these churches heard not only that Paul was gospelizing but that he was gospelizing the faith he once sought to wipe out. What faith was that? The one the Twelve preached — no other. In Jerusalem, the mother church, whither the Twelve often returned, and in all the Judean churches Paul's gospel was acknowledged as the one original faith. What do the Judaizers mean with their falsifications? Here there is another plain example of ἡ πίστις used in the objective sense: "the faith" = the gospel = the doctrine, which contradicts the statement of C.-K. that this word is never used objectively.

24) Instead of running down Paul as the Judaizers in Galatia did all these churches went on glorifying God "in connection with me," ἐν ἐμοί. All these, mark it, were Jewish churches who also had received all their news about Paul from Jerusalem itself, the very seat of the Twelve. What more can the Galatians ask?

Thus by a simple recounting of the historical facts Paul sets before the Galatians what they should never have allowed anyone to make them doubt: he had his gospel directly from God and Christ, by revelation and not at secondhand, the identical gospel of all the other apostles, of all the churches in Judea.

CHAPTER II

2. *How the Other Apostles Acknowledged Paul's Gospel, 2:1-10*

1) Root and branch Paul destroys the allegation of the Judaizers that his gospel is not the original gospel but that of the other apostles, and that he is not a genuine apostle, sent by the Lord like the Twelve, but has come from or through men only. He continues to let the facts speak their crushing language. In chapter 1 the facts reveal that Paul had his gospel by revelation, that during a long period of time he had only fifteen days' contact with Peter and slight contact with James, but that Jerusalem and all the Judean churches glorified God because he preached the very faith he had once persecuted. So much for *the source.*

Now he presents *the contents* of his gospel regarding the very point assailed by the Judaizers, Christian liberty and circumcision in particular. Paul advances to the time of the great apostolic convention at Jerusalem when he came into fullest contact with the other apostles, yea, with all the leaders and with the church officially assembled. This was the decisive occasion when the first Judaizers were publicly and officially discredited and their Judaistic claims rejected. *They* were disowned, *Paul* was most fully acknowledged. Not that he needed such endorsement — he had never needed it. But if anything was wrong with either Paul's apostleship or his gospel of Christian liberty, this wrong would most certainly have been exposed at this convention in Jerusalem, regarding which Paul now presents the pertinent facts.

The Galatians know all about this convention. For, some time after it took place, Paul started on his second missionary journey and began it by visiting the Galatian churches he had founded and delivered to all of them the resolution adopted at the great conference. See the resolution sent out to the Gentile churches, Acts 15:23-29; Paul delivered it in Galatia, Acts 16:4, 5. When he recalls this convention to the minds of the Galatians, Paul needs only to touch the points he deems vital; he does not need to tell the whole story over again. It certainly was preposterous that not so long after the whole Judaistic contention had been utterly repudiated by the apostles and the church as such right in Jerusalem, Judaizers should creep into Galatia and try to make the Galatians believe that Paul and his gospel were repudiated, that the Judaizers were endorsed, that the Twelve themselves were Judaizers.

Thereupon, with an interval of fourteen years, I went up again to Jerusalem in company with Barnabas, taking along with me also Titus.

This is the third "thereupon," and, as in the case of the first in 1:18, a phrase expressing time follows. Διά with the genitive indicates an interval (R. 581) and counts from the time indicated in 1:18, 21, Paul's fifteen-day visit in Jerusalem. Fourteen years after that visit means seventeen years after Paul's conversion. These fourteen years include the eight Paul spent in Tarsus, regarding which we know nothing definite; the years spent in Syrian Antioch, working there with Barnabas in the great church which was chiefly Gentile; the period of the first missionary journey when Paul and Barnabas founded the Galatian churches; their return to Antioch and Paul's further stay in that city until he went to attend the Jerusalem conference.

The supposition that Paul is speaking of the visit which he and Barnabas paid to Jerusalem to bring the relief gathered in Antioch for the poor (Acts 11:27-30; 12:25) is chronologically untenable. This visit antedates the founding of the Galatian churches. At that time the situation in Jerusalem was distressing; James, the brother of John, had been killed by Herod, Peter had fled, Paul and Barnabas saw no apostle. The visit of which Paul speaks here cannot be identified with the one mentioned in Acts 11:30.

Some interpreters count the fourteen years from the time of Paul's conversion on the plea that this is the dominating date for the reckoning of time. It is; but it dominates just as strongly when the fourteen years follow the three as when they include the three. If they include the three, the conversion of Paul is moved forward three years, which upsets the entire chronology. The date of Herod's frightful death (Acts 12:23) is known independently of the Scriptures: the summer of the year 44. Paul is speaking of the time of the convention (Acts 15). All is in order when we accept this date, the beginning of the year 52. But this is not a matter of dates; what happened on this visit of Paul's and Barnabas' to Jerusalem cannot be assigned to a time when it could not have happened.

We see no reason for questioning the force of πάλιν; whether it is retained in the text or not, this was "again" a visit to Jerusalem. The fact that Paul and Barnabas had brought relief to Jerusalem in the fall of the year 44 need not be mentioned because this visit to Jerusalem had no bearing on Paul's gospel. The claim that Paul could not have ignored a mention of this visit is untenable.

We should note the marked difference with which Barnabas and Titus are named. Paul went up "in company with" Barnabas (μετά), with him as his chief associate. They were the two main members of the commission who were sent from Antioch to the Jerusalem conference (Acts 15:2). The Galatians knew all about this; Paul himself had visited them and had brought them the resolution of the conference, which was to be brought to all the Gentile churches.

Paul names Barnabas because Barnabas had helped to found the Galatian churches. Another reason is that Barnabas had stood with Paul in what Paul now tells about the happenings at the time of this conference. This is of importance because the Judaizers were in reality demanding that the Galatians should turn from both founders of their churches. Titus was not a member of the Antioch commission. Paul took him along. We know Titus as being Paul's assistant in the period following the conference. He is mentioned because of what follows; his became a test case at the conference.

2) **Moreover, I went up in accord with a revelation, and I laid before them the gospel which I am preaching among the Gentiles, and in private before those in repute, whether I am running or did run in vain.**

The church in Antioch elected Paul as one of the commission that was to go to Jerusalem for the conference regarding the issue the Judaizers had raised. In Acts 15 Luke reports only that Paul went along. From Paul we now learn more, namely that the Lord bade him go in a revelation. It seems that, although he was duly elected to go, he had some reluctance about accepting. The Lord himself removed his scruples, and he went.

Δέ adds this for the sake of the Galatians. They are to understand that he did not go of his own accord even after being elected; the Lord himself bade him go. The Galatians must not get the impression that Paul was obliged to lay his gospel before others for their approval, or that the church at Antioch perhaps obligated him to do so, or that he at least felt that he ought to do so. The idea that the Lord, who had called Paul as an apostle, wanted him to get the approval of the men at Jerusalem is, of course, preposterous. The Lord's acts are not subject to any man's approval. As his own approved apostle the Lord wanted Paul present at Jerusalem in order to help with the deliberations just as Paul did help.

Nothing is gained by asking whether the Lord gave the revelation to Paul himself or to one of the other prophets in Antioch. The Lord gave so many revelations to Paul that such a question should not be raised. Paul went with the Lord's own assurance that his going would in no way harm his own apostolic standing. He, of course, does not recite the whole story of that conference. The Galatians knew that; Paul and Silas had made a full report to them. Silas was one of the two who were especially commissioned by the conference to carry the written resolution of the conference to the Gentile churches (Acts 15:27). He was Paul's chosen assistant for the second missionary journey (Acts 15:40) and thus officially informed the Galatians of the conference resolution (Acts 16:4, 5).

Paul here presents the test case that was made of Titus and of circumcision. This actual case shatters the whole contention of the Judaizers, shatters it right at Jerusalem to which the Judaizers constantly appealed, and reveals the fact that the other apostles and the whole church stood with Paul.

It was at the first public meeting at Jerusalem that Paul "laid before them (the entire assembly) the gospel which I am preaching among the Gentiles" as also Luke records in Acts 15:4. Luke speaks of "all the things God had done" through Paul and Barnabas; Paul speaks of the means by which all these things were done. We know that the means, namely the gospel Paul preached, was the subject for calling the conference. Means and results naturally go together. In the assembly at Jerusalem the Antioch delegation told the story of the great work that had been done in their city. Paul and Barnabas had their share in that. Then these two told of their first missionary tour to Cyprus and to Galatia. Paul words it well: "the gospel which I am preaching among the Gentiles." It was entirely a story of the gospel which founded the Galatian churches, of the gospel Paul is still preaching. From Antioch it had extended to Galatia and now at the time of Paul's writing was extending still farther. Jesus had ordered the apostles to carry this gospel to "all the ἔθνη" ("nations" or Gentiles).

Paul adds information that is perhaps new to the Galatians, that he laid this gospel of his "in private (δέ, also) before those in repute," the leaders in Jerusalem. This was not in any way a secret conclave; it furnished direct personal opportunity for the leaders to learn from Paul all they might desire to know; we take it that Paul had Barnabas with him. Paul was very glad to tell everything, and, no doubt, James, Peter, and John were equally glad to hear all they could from Paul and from Barnabas. It was a rare opportunity of which all concerned made the most. Whether any others of the elders of Jerusalem were present at this private meeting we cannot determine; it is possible.

Paul calls those with whom he conferred οἱ δοκοῦντες and repeats this expression four times and plays on it in a pointed manner. In v. 6 and 9 he amplifies the designation. The sense is the same throughout. It might be either they who *think themselves* something; or they who *seem* to be something *to others* — the latter with or without the idea of justification. The context determines just what is meant. Here it must be "they who seem to be something to others," they who are considered to be somebody, more briefly, "those in repute."

The very repetition of this designation shows that Paul is quoting it from the lips of the Judaizers in Galatia. "Who," they said, "is Paul when compared with men like James, Peter, and John? These are the men of standing who are considered so in the church."

Paul rubs the word in by his repetitions. The irony of that procedure is directed against the Judaizers. *They* were the ones who thought that repute was the main thing and that it settled everything against Paul. If *they* denied standing and repute to Paul, then Paul counted for nothing, and, of course, the Galatians would accept what *they*, these Judaizers, were pleased to say.

Now Paul is the last man to deny the high repute of James, Peter, and John, or of anybody else. He is also the last man to be jealous of his own repute. All repute among men, whether his own or that of others in the church, is secondary entirely; the essential is something far higher, namely what *the Lord* makes of any man. The business of the church is to consider that and to make its repute correspond to that. That Paul himself held James, Peter, and John in the highest repute is evidenced by the fact that he laid his gospel before these men. He could not have done so if he thought that they did not fully deserve this high repute. He would be a fool for telling the Galatians how he laid his gospel before these men if he at the same time intends to say that in his own estimation these men were nothing.

But the laying of his gospel before James, etc., does *not* mean that he and his gospel were dependent on the verdict of these men because of their repute. Verse 6 leaves nothing to be desired regarding that. Paul is not afraid of laying his gospel before anybody, least of all before these high men of whose great repute the Judaizers sought to make capital against him. Paul's gospel was from God, so was theirs. It was and had ever been one and the same. Any and every time a proper examination is made, this would appear. Paul's repute thus took care of itself. God was back of it as he was back of any true repute that James, etc., enjoyed in the church.

It was solely because of the Judaizers who had appeared in Antioch and with others were now making themselves obnoxious in Jerusalem that Paul (and Barnabas) got together with James, Peter, and John, in order by means of the true gospel, which they all unitedly preached, to crush the Judaistic error most effectively and completely. When the Judaizers of Jerusalem laid their perversion of the gospel (Acts 15:5) before the conference, Peter gave them a crushing reply in his address (Acts 15:7-11). Paul and Barnabas did the same (Acts 15:12), and it was James, who, presiding at this conference, formulated the resolution which the whole conference adopted, put in writing, and sent out to all the Gentile churches (Acts 15:13-32). In this resolution the whole contention of the Judaizers was repudiated. What a farce for any Judaizers now to come to the Galatians with talk of "those in repute" and thereby to throw dust in the eyes of the Galatians! Why are these Judaizers not telling the truth?

Read μή πως as an indirect question: "whether I am running or did run (the English prefers the perfect: have been running) in vain." The implied answer is: "Certainly not!" Both verbs are naturally indicatives, all is grammatically simple. This question does not express a doubt on Paul's part; even πως, "in some way," "perhaps," leaves him without doubt. This question was raised by the Judaizers in Jerusalem; *they* either said outright that all Paul's work was in vain or implied as much. In fact, Paul *was* running in vain if the gospel of the Judaizers was the true gospel. Then all Paul's work was εἰς κενόν, "for emptiness," empty, hollow; it would all have to be done over again. In this indirect question Paul lays the Judaistic contention before the private meeting. James, Peter, and John would have to declare regarding their own work that it has all been in vain if they pronounced this verdict on Paul's work.

Our versions translate: "Lest by any means I should be running or had run in vain." R. 988 thinks that this expresses purpose, "purely final." Let us say that purpose is not acceptable. B.-D. 370, 2 finds a feeling of concern in the main verb: Paul laid his gospel before these men with a feeling of concern "lest he be running," etc. This is not tenable: Paul had a feeling of perfect certainty which rested on God's own direct revelation. Can any man have greater objective or subjective certainty? As the purpose, so the feeling of concern is untenable. R. W. P., regards τρέχω as being subjunctive and explains the aorist indicative ἔδραμον as a sort of afterthought or retrospect and in his grammar adds that in such final clauses the classics expressed unreality by the indicative. R. admires Paul for thus implying that he had *not* run in vain. B.-D. 361 contradicts this: this indicative is "not unreal." This question regarding the modes becomes clear the moment we see that this is an indirect question, one that was precipitated by the Judaizers, the answer to which was beyond a shadow of doubt to men such as James, Peter, and John.

3) So crushingly was the question answered to the complete overthrow of the Judaizers that Paul writes: **But not even Titus, the one with me, although he was a Greek, was compelled to be circumcised even on account of the pseudo-brethren sneakingly brought in, such as sneakingly came in to spy out our liberty which we have in Christ Jesus in order that they might completely enslave us; to whom we yielded no, not for an hour by way of the submission** (they demanded) **in order that the truth of the gospel might continue on for you.**

The Judaizers failed utterly and completely in their contention at Jerusalem. The Galatians have the verdict, the resolution worded by James and formally adopted by the assembly (Acts 15:13, etc.); the failure of the Judaizers was even more complete as we see from the test case of Titus. This was an actual case which occurred right there in the conference. Facts speak even louder than words.

The indirect question asked in v. 2 embodies the verdict of the Judaizers: "Paul had run, was still running in vain!" Ἀλλά is set squarely against this: "On the contrary," and on the contrary to this extent: "not even Titus was compelled to be circumcised." Paul had purposely taken Titus along (v. 1); "the one with me" emphasizes this fact. Paul made Titus an open challenge to the Judaizers. They might have allowed other Gentiles who were living in distant places to remain uncircumcised; they dared not permit this regarding Titus right in the conference itself now that he was thrown into their faces as a challenge by Paul himself. He was a Greek, both of his parents were Gentiles. Paul had never had him circumcised and never circumcised him even later on. His case was entirely different from that of Timothy, whose mother was a Jewess and whom Paul intended to use for mission work among the Jews.

Circumcision was a complete adiaphoron to Paul: it was nothing either way (I Cor. 7:19). He performed it with regard to Timothy because it would prove a help in the work. Since Titus was a Greek, it would prove no help in his case, Jews would always be suspicious of him. Titus was just the man with whom to challenge the Judaizers. When they demanded his circumcision, Paul absolutely refused. He had to. The moment any adiaphoron is demanded as being necessary to salvation, it ceases to be an adiaphoron, it becomes a vital issue on which we dare not yield. *C. Tr.* 1059, etc., elaborates this subject on which so many are confused to the detriment of real Christian liberty.

In the person of Titus the whole gospel as it was preached by Paul, by Peter (Acts 11:1-18; 15:7-11), and by all the apostles came to be embodied. That gospel would have crumbled and fallen if this man would have been circumcised at the demand of the Judaizers. That is why he was *not* circumcised, not even for minor, secondary, innocent reasons. Once the Judaizers made their demand regarding Titus, they destroyed all reasons for his ever being circumcised.

Among the exegetical curiosities we list the one which has Paul say the opposite of what he does say, namely that Titus was circumcised, yet not under constraint but by voluntary action on Paul's part. The emphasis is placed on ἠναγκάσθη, and οὐδέ is regarded as modifying only this verb: Titus "was not even forced" to be circumcised. Even if Paul intended to say this, he would not have put it in the words which he here used. The emphasis is on "not even Titus," and it cannot be shifted to "was forced." "Not even Titus" = he with whom Paul made the challenge, not even he, to say nothing about others who were not made a test case.

4) Δέ emphasizes the διά phrase and does not start a new sentence. Δέ calls on the reader to bear in mind that not even Titus was compelled to be circumcised, compelled "on account of the pseudo-brethren," etc., the very men who so strenuously tried to force his circumcision. We do not have an anacoluthon; this view is due to the claim that δέ is metabatic and starts a new sentence. Zahn removes the anacoluthon by cancelling οἷς οὐδέ from v. 5. The texts, however, are against this procedure, especially regarding οὐδέ.

Zahn's concern is to get another thought; the matter of the anacoluthon is only incidental. We are told that Paul *did yield* for a moment with due subjection in order to conserve the gospel. To whom? To the pseudo-brethren, the Judaizers? That is unthinkable. Some suggest, to the resolution framed by James (Acts 15:13, etc.). But Paul did not yield to that, that was his own hearty conviction; to say that he yielded to it only "for an hour" is unacceptable. Well, then, Paul yielded to the authorities in Jerusalem by laying the clash with the Judaizers in Antioch before these authorities in due submission. This is Zahn's answer.

Aside from the alteration of the text involved, this answer itself is unsatisfactory. It bids us jump from v. 5 to v. 1 and forget about Titus. No reader does that; no writer could expect it. When one says in a preamble that certain men tried to enslave him and then adds that he yielded, every ordinary reader will understand that he yielded to these men — he *must* so understand. Textually and in every other way the negative stands: "I did *not* yield for one moment!" Add to this the fact that Paul was *not* subject to any authorities in Jerusalem, that he repudiates this assumption throughout, most decidedly in v. 6. He was subject only to God and to Christ, was on a perfect equality with the Twelve. To make Paul subject to James is unwarranted.

Paul says that what set everybody against circumcising Titus for any reason was the attitude of "the pseudo-brethren," a term that is like "pseudo-apostle" found in II Cor. 11:13. In forming our estimate of them we should not forget Acts 15:5 and paint them too black. Luke calls them "Pharisees who believed" yet demanded "that it was needful to circumcise them and to command them to keep the law of Moses." They were not *dis*believers but *mis*believers, errorists, but such as had become fixed in their error. They accepted Christ yet added the Mosaic law to Christ and thus falsified Christ. From Paul we learn more. First the adjective "brought in on the side," surreptitiously, sneakingly. They should never have been brought into the church as members. Somebody was to blame for bringing them in; who is not said, but it surely was not any of the apostles.

"Such as came in on the side," sneakingly, adds the thought that they were of this type. The real blame lay on them; they deceived those who brought them in. This is evidenced by what they proved to be, not brethren whose aim it was to let go their Pharisaism and to accept the free gospel wholeheartedly, but men who were determined to cling to their Pharisaism, set on "spying" out our liberty which we have in Christ Jesus."

They are not to be identified with the Judaizers who appeared in Antioch and first caused the Judaistic question to be raised. They were not the same men, for we must conclude from Luke's account that the Judaizers in Antioch did not send a delegation to Jerusalem at the time of the conference. The pseudobrethren in the mother church made it their special business to pry out whether one or the other of the delegation that came from the church in Antioch was perhaps uncircumcised. Of course, they soon found Titus and centered their general demand for circumcision (Acts 15:5) on him. It was entirely a matter of liberty whether a Christian man wanted to remain uncircumcised or not. Paul writes *"our* liberty," for the matter concerned the entire delegation from Antioch irrespective of how many were or were not circumcised. "Which we have in Christ Jesus" declares this to be the true Christian and gospel liberty.

Paul adds that the purpose of the spying out was "that they might completely enslave us," κατά in καταδουλώσουσιν, a future indicative after ἵνα (R. 984), the verb itself being causative (R. 802). "Enslave" matches "liberty." Acts 15:5 accords with what Paul says here. It would be the worst kind of spiritual slavery again to be forced under the old Jewish Mosaic ceremonial regulations. With these again in control, works and outward observance would destroy the doctrine of "by faith alone." And that would mean loss of justification and salvation. Even on account of these men, who, in their Pharisaic zeal, surely made the most strenuous efforts, Titus was not compelled to be circumcised. James, Peter, John, and the great body of the church were not moved an inch.

5) Οἷς, like other relatives that are attached at the end of a longer statement, has demonstrative force, cf., Rom. 1:25; 3:8, 30. It is like saying: "These fellows to whom we yielded no, not for an hour by way of the submission" (i. e., the one they demanded). "We" refers to the entire delegation from Antioch (Acts 15:2). "The submission" was not "the submission which Paul and the delegation owed to James," etc. Τῇ ὑποταγῇ is the dative of mode, and the article refers to the submission or obedience in question. Not for a moment did we yield "by way of *the* (demanded) submission" to the enslavement proposed by the pseudobrethren and give up our liberty in Christ Jesus.

Paul states why "we did not yield for an hour (we say: for a moment)." He and Barnabas together with their fellow delegates thought of the Galatians to whom they had brought the truth of the gospel. If they had yielded, that truth would have been lost to the Galatians. Paul and Barnabas would have had to go back to Galatia and undo all that they had done. They stood solid "in order that the truth of the gospel (its verity and reality) might continue on (on through, διά) for you." Πρὸς ὑμᾶς is not "with you"; it is the face-to-face preposition: the truth of the gospel facing the Galatians, they facing the truth. "For you" is a most effective touch when Paul now writes to the Galatians. We can almost see Paul and Barnabas at the convention talking about their Galatian congregations and showing how the point at issue regarding Titus affected them all, and, of course, any other Gentile congregations yet to be founded.

It was only the circumcision of Titus — many shortsighted and weak-kneed preachers would have yielded and then perhaps justified themselves by a reference to their love. But Paul and Barnabas and their associates saw that in this one case "the truth of the gospel" itself was at stake, its very heart was at stake. If the pseudo-brethren gained their point, "by faith alone" would be overthrown right in the mother church in Jerusalem. What was that bound to do to all the other churches?

We add that if οὐδέ is cancelled, if Paul says that he did yield, the purpose clause: "in order that the truth of the gospel might be conserved for you," becomes unintelligible. The idea that Paul submitted to the authorities in Jerusalem in order to secure a favorable verdict, in order that the Galatians might keep the gospel truth, is strangely involved, and the main point is introduced from the outside. Such an exegesis will not meet universal approval.

The situation obtaining at the conference in Jerusalem is a kind of parallel to the one now obtaining in Galatia. There, as here, the Judaizers tried to destroy the liberty of the gospel with their legalism; there, as here, Paul yields not an inch. We may add that there the truth of the gospel was maintained against all legalism. Would that we could say: "It has always been so maintained." Alas, there are many legalists today. Paul's fears that he expressed in Acts 20:29, 30 have become reality. His warning uttered in Rom. 16:17, 18 is not heeded. But note: if the Judaizers in Galatia who opposed Paul's doctrine claimed the support of the apostles and of the mother church, the very opposite was the fact: all of the latter stood solidly behind Paul in the test case of Titus. The force of this truth must have been powerful, indeed, for the Galatians.

6) Paul has facts in connection with the conference, both negative and positive, that are so powerful as doubly to close any Judaizer's mouth. No change in the work of Paul was proposed; on the contrary, James, Peter, and John gave Paul and Barnabas the right hand of fellowship, each acknowledging the other. No right hand of fellowship for the Judaizers! This is what happened at that notable conference.

Moreover, from those reputed to be something (whatever kind they were makes no difference to me — God does not accept a man's face) — before me, then, those in repute placed nothing; on the contrary, the very opposite, etc.

Here we, indeed, have an anacoluthon, and a beautiful one at that. In the middle of the sentence Paul changes from the expected passive ("there was placed before me") to the unexpected active ("they placed before me"). Why did Paul write an anacoluthon, and why did he retain it? It was not due to the rapidity of his mind. That very rapidity saw where he was going when he began the sentence. R. 438 states that the parenthesis led Paul to change the construction. But that view is unsatisfactory. Paul uses the anacoluthon as a legitimate form of expression; it is as "regular" as what the grammarians call regular.

That is the formal side. The material is more important. Paul's anacoluthon is used for a reason: to express what would otherwise not be expressed, what would otherwise require several statements. In the present instance this is quite apparent. The literary beauty of this anacoluthon shows the mastery of Paul in fitting language to thought. We shall explain.

"From those reputed to be something" repeats the designation that was used by the Judaizers when they pitted James and the Twelve against Paul, see v. 2. He now amplifies the designation as the Judaizers themselves did who said that these men really amounted to something while Paul amounted to nothing. To be sure, these men did amount to something, for which reason Paul also laid his whole gospel and his work before them. But if Paul amounted to nothing in comparison with these men, then they would, no doubt, point out to him certain things that he had overlooked, certain mistakes that he ought to correct, errors that he must avoid, in particular that he must insist on circumcision and on the legal regulations of Moses (Acts 15:5). What are the facts? The very contrary. These authorities that enjoyed this high repute laid absolutely nothing before Paul, not a thing regarding those mentioned, and not a thing concerning other, even lesser, matters. This is only the negative side, but it speaks volumes. It declares that in the finding of these very authorities, of whom the Judaizers made so extravagantly much, Paul's gospel and his work were in literally every respect as perfect as their own.

But it is now time to add a remark or two on the designation used so pointedly by the Judaizers: "those reputed to be something." Paul does it in only two brief, parenthetical remarks; no more is necessary: "whatever kind they (actually) were makes no difference to me — God does not accept a man's face." Ὁποῖοί ποτε should not be separated (B.-D. 303: *welcherlei Leute immer*), "whatever kind," R. 732; the adverb merely makes the adjective indefinite. It, of course, made no difference to Paul (*verschlaegt mir nichts*) what high repute James, etc., enjoyed; they might have enjoyed a still greater repute. Paul had received his gospel from far higher authority, from God himself. It is necessary to remind the Galatians of the fact that human repute does not count and did not count at the Jerusalem convention in the case of Paul.

But such a limited statement may seem derogatory to James and to the Twelve as though Paul cared nothing for them or their standing. It is not intended in this way. Paul does not wish to detract from them in the least, for is he not telling the Galatians that these men acknowledged him and his gospel? So he adds a second parenthetical statement: "God does not accept a man's face or person." The emphasis is on πρόσωπον and then on "God" and "man's," which are placed in contrasting juxtaposition: With *God man's* face does not count. The fact that Paul was only Paul, once a persecutor of the church, an abortion when he was called to be an apostle (I Cor. 15:8, 9), was of no consequence to God in comparison with Peter and John and others who followed Jesus from the beginning. God is able to make an apostle of whomever he will. Faces, names, persons are not decisive for him. Any wrong deductions that might be made from the first part of the parenthesis are thus removed.

Paul has begun as if he intends to say, "From them I on my part received nothing." But if he had finished thus, it might sound as though these men of repute tried to impart something to him. Yet they assumed no superior airs toward him, they did not even attempt to lay anything before him which, in their opinion, he ought to accept. He wants to deny both ideas. Most skilfully and with great delicacy he achieves this double denial by using an anacoluthon. The thought that they might possibly have wanted to lay something before him is thereby left only as a mild implication. It is kept down to that by the phrase: "from those reputed to be something," i. e., who might feel they had a right to dictate to me. By leaving this incomplete he brushes away the implication. The anacoluthon, starting the sentence anew with a nominative: "before me, then, those in repute," etc., constitutes only an easy turn in the construction, especially after the two parenthetical insertions.

This is made still easier by placing the dative forward: "— before me on my part 'those in repute' placed nothing." Count my repute what you will — such as I was and still am, these men in high repute, according to the phraseology of the Judaizers, strange as they may deem the fact, "before *me* they placed nothing" that I should accept. The aorist states the fact as a fact. Thus two birds are killed with one stone: the suggestion that "from them" something at least in the way of correction should surely have been placed before Paul; and the cold, solid fact that they did nothing of the kind. Verily, anacolutha are excellent means for expressing thought if, like Paul and other good writers, one knows how to use them.

Γάρ is another delicate touch. It connects the new turn of the sentence with the parenthesis by implying that those in repute fully deserved their repute far beyond what the Judaizers realized. These men in repute understood perfectly what Paul here says, that with God there is no respect of persons. They never dreamed of letting Paul feel their authority by putting at least something before him. That is what men in repute so generally like to do. They want all others to feel that they *are* in repute; hence they insist on something even if it be only a triviality in order to have their authority noted. James, etc., were far above that. Catch this effect from the way in which "those in repute" is once more inserted — they truly deserved to be in repute! We translate: "Before me, then." "I say" (R. V.) is not so good; "for" in the A. V. is better. Προσανέθεντο has the dative as in 1:16: to lay something before another either in the way of counselling with him (thus in 1:16) or in order to have him accept it (so here).

7) Beside the negative, which already says so much, is placed the still stronger positive: **on the contrary, the very opposite, having seen that I have been entrusted with the gospel for the foreskin even as Peter** (with the gospel) **for the circumcision (for he who wrought for Peter with regard to an apostolate for the circumcision wrought also for me with regard to the Gentiles), and having realized this grace given to me, James and Cephas and John, those reputed to be pillars, gave to me and Barnabas the right hand of fellowship that we on our part (go) to the Gentiles, and they on theirs to the circumcision, only the poor, that we keep remembering them — the very thing I also hastened to do.**

How mightily the facts do speak! The whole is one grand sentence. While after a negation ἀλλά means "on the contrary" and might thus suffice, here it is reenforced, for this contrary is the direct opposite. Those in repute did the complete opposite of making any demand on Paul, they endorsed him by a solemn public act and agreement. Can anything that is more crushing to the Judaizers be imagined?

The construction is simple: "having seen — and having realized — they gave." Here, for once, Paul's whole teaching and his work were fully examined and competently compared with those of the other apostles. Hitherto no occasion for such a comparison had arisen. Now that the occasion had come, these men saw what was so apparent, that Paul had been entrusted with the gospel for the foreskin just as Peter had been entrusted with the gospel for the circumcision.

The abstracts "foreskin" and "circumcision" generalize and in this sense stand for Gentiles and for Jews. We regard the two genitives as objective: "for the foreskin," etc. God entrusted the one as he did the other. The perfect refers to a past act with continuous effect: the trust given remained. This passive is not intransitive although the active is (R. 816); hence it takes the accusative like other transitive passives.

This does not indicate a difference in the contents of the gospel. It is identical for all nations and all times. The idea that our modern times need a different gospel, or that in mission work the gospel should be changed for this or that nation is unwarranted. Any change loses the gospel to the extent of the change attempted. The gospel is fixed and permanent in the Scriptures, in particular in the New Testament. These men naturally had nothing whatever to lay before Paul just as he had nothing to lay before them.

The remarkable thing is that Paul and Peter are placed on a par. John is not mentioned in the statement. This is scarcely due to the fact that the Judaizers claimed Peter as their patron; for the term Paul borrows from their lips is a plural: "those in repute." Peter is not named with the idea of excluding the eleven but as representing them. The division of territory can also not be meant in an exclusive sense. Paul always began his work in the synagogue; Peter preached to Cornelius and to other Gentiles in Caesarea. *A fortiori fit denominatio;* the distinction and the division of work was made on broad lines. In Acts 23:11 the Lord orders Paul to do the great mission work among the Jews that was waiting to be done in Rome. Yet, beginning with Paul's original appointment, especially he was to be the apostle of the Gentiles (Acts 26:17, 18). This is what the men saw at Jerusalem.

8) They compared what God had done. Paul adds this in explanation by means of γάρ; by placing it in a parenthesis the statement is made the more objective: "for he who wrought for Peter with regard to an apostolate for the circumcision wrought also for me with regard to the Gentiles." The two are closely paralleled. As Peter was placed in the Jewish work by God, so

Paul was placed in the Gentile work. The datives are indirect objects (R. V.) and are not due to the ἐν in the verb; "in Peter — in me" (A. V.) The place referred to by this verb is indicated by an ἐν phrase. "Also for me with regard to the Gentiles" is only a briefer form of expression that uses the concrete "Gentiles" instead of the abstract "foreskin." How God wrought is not stated. The fact that he wrought the same miracles for both apostles seems too narrow a conception; also that he bestowed the charismata of the Spirit equally on converted Jews and Gentiles (Acts 15:8, 9). God wrought alike for Peter and for Paul by grace and by providence in the widest sense so that one came to work mostly among the Jews, the other among Gentiles. The credit for what was done by each is given wholly to God. Regarding himself Paul says in I Cor. 15:10: "Yet not I, but the grace of God which was with me."

9) The men at Jerusalem *saw* what the facts were and then also *realized* what these facts involved regarding Paul, namely, "the grace given to him" by God. Here it is again best to take this grace in its widest sense as including Paul's office, his ability, and his marked success. Although the participle already has its subject, "those in repute," Paul now names "James and Cephas and John" and adds "those reputed to be pillars." The latter is the most specific designation which the Judaizers employed. A few others are perhaps to be included in those of repute. It is immaterial. No other apostles at least were present at this conference, for they would either be named as Cephas and John are or be indicated in some plain manner. The figure suggested by "pillars" states outright what being "something" means in v. 6: columns that support the οἰκοδομή of the church, that are at once essential and ornamental. If they are broken, the building would be wrecked. The men named were pillars indeed although

the Judaizers used the expression to deny such importance to Paul.

James we meet already in 1:19. He is rightly named first although he is not an apostle; he presided at the conference (Acts 15:13). Cephas is next because, aside from all else, he was most prominent at the conference (Acts 15:7). The fact that John was present we know only from what Paul states here. Yet we are not surprised to find Peter and John together also on this occasion. Though each had a brother, we find Peter and John together in John 20:2, etc.; 21:20, etc.; Acts 3:1; 8:14. The two were evidently most intimately attached to one another. The three named here were certainly the foremost pillars of the Jerusalem church; although at the time of the conference they were absent from Jerusalem because of the work, also the rest of the Twelve deserved to be called pillars.

Behold, what these three did! "They gave to me and Barnabas the right hand of fellowship." And this was not merely fraternal fellowship such as is extended to brethren in the faith; κοινωνίας is placed last in order that ἵνα may define it: "of fellowship, that we on our part (go, the verb understood) to the Gentiles, and they on theirs to the circumcision." This was the fellowship of the apostles, the fellowship of the apostolic work. Three pillars acknowledge two others. This is what James, Peter, and John did at the great conference; behold what the Judaizers were trying to do in Galatia!

This giving of the right hand must have been a public act, one that was performed before the entire conference. The most likely moment must have been after the resolution offered by James was adopted. Note that the drafted resolution which was to be sent out to all the Gentile churches contains the words: "our beloved Barnabas and Paul, men that have hazarded their lives for the name of our Lord Jesus Christ," Acts 15:25, 26. That this giving of the hand occurred only at the private consultation is highly improbable. In the Greek the first person is named first, in English last; hence here: "to me and Barnabas." As James is concerned in this, so also is Barnabas. Paul and he were the ones who had gone out from Antioch on the first great missionary journey among Gentiles; they were the heads of the delegation sent to the conference from Antioch (Acts 15:2); they were the ones who would lead in the continuance of this work. The Spirit named Barnabas in Acts 13:2.

Regard both ἵνα clauses as subfinal, as defining the terms of the fellowship here solemnly published. R. 1000 thinks that the first ἵνα = "on condition that," and that the second is an expletive with a voluntative subjunctive (933). Both are alike, the second is added to the first, and neither denotes purpose.

The first stipulation was in regard to fields of work, the Gentile field was assigned to Paul and Barnabas, but not as being just a human arrangement, no, as one that was most plainly indicated by God himself. This implied the fullest endorsement of the work done in Galatia, of all the liberty of the gospel Paul had been and was preaching, and complete repudiation of all the contentions of the Judaizers. What more could Paul's soul desire?

10) In the second ἵνα clause: "only that," etc., the genitive object is placed first: "only the poor, that we keep remembering them." This prolepsis is used for the purpose of emphasis and occurs frequently in connection with ἵνα. These are the poor among the Palestinian churches to whom already on a previous occasion Antioch had sent help by the hands of Barnabas and Saul (Acts 11:30). Zahn rightly says that the pillar-apostles were not begging, nor were they using this

great occasion for begging. The fellowship in the division of labor included the fellowship of love and of loving aid.

When Paul adds: "the very thing I also hastened to do," i. e., carry out, this must refer to collections he took up during the year immediately following the conference; for it was at the end of this year that he wrote this epistle in Corinth. We know nothing further about these alms. The great collection which he later gathered in all his Gentile churches can thus not be referred to here. But we see how Paul got the idea of such a great collection, the object of which was not merely most materially to help the poor but also to cement the "fellowship" between all his Gentile churches and the mother church in Jerusalem from which the gospel had first gone forth into the world.

3. *How Paul Corrected even Peter, and how Peter Accepted this Correction, 2:11-21*

11) *Ad summa venit argumentum.* This is, in-indeed, the climax. Paul corrects no less a man than Peter himself, and Peter accepts the correction! Is it possible? It was done in public before scores of witnesses. Again Paul lets only the facts, the straight historical facts speak. The secret of all his work is that he is a theologian of fact. He meets the Judaizing movement in its attack upon his person and his apostleship by a few facts, incontrovertible facts. This part of the attack is thereby literally crushed.

When did this episode occur? Before or after the public acknowledgment mentioned in v. 9? No indication of time appears. Such a temporal particle ought to appear if this happened earlier. Otherwise the natural thing to do is to follow the previous narrative where one episode succeeds the other in time, and to understand this last as likewise occurring later than the preceding. Yet, starting with Augustine, a few writers assume that this event antedates the one mentioned in v. 1-10. They tell us that Peter came to Antioch, then the strict Jewish Christians from James, then the pseudo-brethren who made the Jerusalem conference necessary. This is thought to make the case against Peter and for Paul much stronger. But the reverse is true; for then the matter was still subject to a final decision on the part of the church. Summary: Paul follows the chronological order up to 2:10, the natural expectation is that he continues thus in the final episode. If Paul now reversed the order of time, this would necessitate an indication to this effect. Besides all this, it is incomprehensible that Paul could use this episode regarding Peter as the climax of his historical proof if it had occurred at an earlier date. Then, most assuredly, the conference would form the climax.

Now when Cephas came to Antioch, I withstood him to his face because he (already) **stood condemned.**

Δέ is transitional. The terse way in which Paul states the fact that he withstood Peter shows that the Galatians had already heard of this affair, that Paul is now merely recalling it to their minds and emphasizing the features that bear on the present issue in Galatia. It is also probable that the Judaizers made capital of this incident and twisted the facts so as to make it appear that Paul turned against Peter, forsook the old, original gospel that Peter preached together with its legal requirements, and was swept into his liberalism so that he might please the Gentiles. The exact reverse was true.

There is no need to say what brought Peter to Antioch for this visit. In the absence of all information it is gratuitous to say that he had no business there. The apostles did not run around where they had no business. Nor is it necessary to try to save Peter's reputation by assuming this Cephas to be some other man who had this Hebrew name. Paul has been speaking of the Cephas who is Peter and is reputed to be one of the pillars. The main point is stated at once: "I withstood him to his face." That must have occurred in public as also the following shows. It occurred in connection with the agape, before the whole congregation at Antioch. Picture the scene; it was surely dramatic in the highest degree. We know of no other case after Pentecost when one apostle corrected another. The aorist is significant and implies that Paul withstood successfully, that Peter had no defense, that he yielded. Think how this smashed the Judaistic contention which would have Peter correct Paul and never Paul correct the great Peter.

What makes the statement about Peter so severe is the clause: "because he stood condemned." Peter himself stood so by his own act. Anybody could stand against him, and Peter had no defense. Paul did it in Antioch; we shall see why Barnabas failed. R., W. P., regards the verb as a paraphrastic past perfect passive. C.-K. 259, and others consider the perfect participle the predicate of the imperfect $\tilde{\eta}\nu$; it does then not mean, "because he had been pronounced against," but, "he was a person who had a pronouncement standing against him," one that had been made some time ago and was still in force (perfect tense). Paul says that Peter was in this unfortunate position. We shall see that this was due to Peter's own act. The term Paul employs is legal, in the active it means *wider jemand erkennen*, so that nothing is left but the fixing of the penalty by the judge. Outside of that the case had been closed. All that Paul did was to point out this fact.

This verb never means "to accuse" in Biblical Greek. When it is used in this sense in secular Greek, the charges are always added. The mere accusation of

Peter would leave the question open as to whether he was guilty or not. Accusation would also call for a competent judge to try Peter; the judge might find him innocent. Paul does not use κατακρίνειν, for that would imply that Peter had had an adverse trial; he uses καταγινώσκειν: an adverse judicial pronouncement stood against Peter.

This fits the situation exactly. It was the pronouncement made by the Jerusalem conference in Acts 15:13, etc. Peter himself had helped greatly in making that pronouncement. If this affair at Antioch preceded that pronouncement, we are left to imagine some pronouncement against which Peter was now sinning and to invent some proper authority who could have so pronounced. All is clear if the conference preceded. For this reason, too, Paul does not need to name the court here involved; it was the conference and its finding against all Judaizers. Here at Antioch, Peter placed himself among these already condemned Judaizers. The moment he did that he stood condemned, condemned by the pronouncement he himself had helped to issue. All defense and even the right to enter a defense had been removed.

Barnabas and all the others at Antioch who acted as Peter did were certainly under the same verdict. Paul took Peter to task, not because he intended to leave out these others, but because Peter was the great apostle, the one who was blameworthy in this instance. When he was convicted, all those who stood with him were convicted. Peter misled even a man like Barnabas. We see at a glance what a calamity was threatening because of Peter's act of Judaizing. It was a God's blessing that Paul was there and withstood Peter to his face.

We see why Peter made no defense. It would have been preposterous for him to make even the attempt. To deny or to contradict the finding of the conference would have included a denial of the central part of the gospel. Peter was erring. But his greatness is evident: he accepted public rebuke in all humility, he mended his ways. How many men, high in the church, have done the same when they were in the wrong?

Do not ask how a man like Peter could have done what he did. Just ask yourself how you at times can and do sin even against better knowledge. That is the answer. Peter's erring at Antioch has been mentioned in connection with his inspiration. Instead of hurting the inerrancy of inspiration, Peter's erring helps to establish the inerrancy. Save for inspiration errors such as that of Peter here at Antioch would have spoiled many a page of Scripture. The assumption that every holy writer was constantly under inspiration in every word he uttered down to "Good morning!" and "How are you?" was infallible also in every act and movement, is contradicted right here. Inspiration is that act of God's when he speaks through the voice or through the pen of chosen men (see Matt. 1:22). This is the Biblical definition. God spoke "at sundry times" (Heb. 1:1); *then* there was inspiration, then only. And then error was excluded, for *God* spoke "through" (διά) his human instrument.

12) Paul explains what Peter did so as to make him stand condemned. **For before certain ones came from James he went on eating in company with the Gentiles, but when they came, he began to draw back and to separate himself, fearing those of the circumcision. And there acted the hypocrite with him also the rest of the Jews, so that even Barnabas was carried away in their hypocrisy.**

Here we have a graphic description of the situation brought about by the wrong action on the part of Peter. How long a time elapsed until certain ones from James arrived in Antioch we do not know, yet it was long enough to justify the imperfect: "he went on eating in company with the Gentiles," i. e., the Gentile Christians. This occurred at the agape where the congregation dined together. All the members save the poor brought their own food. They dined in groups, families together with friends, many groups in natural formations. Until those from James arrived, Peter ate regularly with Gentile groups.

To understand this aright we must remember that these Gentile Christians had joyfully received the resolution of the Jerusalem conference (Acts 15:30-32) and brought no meat that had been a part of the sacrifices to idols, or had been taken from strangled animals, or food that was made with blood (*Blutwurst*). Their food was not kosher, but it complied with the omissions the conference asked in order to keep harmony between Jewish and Gentile church members. In their groups the Jewish Christians brought only kosher food such as they had always eaten. They, too, did this in entire Christian liberty, condemned no Gentile Christian for eating other kinds of food. Some Jewish groups perhaps also gave up kosher eating; some Jews and Gentiles ate together in certain groups just as Peter did.

All went well until some came to Antioch from James. "From James" is scarcely the same as "from Jerusalem." These people were not sent by James, did not represent him. They were from the circle about James, in close association with him. When they came to the agape they naturally ate kosher as many Jewish Christians at Antioch did, which was their privilege. Paul hints at no disturbance that they made about Peter's eating in Gentile groups. Paul pictures them as the innocent cause of Peter's wrong action, for he says: "When they came," Peter changed. He "began to draw back" from all Gentile groups, "began to separate himself" from these groups.

The inchoative imperfects are also descriptive; at the same time they point forward to the outcome mentioned in v. 14, to the aorist used there. Peter's change was marked; all noted the reversal in his conduct. If he had eaten in Jewish groups in the first place as was his privilege, all would have been well; if at first he had only occasionally eaten with Gentile groups, it would not have been so bad. But to eat so long a time with Gentiles and then, the moment a few from the circle of James arrived, to eat only with Jews — that was bad.

What was the matter with Peter? He "feared those of the circumcision." Peter turned coward. Fear made him act against his own better convictions. "Those of (the) circumcision" is a specific designation. It might refer to any Jewish Christian, Peter, Paul, Barnabas being among them. It is far narrower here and signifies the Judaizers, those at Jerusalem. Yet "certain ones from James" were not Judaizers; the very phrase "from James" forbids this idea. For James presided at the conference and himself formulated the conference resolution which was adopted in order to disown the Judaizers, and which, when it was sent out, pleased the Gentile church at Antioch and all others exceedingly. Peter's fear was that, on returning to Jerusalem, these friends of James' might report that he ate steadily with the Gentile Christians in Antioch, that the Judaizers would get to hear of it and be enflamed against him. This was the brave Peter who was thrown into a panic in the courtyard at the time of the trial of Jesus. "They that were of the circumcision" (the same designation as here) had assailed him in Jerusalem after he had eaten with Cornelius (Acts 11:2, 3). At that time he had successfully defended his action.

One wonders why he should now be afraid of such Judaizers. Did he now intend to act prudently, to use his Christian liberty first in one way by eating with the Gentile Christians in Antioch and then in another way by eating only with the Jewish Christians? That was false prudence which was dictated by fear and not at all Paul's principle of love (I Cor. 9:19-23) but wretched concern for self. Fear produces strange actions. Calm reason must declare that Peter was wrong, totally wrong. Many wrong acts are devoid of a sensible, reasonable explanation. So it is with Peter's action on this occasion. The fact that an apostle like Peter should become guilty of a grave wrong at this time of his career should be a grave warning to us all (I Cor. 10:12). It is a wonder that he did not lose his apostleship.

13) The worst feature of his action was the evil effect it produced at Antioch. Why did Peter not fear that? He thought only of himself and of possible attacks from already completely discredited Judaizers. The position he held caused the other Jewish Christians, of whom there was a large number in Antioch, to act the hypocrite with him, i. e., to herd off by themselves at the agape and eat only kosher food. An evil rent was being made in the church. The whole question which had been settled at much pains in the Jerusalem conference, threatened to be opened again in a way that was worse than before. What must have pained Paul especially was the fact that even staunch Barnabas who, with Paul, had founded the Galatian congregations, who had been his fellow delegate to the conference, to whom he had been a bosom friend since Barnabas called him from Tarsus to Antioch, that even he should be carried away with the hypocrisy of all the rest (dative of means, R. 532, and not just after σύν in the verb). Ὥστε with the indicative is one of the two instances of this classic construction found in the New Testament to indicate actual result.

Peter, of course, did not set out to act the hypocrite, nor did the Jewish Christians of Antioch, nor did Barnabas. But Peter and those Christians did so act.

Paul states the cold fact. He is more considerate with regard to Barnabas: their hypocrisy carried him away; he should have remained firm like his friend Paul. But that is the sad result when high and revered men head into a wrong course: they often sweep most excellent lesser men along with them. Barnabas is a warning to us. The church is full of great names that are still constantly quoted in support of some false doctrine, false practice, false principle, false interpretation. Their very names stop lesser men from testing what they advocate, and so they, like Barnabas, are carried away.

But is Paul not too severe when he labels their acts hypocrisy? Note that he deliberately uses the word twice, once the verb (an aorist at that!) and then the noun. This duplication serves notice that Paul means just what he says. These men acted as if they believed one thing when at heart they believed another. They all believed as Paul did, that all outward observances were unimportant as far as Christianity is concerned, but here they acted as if, after all, outward observances in regard to meat and drink were an essential, at least a very important thing in Christianity. Both verb and noun are used with reference to show acting; the ancient actors wore masks. These men were playing a part: their action was done for effect, it was thoroughly insincere.

But could Paul look into their hearts? He did not need to do that. At Jerusalem, Peter and Barnabas and the rest of the Antioch delegation had solemnly subscribed to the *modus vivendi* established for Gentile and for Jewish Christians; but here all of them were by their actions denying what they had solemnly affirmed and what the whole church at Antioch had heartily accepted. They acted as if eating with Gentile Christians was defiling and yet knew it was nothing of the kind, such a thing as ceremonial defilement no longer existed for them. Indeed, hypocrisy is the proper term. How could they stoop to it? All sins against better knowledge lack a rational explanation; they are committed against right reason, are irrational.

14) Paul now states how he withstood Peter to his face. **But when I saw that they did not walk uprightly with regard to the truth of the gospel I said to Cephas in the presence of all: If thou who art a Jew livest Gentile-like and not Jew-like, how compellest thou the Gentiles to eat Jew-like?**

Paul did not act hastily; he waited until he saw things clearly. He had just stated when this moment came, namely when even Barnabas was carried away with the hypocrisy. Then it was, indeed, plain "that they are not walking uprightly." The Greek does not change the present tense of the direct discourse to the past as we do after a main verb in the past. The verb is derived from ὀρθόπους, one with straight feet, who is able to stand and to walk accordingly. Πρός, face-to-face with the truth of the gospel, has the idea of comparison and of a reciprocity in this regard: their conduct did not match the truth of the gospel, nor did that truth match their conduct. The two were out of line, badly so. "The truth" of the gospel is its substance, the divine reality it embodies. This is one grand unit. Peter was in conflict with that truth and was putting others into danger.

Then Paul acted and did so effectively. He rebuked Peter, the one who was chiefly guilty, "in the presence of all." Should he not have gone to Peter privately? We have found that men who have committed some grave error are very particular not to have those who rebuke them commit the least error in the place and in the manner of the rebuke otherwise they become the guilty ones and the errorists persecuted martyrs. Well, Paul gave Peter a public rebuke, public not as a deserved punishment for him but so that all might hear it for their own good. Even Pelagius says: *Publicum scandalum non poterat privatim curari*. Augustine, otherwise his opponent, agrees: *Non enim utile erat errorem, qui palam noceret, in secreto emendare*. A public wrong is not to be corrected in private. We certainly do not hang our dirty linen in the front yard. It was Peter who sinned as a public man in a public way; *he* forced the public rebuke from Paul, *he* made it necessary that all should hear.

Paul puts his rebuke into the form of a question. He throws the onus of the answer on Peter himself. No legitimate answer can be given save one by which Peter condemns himself. Peter stood as having been condemned (v. 11), not by Paul and by what Paul now says, but by the Jerusalem conference in which Peter had taken a leading part. Paul merely asks Peter whether that is not the fact. The moment he asked this, Peter saw it, had to see it, and all the rest who were present likewise saw it.

It was masterly in every respect to use the question. But the point of importance in this epistle is the fact that Peter deflected from the gospel truth and not Paul. This the Galatians are to see. The Judaizers of Galatia tried to play Peter against Paul; such a procedure was farcical in view of what happened at Antioch. All Judaistic falsehoods which tried to use Peter as a shield are exposed by the episode at Antioch as they are already by what Peter did in conjunction with James and John at the Jerusalem conference (v. 9, 10). Here perishes the Catholic contention that Peter was the first pope, on which much more may be said.

Peter was a Jew by birth but had lived in Gentile fashion when, on first coming to Antioch, he had steadily eaten with the Gentile Christians. The present tense, "livest Gentile-like and not Jewish-like," describes Peter's conduct without reference to time. It was not the first time Peter had done this; he had done it years before this at Caesarea after that special revelation at Joppa when he remained at the house of the Gentile Cornelius. How often Peter had repeated this we do not know; he must have done so on a number of other occasions.

In the apodosis, which is put into the form of a question, the deduction to be drawn from the "if" clause at once advances to the ultimate deduction. Paul does not stop and ask, "How, then, canst thou now so significantly separate thyself from the Gentile Christians?" He leaps to the conclusion which this wrong conduct involves for all Gentile Christians: "How compellest thou the Gentiles to act Jew-like?" for that was what Peter was really doing.

Peter may not at this time have realized that his action involved so much; but it is undeniable when Paul now points this out to him. It often happens so: the judgment is beclouded in erring conduct. The decisive things which should be seen at once to make us recoil from such conduct are not seen or are placed into a false light. Then, too, many refuse to see when the true light is brought to bear upon them. Paul was right in speaking out publicly. If Peter did not now see, many, if not all the rest, would see. All the Gentile Christians who beheld Peter's marked withdrawal, which was followed by that of the other Jewish Christians at Antioch, including even their pastor Barnabas, could not help but conclude that they, too, in order to be Christians in the full sense of the word, should henceforth, like Peter, stop living Gentile-like and live Jew-like. "Art compelling" refers to silent, moral compulsion which was, however, effective.

The wrong which Peter perpetrated was not that he at one time lived Gentile-like and at another time Jew-like. That was a matter of liberty. The revelation which he had received at Joppa did not imply that he was henceforth to live only Gentile-like. Paul became a Jew to the Jews, but note, only in order that he might gain the Jews, gain them for this truth of the gospel and its liberty (I Cor. 9:20); he also did the same and for the same purpose with regard to the Gentiles. What the revelation granted him at Joppa made a wrong for Peter was any conduct that cast reflection on Gentile-like living. Of that conduct Peter had made himself guilty here at Antioch. "Those from James" were not guilty, nor does Paul in the least imply this. They exercised their liberty by eating kosher and thereby cast no reflection on Gentile Christians for eating otherwise.

15) Is the section, v. 15-21, the continuation of the rebuke administered at Antioch or some reflections on that incident which Paul now adds as he writes about it? In support of the latter view we are told that σύ or ἡμεῖς do not occur in these verses. But the very first word is a plain "we" which is followed by an emphatic ἐγώ. The absence of a connective is to be expected. Paul paused after stating his question, and when Peter offered no answer as he, indeed, could not, Paul continued to speak.

The assertion that "stood condemned" in v. 11 requires no more than the pointed question of v. 14, is not convincing; all ordinary readers expect more, for Paul surely did say more. The fact that Paul reproduces at length what he said to Peter is certainly exceptional; but this entire incident is exceptional, in fact, this whole part of the epistle is so, for it is entirely historical. Just because it is historical, an extended discourse may be reproduced in it; histories abound in such discourses.

At Antioch, Paul stated the doctrinal principles on which his rebuke rested. Peter needed reminding, but so did all others. These principles were the main factor, "the truth of the gospel." The fact that Paul did not interrogate Peter beyond that first painful question shows his consideration and his tact; yet in a fine way he includes Peter in ἡμεῖς, and when he uses ἐγώ he does it so as to voice what must be the conviction also of Peter and of every Jewish Christian.

Paul's reproduction of just what he said at Antioch is admirably suited to the Galatians; this is just what they want to hear. Paul could not tell them anything that would be more necessary, for what Paul said to Peter contains the very gospel that both he and Peter preached, for which Paul was assailed among the Galatians. Finally, the reproduction of the address delivered at Antioch is a perfect transition to the next part of the letter, which is entirely doctrinal.

First a solemn and a complete statement to which every truly believing Jew assents. **We, by nature Jews and not sinners from the Gentiles, yet having come to know that a man is not declared righteous in consequence of work of law but only by means of faith in Jesus Christ, even we came to believe in Christ Jesus in order that we might get to be declared righteous in consequence of faith in Christ and not in consequence of works of law; because no flesh will be declared righteous in consequence of works of law.**

We do not divide this sentence by supplying "are" with the first "we" and letting the second "we" begin a new sentence. The second "we" emphatically takes up the first one: "we — even we."

"We on our part, by nature Jews," characterizes Paul, Peter, and the other Jewish Christians according to their nationality. The apposition makes them "by nature Jews" (R. 532 dative of means) who were born so, trained so. Paul adds the contrast: "and not sinners from the Gentiles." He uses the expression that was current among Jews who denominated all Gentiles ἁμαρτωλοί, "open, plain sinners." The idea contained in this expression was the thought that the Jews strove after righteousness, something that did not occur to Gentiles. The Jews had their νόμος or law and labored to produce "works of law" in order thereby to become righteous; the Gentiles were ἄνομοι, devoid of this law. Paul is simply using Jewish language. He is not calling Jews saints and Gentiles sinners; he is not saying Jews are righteous, Gentiles not. Who is righteous before God he says in the next breath. All he says is that we native Jews are not like the common run of Gentiles who are called "sinners" by Jews because they are not Jews.

16) Δέ marks a contrast and singles out one class of native Jews, the believing, Christian Jews who "came to know that a man is not declared righteous ἐξ ἔργων νόμου, in consequence (as a result) of works of law but only by means of faith in Jesus Christ." The participle is the ingressive aorist: they got to the point where they knew this. The gospel brought them to this point. Jews though they were who throughout their entire lives banked on the Mosaic law and on works of law as the source (ἐκ) from which to obtain true righteousness before God, they finally discovered their terrible mistake, namely, "that a man is never pronounced righteous (by God) as a result of works of law," no matter how many of such works he may muster; they discovered that a man is not declared righteous thus "but only by means of faith in Jesus Christ." In a succinct statement Paul formulates the old Jewish error which was so fatal to his nation and the simple gospel truth. "A man" is universal: be he Jew or Gentile, it is the German *man*. The Greek keeps the negative with the verb, a construction which we can imitate in English although our common idiom is: "no man (*niemand*) is justified."

Here would be the place for a full discussion of δικαιοῦν and its cognates, which, however, would require many pages. We must refer the student to the best and the richest source: C.-K. 296 (δίκαιος), 311 (δικαιοσύνη), 317 (δικαιόω). See the author on Rom. 1:17. We content ourselves with a summary.

The passive δικαιοῦται has God as the agent. The verb, the noun, and the adjective are always forensic; so are the opposites; so are the synonyms, in Hebrew, in Greek, in the Old Testament, in the Apocrypha, in the New Testament. The sense is, "to *declare* righteous" and never, "to *make* righteous." This is the sense in even secular statements. Always a judge is involved who pronounces a verdict. When the judge is God, the verdict establishes a relation to God and to his judgment, to his δίκη or norm of right. A δίκαιος is "righteous" because God so declares in his judicial verdict. Δικαιοσύνη is the quality of "righteousness" possessed by him whom the heavenly Judge pronounces righteous. The passive is to be understood in the same sense: "to be pronounced righteous," and is never converted into the middle "to become righteous." True, some passive forms found in the Koine are to be understood in a middle sense; a few German commentators translate the passive *gerecht werden* and quote Luther in support of their translation. When certain modern interpreters translate δικαιοσύνη "uprightness" or "goodness," or employ a term that denotes a virtue to be found in us and not a forensic relation established by God as the Judge in a verdict pronounced by him, they depart from the Scriptural use of this term and eliminate the central doctrine of Scripture.

Ἐκ pictures God's verdict as arising out of works of law so that these would call forth the verdict in the court of God. In "works of law" neither noun has the article, which makes the quality of each stand out; the two are a practical compound, *Gesetzeswerke*. Paul is speaking of Jews, hence he has in mind the law of Moses and the corresponding works. Yet "works of law" is general, any law and any works of any law are included as being completely barren in eliciting a declaration of righteousness from God. The Jews of whom Paul speaks, "we," including himself, have discovered this fact, hence no argument is necessary, and none is appended.

Ἐὰν μή is elliptical and is really a case of brachylogy (R. 1204) because it follows a negation. It states how alone a man is justified. The sense is offered by the translation of the American Committee of the R. V.: "but (or: but only) by faith." The genitive is objective: "by faith in Jesus Christ." Διά denotes the subjective means. Πίστις is a correlative term that involves the object on which faith or trust rests, which is here "Jesus Christ," his person as the Savior together with his office and his redemptive work.

It should not be necessary to say that "faith in Jesus Christ" is wrought entirely by him who kindles this confidence by coming in contact with us through the gospel. The only means by which we may obtain the divine verdict in our favor is faith, *fiducia*, in Jesus Christ. He who comes before the judgment seat of God with Jesus Christ is instantly pronounced righteous. "We," Paul says, "have come to know this." Hence he adds no more.

What Paul has stated as a truth that he and the others came to realize he now restates in other words; in fact, he states the negative side two additional times: "not in consequence of works of law — not in consequence of works of law," driving this fact in deeply. "Even we" emphasizes the thought that we Jews, we who once thought we had righteousness by works of law, became exactly like the sinners from the Gentiles who never knew anything about such works of law. "Even we," just as they, "came to believe in Christ Jesus in order that we might be declared righteous in consequence of faith in Christ Jesus and not in consequence of works of law."

"Came or got to believe" is the ingressive aorist and marks the first instant of faith; we may say the same regarding the aorist passive: "might get to be declared righteous." In the former instance Paul used "faith" but now he uses the verb "we believed." He turns his expressions over and over in order to make them register the more. "Once," Paul says, "our trust rested in our own works of law, now all our trust has come to be utterly removed from all such works and rests only in Christ Jesus. Such Jews are we now."

He even changes the phrase διὰ πίστεως to ἐκ πίστεως and thus makes it the exact opposite of the repeated phrase ἐξ ἔργων νόμου. See the exposition in Rom. 1:17. "Faith" is both means and source of justification. The latter should not be more startling than the former unless we still have a synergistic conception of faith. It is ever the contents of faith that justifies and saves, and never faith apart from its contents. It is the Christ in the faith and not the faith devoid of Christ. All the believing in the world secures nothing but damnation from the Judge, but the tiniest believing in Christ secures acquittal on the instant. The Scriptures attribute everything to faith because they know only a faith that is filled with Christ, only a faith that is wrought by Christ. Now Paul writes "Christ Jesus," office and person, the sense is the same.

So faith in Christ Jesus is the opposite of all works of law; they exclude each other: to be justified "as the result of faith" = to be justified *not* "as a result of works of law." The two will not mingle. He who would put one foot on faith and the other on such works plunges into the gulf. Make Christ the bridge, all save the last inch, use works of law for that, and the bridge crashes the moment you step upon it.

Enough has been said, and yet Paul repeats once more as though enough cannot be said. Διότι = *denn*

(B.-P. 310): "because (this fact stands forever) no flesh will be declared righteous in consequence of works of law." This negative is so important because of Peter's dangerous action. For the third time "works of law" are excluded; for the third time we have the verb "to declare righteous." In all three instances the passive is used with God as the agent. The road to righteousness by way of works is triply barred.

The future "shall not be declared righteous" means that no case of this kind will ever occur although blind fools refuse to be convinced and try again and again. Instead of the previously used ἄνθρωπος we now have πᾶσα σάρξ, which has the same sense but is more emphatic and emphasizes man's frailty; we may translate "every mortal." The Greek idiom construes the negative with the verb: "every flesh shall not be justified"; we negative the subject: "no flesh, no mortal shall be justified." The negation in οὐ — πᾶς is absolute (R. 752). Is Paul quoting Ps. 143:2: "In thy sight shall no man living be justified"? He has no formula of quotation, and the words are not identical. It is enough to assume an allusion just as we also often use expressions that are more or less Scriptural.

We are perfectly satisfied to let Paul write: "Having gotten to know — we got to believe — in order that we might be justified." That succession and that order are correct. In the case of adults it is always thus. We gain nothing by philosophizing, by letting Paul look back over his past life and by asking how and why he came to faith; for even then he is telling us his exact experience: knowledge — faith — purpose of the faith. No adult arrives at faith except through knowledge of the very fact here emphasized by Paul. And no adult believes except for the one purpose that he may be justified. To say that Paul speaks so but does not mean so is to employ dangerous language. True knowledge merges into faith, and faith's vital intent is justification.

17) In v. 15, 16 Paul states what we Jews discovered about works of law and about Christ; what we did, we left the works of law and believed in Christ. Why? So as to be justified, since no mortal can possibly be justified by works of law. Now there follows a thrust at Peter's action and at that of Barnabas and the other Jews who followed their lead: If after all this we only dropped to the level of sinners like the Gentiles and now still have to go back to works of law, must we not then say this blasphemous thing that Christ has ministered nothing but sin to us? Do not Peter and the rest see that their present action necessitates this conclusion?

But if by (our) **seeking to be declared righteous in connection** (only) **with Christ also we on our part came to be found** (nothing but) **sinners** (after all), **is Christ a minister of sin? Perish the thought!**

The condition of reality argues the matter as though it were a fact although, of course, it is not. To put it thus makes the point clearer and stronger. The participle "seeking to be declared righteous in connection with Christ" repeats the preceding purpose clause: our believing "in order that we may be declared righteous in consequence of faith in Christ and not in consequence of works of law." That was our purpose, that was what we were seeking. Paul has said that we were sure we should be righteous in that way by simply believing, by giving up all work of law.

But if, after all, we were mistaken, if our purpose was not attained, if our seeking did not bring us what we sought, if our connection with Christ (ἐν, by faith) did not get us declared righteous by God, if despite this our seeking "we were also ourselves found (nothing but) sinners," we who once were Jews but had given up Jewish works of law and thus sank to the level of "the sinners from the Gentiles": — what good, then, is Christ to us? "Is he (only) a minister of sin?" Is that all he amounts to? The very idea is blasphemous. "Perish the thought!" But this conclusion that Christ *is* only a minister of sin automatically follows if the action of Peter and of these other Jewish Christians is right, their action of separating themselves from the Gentile Christians who do not eat kosher and of eating only with those Jewish Christians who do. Then kosher eating and, of course, other Jewish observances have to be added in order that we may escape being such "sinners," in order to be declared truly righteous by God. What a reflection on Christ! See what it makes of him! And we Jews believed that faith in him would get us the declaration of righteousness from God!

Most of the manuscript have the reading ἆρα, the interrogative particle; some have the reading ἄρα, "then" which marks a natural conclusion. The thought is the same; the question is more dramatic. The genitive in "a minister of sin" is objective. It does not imply that Christ ministers to sin as his master (διακονεῖν τινί) but that he produces sin (διακονεῖν τι) with his ministry. The thought is that he makes us do nothing but drop law and works of law so that we are "sinners" who are on the same level with the Gentile sinners who are called ἁμαρτωλοί by all Jews. We must construe together "sinners from the Gentiles" (v. 15) — "ourselves also sinners" ("also" like the Gentiles) — "of sin."

Paul's question is directed straight at Peter and those whom he was misleading, at what their action involved: that faith in Christ would not give them the righteousness they sought, would only make them the same as Gentile sinners, would turn Christ into a minister of sin. Here we have another instance in which Paul's thought does not halt halfway but advances to the end, to Christ, to what Peter's action makes of Christ.

We are told that this interpretation is wrong. From v. 15 onward Paul is writing in general terms; these verses do not contain what he said to Peter and to the rest at Antioch; if Paul is addressing anybody, the Judaizers are referred to. But Paul never stoops to argue with the Judaizers, he denounces them. That all of this belongs to Paul's address at Antioch we have shown in v. 15. More serious is the assumption that Paul is speaking of what Jesus makes of every Jew *before* his justification, namely that he reduces all Jews to sinners like the rest of mankind. But then Paul ought to exclaim: "Thank God!" not: "Perish the thought!" If this makes Jesus "a minister of sin" in this general sense of revealing all men and thus also all Jews as sinners, Paul could not be shocked at the thought, in fact, he could not use the expression: "Perish the thought!"

In addition to this, by making Jews sinners in the general sense of the term sinners Jesus would bring them to salvation; for God justifies every contrite and believing sinner. No, no; Paul here speaks of believing Jews. If *after* believing in Christ they are found sinners, not merely sinning daily as Christians still commit sins that must be pardoned daily by God, but "sinners" as the Jews called all Gentiles "sinners" because they had no works of law: then, indeed, the awful conclusion follows that Christ is a minister of sin, that he reduces law-abiding Jews to the low level on which the Jews placed all Gentiles.

This question of Paul's rests on Peter's action in turning from all the Gentile Christians to live in Jewish fashion. If that is necessary, then all believing Jews are not justified, are only Gentile "sinners" until they do what Peter now did; and Christ would be nothing but "a minister of sin" who aided sin — frightful thought. In μὴ γένοιτο we have the optative of wish, one of the few optatives left in the Koine: "May it not be!" in our idiom: "God forbid!" or "Perish the thought!"

18) Paul explains with γάρ by stating the matter in a different way. Peter's action would make all believing Jews nothing but Gentile sinners and Christ a minister of sin. But see what it would make of every apostle if Peter's action is right, if every apostle should do likewise.

For if these very things which I tore down I start building again I prove mine own self a transgressor. For I on my part by means of law died to law in order that I might become alive to God.

"I" is unemphatic, being found only in the verb suffix; no contrast with another person or persons is intended. Paul uses the first person to soften the rebuke to Peter; hence he also uses the conditional form. The singular "I," it seems, refers especially to an apostle, for his was the special work of tearing down and of building up. The condition is again one of assumed reality even as Peter was actually doing what is here stated. What is said fits Peter so accurately that Paul must be writing what he said at Antioch.

When Peter ate regularly with the Gentile Christians in Antioch he certainly tore down works of law, the conception that any Christian needed anything whatever besides faith in Christ for his justification by God; he held true to what v. 15, 16 say of all Jewish Christians when they came to faith. But when Peter turned back, separated himself so markedly from all Gentile Christians, and began to live strictly Jew-like (v. 14), he started to build up again (inchoative present tense) the identical things he had torn down.

Actions speak louder than words. They spoke to the entire congregation at Antioch. Peter contradicted all that he had heretofore taught and done. He acted as though he had undergone a second conversion. His action proclaimed that some Jewish ceremonial works were after all necessary — of course, also for Gentile Christians (v. 14b). Paul loves the figure of building and uses it aptly here.

Συνίστημι (some texts read συνιστάνω) = *ich stelle dar*, yet not in order to reveal what one really is or has in mind but to present and thus to prove and to establish what is otherwise doubtful or hidden. "I prove mine own self a transgressor," i. e., of the law, means a guilty transgressor in all my previous action of tearing down. My present building it up again is proof positive of my past transgression. I should never have torn down, should never have relied on faith alone. Although Paul softens the rebuke by predicating it of himself, he nevertheless aimes it squarely at Peter. And Peter understood. If Peter now continued the course of conduct he had entered upon, he would be a Judaizer. If he was afraid of the Judaizers (to be afraid of whom was foolish), Paul here points him to something of which to be afraid. "So," Paul says, "thou now standest forth as having been a miserable transgressor of the law during all these past years and art now just coming out of thy long transgression! So this is the kind of apostolic builder thou art!"

19) With the emphatic ἐγώ Paul now refers to himself. He for his part had not become a transgressor of the law in the sense in which Peter was now proving himself one. "For" adds as an explanation how he had used the law in order to be forever done with the law. The reference is to the three phrases used in v. 16: "not in consequence of works of law." Paul states what he does with regard to him-

self, but every true Jewish Christian will second this as being equally true of himself. "I on my part by means of law died to law." This is purposely paradoxical: "by means of law to law I died." The thought is at the same time concentrated. Paul used law in order to be forever rid of law. Peter is not done with law, he has started to go back to it as though he had been a bad transgressor because he ever left it. Paul writes "law" without the article; R. 796 thinks that this refers to the Mosaic law. Anarthrous νόμος includes everything that is "law," Mosaic or otherwise.

The right, the first and foremost use of law is to use it so as never to respond to it again, so as to die to it. Let law bring you to the realization of sin (Rom. 3:20), to despair that any and all work of law can ever do even the least toward securing God's verdict of righteousness. Let law make you a sinner indeed and not merely in the sense of the self-righteous Jews who called Gentiles "sinners." Let law make you give up all hope in law and by faith place all your hope in Christ Jesus. The moment you do that you are rid of law forever unless you blindly return to it as Peter was doing. You are dead to law. You are like a corpse, at which law can thunder with all its might and get in response not even the stirring of a finger or the flicker of an eyelash. Why? Because you have found the righteousness of faith. Believing in Christ, you are justified, "justified from all things from which you could not be justified (even) by the law of Moses" (Acts 13:39). There is no verdict of condemnation against those in Christ Jesus (Rom. 8:1). The servitude "under law" is ended. No master is able to give orders to a dead slave.

Of course, this is only the negative side which is never without the positive. Paul utters both in one breath: "Died to law in order to become alive to God."

His statement is again a paradox but gloriously true. This death makes alive. But note that the subjunctive is an aorist, punctiliar, to designate the moment in which the life enters. It is the moment of God's acquittal, and that is the moment of faith, and that faith is life, spiritual life. Once kindled, that life goes on unless, like Peter, we again endanger it. "Alive to God" means in Christ Jesus, responsive to all God's grace, children, sons in his household, etc.

20) Paul adds only the main part of it. Verse 20 is an expanded and elucidative parallel to v.19. **With Christ have I been crucified; and there is living no longer I, but there lives in me Christ. Moreover, what I am now living in flesh, in faith I am living, the** (faith) **in the Son of God who did love me and did give himself up in my stead.** In this way Paul died to law to become alive to God.

The first two sentences are phrased in mystical language, especially the first: "With Christ have I been crucified." Symbolical language is something different. What occurred in a physical way in the case of Christ, Paul predicates of himself in whom it occurred in a spiritual way. We have no figure, no symbol, no verbal beauty, but concentrated facts.

Paul says more than that Christ was crucified for him, and that Christ's crucifixion is regarded as though Paul himself had been crucified, or even as if all the benefits of Christ's crucifixion were personally made Paul's own. The spiritual effect produced in Paul is at once included: "crucified together with." The interval of time is disregarded. Yet this difference remains: Christ's crucifixion was sacrificial, vicarious; Paul's crucifixion spiritual only, escape from law and sin and from the dominion of both. This concentrated predication rests only on the verity of this difference. Of course, the next step follows, the joint life. See Rom. 6:4 and the following mystical statements: entombed with, died with, living in. Note the force of the perfect tense "I have been crucified": having been once crucified, Paul remains so, the effect is permanent.

This state of crucifixion is the state of death Paul entered when he died to law. Only by being crucified with Christ does one die to law. It is the one avenue of escape. Otherwise law has us by the throat and will destroy us. Σύν in the verb denotes faith, for it alone joins us to Christ crucified to be crucified "with" him.

Paul might have continued to use the same completely mystical language: "and with him have I been raised up." He uses modified mystical expressions: "and there is living no longer I, but there lives in me Christ." The first δέ is not adversative (our versions: "yet"), for this living is the normal effect of being crucified with Christ and not its opposite. The verbs are placed first, subjects last, both are emphasized. "And there lives no longer I"; Rom. 6:6: "our old man was crucified with him." Paul was dead, his old personality was in the bonds of sin, vainly striving for righteousness by means of works of law.

It was the same Paul and yet not the same, the same being, yet one that was utterly changed. "No longer I" is true. Elsewhere the change is called the new birth, regeneration; here Paul says: "there lives in me Christ." Christ, the Life, lives in Paul. By faith Christ fills Paul's heart, soul, being. That means, first of all, Christ as Paul's righteousness. His expiation on the cross became Paul's own when he was crucified with Christ, and this expiation gave him God's verdict of acquittal. Thus Christ lived in him. Secondly, Christ lives in him so that his mind and will ever respond to Christ in thought, word, and deed. The former is justification, this latter is sanctification, the two are never separated just as life and its manifestations always occur together and are inseparable.

"No longer I, but Christ in me," is correct. "In me" is mystical. Hence he adds the further (δέ) entirely literal statement: "Moreover, what I am now living in flesh, in faith I am living," etc. Paul is speaking of his life in the body since he was first crucified with Christ. The neuter "what I am living" is the whole of this life as it manifests itself day by day. The Greek needs no article with phrases such as "in flesh." "Flesh" is used much as it was in v. 16, to denote our frail, mortal nature and earthly form of existence; here the word is not to be understood in the ethical sense. Paul's whole present life is "in faith," in this blessed sphere of trust. He thinks and acts as faith ever guides and controls him. At one time this was the case; at one time he was dominated by law and works of law, his whole life was vain and empty.

The article adds the object of faith attributively: "the (faith) in the Son of God," etc., the genitive being objective as in v. 16. The emphasis is first placed on the phrase "in faith" and secondly on "the Son of God," etc. Here the wonderfulness of justifying faith becomes evident. This lies entirely in its object. We have had this named as "Jesus Christ" — "Christ Jesus" — and then "Christ." Now his deity is added: "the Son of God." Again and again Paul calls Jesus "the Son of God."

Two participles are added with one article, thus indicating that the two acts belong closely together. The whole is thus a unit designation: who he really is and what he did. It was the Son of God, he that loved me and gave himself up in my stead. The all-sufficiency of his loving expiation is assured by the deity of his person. Both participles are aorists. The great, supreme act of his love is referred to when he gave himself over into death. Compare 1:4: "he who gave himself for our sins," etc. The motive and the deed are combined.

Ἀγαπᾶν denotes the love of intelligence and comprehension coupled with corresponding purpose, the love with which God loved the world, John 3:16. This love sees the sinner in his doom and resolves to deliver him. It passes all human understanding. It moved God's own Son to give himself up for us on the cross. This God's Son did after he had become incarnate in our human nature. Here he is named according to his deity alone, and yet his dying on the cross is predicated of him, an act that became possible only by means of his human nature. The Scriptures often speak thus. Without Matt. 1 and Luke 1 and 2 all these and other statements become incomprehensible. Yet some think that if Matt. 1 and Luke 1 and 2 can be discredited, the incarnation would be removed. It is woven clear through the New Testament and appears even in the Old. Remove those chapters from Matthew and from Luke, and we should have to supply their main substance from the rest of Scripture. Παραδίδωμι is the verb that is regularly used to designate this act of the Son's self-sacrifice.

Here we have one of the numerous cases in which ὑπέρ plainly denotes substitution: "instead of me." Translate, if you wish, "for me," "in my behalf," these phrases convey and must convey vicariousness, substitution. Linguistically this is settled by R. 632 and his *The Minister and his Greek New Testament* with its chapter on this preposition. In many connections an act cannot be *for me* or *for my benefit* unless it is so by being done *in my stead*. The statement that this latter thought must be expressed by ἀντί is unwarranted; in fact, the Greek prefers ὑπέρ although it may use either. Those who deny Christ's substitutionary act do so in the face of ὑπέρ.

When Paul writes: who loved "me" and gave himself up "in my stead" he voices his own faith which appropriates to him personally this love and sacrifice. This is the very function of your faith and of mine. He loved *me*, he gave himself instead of *me*! This faith is forever done with the intolerable and hopeless burden of works of law; it rejoices in the certainty of justification and righteousness which is assured to it through Christ's loving self-sacrifice.

21) The closing statement clinches all that precedes. **Not nullifying am I the grace of God. For if by means of law** (there is) **righteousness, then did Christ die for nothing.**

Who is nullifying the grace of God, setting it aside, that grace which gave us the Son to die for us so that by faith in him we might be declared righteous? Who? Not Paul! We know who: Peter and those who were following his lead were beginning to make God's grace void. Paul is not answering a charge made against himself; nobody in Antioch is charging anything against him. Paul is washing his hands of what Peter is doing. The stress is not on "I," for which we have only the verbal ending, but on this nullifying: *none* of it for Paul.

The reason is mighty, indeed. If by means of any law whatever the quality of righteousness could in any way be obtained in a divine pronouncement and verdict, then (inferential ἄρα) Christ died for nothing, his death and sacrifice were unnecessary. Since the grace of God climaxes in the sacrificial death of his Son, if his death were for nothing, this grace would be abolished with a vengeance. That is what Peter was starting. That is what the Judaizers had finished. Either God's grace is all, or it is nothing. Either

Christ's death is all, or it is for nothing. If the verdict that one is righteous is gained by means of law, then law and works of law are the means and not Christ and his death. Paul states this thought in the negative. We may add the positive: Christ did die. It is impossible to believe that God's Son should die for nothing. He died because no law could gain God's acquitting verdict. God's grace is forever established by Christ's death. Amen and Amen!

Paul says nothing about the effect produced by his action in opposing Peter face to face. He does not need to. Peter dropped his wrong course. His mistake was one of the moment, one of conduct and not one of principle. If Peter had rebelled, Paul would be compelled to say so. Paul is not lowering Peter's standing in the eyes of the Galatians. But he *is* proving that he has the old, genuine gospel, proving it by showing that he had at one time to maintain it even against the Peter whom the Judaizers tried to make their patron. Now Judaizers, men who on principle nullified grace and Christ's death, were trying to sweep the Galatians away to join in this nullification. Peter swiftly recovered from the first step in his wrong course. The Galatians would surely do the same.

CHAPTER III

PART II

The Gospel of Christian Liberty Unfolded Anew for the Galatians, 3:1-5:12

Paul has brought the Galatians the true gospel which was given to him by revelation, acknowledged by the Jerusalem conference, attested in correcting Peter himself. This precious gospel Paul now unfolds anew for the Galatians in such a way as to destroy the Judaistic error that was creeping in among them. The body of this letter consists of doctrinal exposition which is shot through with dramatic application to the Galatians. It covers 3:1-5:12; some stop at the end of chapter 4. There are three circles of thought in this main body of the epistle.

In the first place, like Abraham, the Galatians were declared righteous by faith and not by law, 3:1-14.

In the second place, this becomes very clear when the relation of faith and law is understood, 3:15-4:7.

In the third place, the Galatians are earnestly admonished not to return to law, 4:8-5:12.

---

1. *Like Abraham, the Galatians Were Justified by Faith and not by Law, 3:1-14.*

O foolish Galatians, ask yourselves a few things!

Expression and thought show that a new section begins at this point. Paul pours out a flood of questions upon the Galatians, questions they should have asked, should now ask, the answers to which would certainly help to open their eyes.

First, the question of shocked surprise. **O thoughtless Galatians, who bewitched you, you for whom, plain to the eye, Jesus Christ was publicly placarded as having been crucified?**

The address fits the question; "brethren" would not do so. Paul's feeling is the same as that which is in evidence in 1:6. It is almost unbelievable that, having Christ crucified before their eyes, the Galatians should start to Judaize. The Greek is sparing in its use of "O" with vocatives, which makes it more effective when it is used. Paul says "Galatians" much as he uses "Galatia" in 1:2. It is a general term that is taken from the Roman province and includes all the members of the churches of whatever nationality they may be, Phrygians, Lycaonians, Roman colonists, or Jews. This word was a convenient term when only these people as such were addressed. Paul calls them ἀνόητοι, "thoughtless" or "foolish" people who were not using their νοῦς or mind, who were not stopping to think. The relative clause states of what they should at once have thought, namely of Christ crucified. Where were their minds?

"Thoughtless" cannot be understood as a reference to a national characteristic of the Celts as though these Galatians were for the greater part Celtic. A few ancients describe the Celts as being fickle and easily moved. If these Galatians were predominantly Celts, and if Paul intended to score them for their national failing, he should have written: "O thoughtless or fickle or unstable Celts!" While "Galatians" is derived from Κέλτοι, Galatia and Galatians designate the Roman province and any or all of its inhabitants irrespective of their extraction. All these Christians in Galatia were acting thoughtlessly, phenomenally so.

The church has known such waves of thoughtlessness in its history from time to time. People are just swept along. Those who do think are cried down and ignored. People seem to have a spell cast over them. "Who bewitched you?" uses this figure. The question is rhetorical, exclamatory, and asks for no answer. It is like our: "What has gotten into you?" The verb is to be taken in the general sense although some think of the evil eye; the idea of envy does not apply here (R. 473). The point to be noted is that when well-instructed Christians go wrong, they act unreasonably. They need a severe jolt to start them thinking sanely again. Paul supplies the jolt and even the right thoughts to which the Galatians must return.

This does not imply that Paul "believed in witchcraft," i. e., that it produces supernatural effects. The Bible condemns witchcraft; every form of it is devilish, and all its forms run back to paganism in their roots. The devilishness lies in the deception; the devil deceives all who resort to witchcraft. No miraculous effects are produced by it. It is the delusion that such effects are and can be produced that keeps these occult arts alive. Churchmen have ignorantly, sometimes learnedly, held this view and have thus supported the practice of witchcraft. Those who do so today will challenge what is said here. Let them know that the writer does not speak hastily; he speaks after a long and thorough investigation of the entire subject.

The relative clause states that the Galatians should have been the last persons to allow themselves to be deceived. Textual authority is against the insertion of "not to obey the truth" and ἐν ὑμῖν. Sometimes the latter is still retained because of its difficulty, and because its insertion is hard to explain. The clause is sometimes divided: "before whose eyes Jesus Christ was? — He was painted among you," etc. Few will agree to do this. Difficult readings are not *eo ipso* correct, nor is inability to explain a variant a cause for its retention.

The relative οἷς is emphatic: "you for whom," etc. The κατά phrase is also emphatic, the sense of which is: "plain to the eye." It would fit the context well to translate: "was painted before your eyes"; but while the simplex is used with regard to depicting, the compound is never so used. It is common as a designation for posting placards (M.-M. 538), for instance, a father posts a proclamation that he will no longer be responsible for his son's debts. We need not think that Paul refers to writings which he had sent to the Galatians. The term is figurative for all Paul's public preaching in Galatia, Barnabas helping him. All of it was like public placards, plain to the eyes, announcing "Jesus Christ" and him "as having been crucified."

In I Cor. 2:2 Paul uses the expression: "Jesus Christ and him crucified" which has the same perfect passive participle. The tense points to the enduring effect of Christ's crucifixion. As for the Galatians, so for us to this day every gospel sermon placards Jesus Christ as the One crucified. Read Paul's placard in 2:20, where the word occurs, and in 2:21 where again, plain to the eye, he writes, "Christ died." In that one perfect participle which is here predicative the entire gospel is concentrated as abolishing all salvation by law or works of law. This participle destroys all Judaistic teaching; it does so today with regard to all the modern forms of this teaching.

This is the indictment against the Galatians: all this placarding was so plain to the eye, and yet they acted as though they could not see, had no sense to read, could not think what this meant. "Crucified — crucified — crucified!" — even a little thinking should suffice to turn the Galatians against all Judaizers. The entire Scriptures are so placarded, yet men even preach on them and see nothing in the cross except noble martyrdom. II Cor. 4:3, 4.

2) The first question is asked regarding the objective substance, Jesus Christ crucified; now Paul asks questions regarding the great subjective effects produced in the Galatians. He pours out question upon question. He wants no answer for himself, *he* needs none; the Galatians need them for themselves. It is high time they did a little plain Christian thinking.

This alone do I want to learn from you: Was it from works of law that you received the Spirit or from the hearing of faith?

"Think for a moment," Paul says, "look back at your own selves! I want to learn just one thing from you because it is decisive, must be decisive for you. You are all Christians, you all received the Spirit, when he entered your hearts you became Christians." On this there is no question; it is the basis of Paul's questioning. The question is: "*Whence* did you get the Spirit? From what source (ἐκ)? Was the source 'works of law' or was it 'hearing of faith'?" It requires practically no thinking on the part of a Christian to give the answer.

The majority of the Galatians had been Gentiles and thus ἄνομοι, people who paid no attention to law as a source of salvation. Paul's question does not imply that they at one time relied on works of law. Paul refers to his own preaching in company with Barnabas. They were not Judaizers, they brought no "works of law," they brought the very opposite, namely "hearing of faith." Through that the Galatians received the Spirit. So did the Jews among them who, while they were in their Judaism, had practiced works of law, but had failed utterly to receive the Spirit until Paul brought them to the hearing of faith. The gospel is true apart from our experience; yet all Christian experience corroborates its truth.

On the phrase "from works of law" see 2:16 where it is used three times. Some interpreters think that receiving the Spirit refers to the reception of charismata, wonderful charismatic gifts. They point to λαμβάνειν as the verb that is used in connection with such gifts and refer to Pentecost. But at Pentecost the 3,000 received no such charismata; the 3,000 did not speak with tongues. I Cor. 12:8-10 and Rom. 12:6, etc., list as "gifts" abilities that are devoid of miraculous powers, especially Romans 12. Thousands of Christians in Galatia and elsewhere possessed no miraculous charismata.

Paul addresses all the Galatian Christians; they had received the Spirit when they came to saving faith in the gospel. The reception here referred to occurs at the moment when the Spirit enters the heart by faith and regeneration henceforth to control heart and life. Paul's question is one that every Christian must answer to this day. Regarding the question of miracles in Galatia see v. 5. They should not be introduced at this point. But every Galatian knew that the Spirit had entered his heart with saving power.

"Works of law" and "hearing of faith" are exclusive opposites; neither tolerates the other. "Works" are such as *we* do, and they are many so that no man can know whether he has done enough of them. The opposite is ἀκοή, but not in the active sense, the *actus audiendi*, but as C.-K. 106, etc., shows, in the passive sense: "being made to hear" what *God* wants us to hear.

The genitives are also opposites: "of law" — "of faith," but both are possessive: "works which belong with law" — "a being made to hear which belongs to faith." Both expressions are practical compounds. Yet we question the view of C.-K. when he has ἀκοή = κήρυγμα but adds the exception that the former is also subjective: *Kunde vom Glauben* (objective genitive); R. V. margin has "message" about faith. Also when, despite the few times the word is used, ἀκοή is made a technical term. The genitives are alike. "Being made to hear" involves the thing God brings to our ears (Christ crucified, v. 1). This belongs to faith in the sense of being intended for us to believe. When God speaks and makes us hear he wants us to believe. As law calls for works, so our being made to hear calls for faith. Compare Rom. 1:16, 17; also Heb. 4:2.

God made the Galatians hear about Christ crucified so that they came to faith, and thus, thus alone, they received the Spirit and became the Christians they have been.

3) **So thoughtless are you? Having begun with spirit, are you now finishing up for yourselves with flesh?**

More surprising thoughtlessness. The double question is in reality one. There is nothing in v. 2 to which οὕτως can refer, it points forward. So foolish as to try to complete in a fleshly way what you began in a spiritual way? In v. 2 Paul refers to the beginning, to the time when the Galatians first received the Spirit, and asks from what source this came; now he refers to the ending the Galatians are proposing to make. One may begin well but end ill. The Galatians had, indeed, begun well (v. 2), but what about now ending altogether otherwise? That would be folly, indeed!

The two datives of means πνεύματι and σαρκί are paired opposites, hence the former cannot be the Holy Spirit (our versions). If he were referred to, the article would be necessary. Both datives lack the article, both stress the quality expressed: "with spirit," in a truly spiritual manner — "with flesh," in a fleshly manner. Note also the analogy of Scripture: the Holy

Spirit is never said to be the means which *we* use. Again, the Holy Spirit, this divine Person, is never and can never be paired with an opposite such as flesh.

Paul advances the thought from our reception of the Holy Spirit mentioned in v. 2 to the true spirit that animates our hearts and our lives, the spirit wrought in us by the Holy Spirit. The word "spirit" refers to "faith" mentioned in v. 2, and "flesh" to "works." The latter is not to be taken in the ethical sense: the sinful nature of man, but far more concretely: the outward deeds which belong to the bodily nature of man. For all works of law have to do with physical, bodily matters, circumcision, kosher eating, Sabbath resting, and all manner of ceremonial observances.

Pray, what are you Galatians thinking to start in one way and to conclude in the exactly opposite way, to start in the right and most blessed way and to end in the utterly wrong and ruinous way? This is not even sane thinking. But note that, while the participle is the aorist to indicate the beginning made, the main verb is the present tense, the concluding has not yet been completed, it has only begun. The damage can still be corrected; Paul is doing his utmost to prevent this present tense from becoming a fixed and final aorist.

Is the verb middle or passive? One might say passive because the Judaizers were working on the Galatians; but the middle is very good, for by listening to the Judaizers the Galatians were doing the concluding for themselves. If they actually ended wrongly they could not shift the blame. Ἐπιτελέω = to bring to an end, to finish or complete.

4) First we have a question as to how the Galatians began (v. 2), next a question as to how they propose to finish (v. 3), now a question as to what lies between. **So much, did you suffer it in vain?**

if, indeed, also (as I cannot believe) **in vain!** Again the question and its appendix are exclamatory. "So much" is placed emphatically forward and marks either greatness or quantity. Those who think that these were northern Galatians assume that they, too, suffered persecution; but regarding the southern Galatian churches we know what Paul suffered when he and Barnabas founded them (Acts 13:50, etc.; 14:2, 5, 19, 22: II Tim. 3:11). Acts 14:2 states that "the brethren" were involved. They would naturally be so in every instance. We cannot say positively whether the Galatians were made to suffer more later on; yet we know that in Acts 14:22 Paul tells them they must expect as much.

Do they now intend to say that all of that suffering was in vain, a great mistake, all to no purpose? But he himself adds that he can scarcely believe that they now think so. Εἰ is strengthened by γε: "if, indeed"; but καί is not to be construed with εἰ because γε intervenes, nor is it to be construed with the adverb "in vain." The thought is not that this is something bad enough, namely "in vain," beyond which lies something worse, namely actually falling from the faith. Such an idea is remote from those sufferings. At times Paul uses καί to intimate a contrary supposition that is in his own mind, here one that is indicated by the "if" clause itself: *wenn denn doch wirklich vergeblich*, which is something Paul cannot bring himself to believe. "If, indeed, in vain" already expresses the doubt about its all being in vain, and καί increases this: Paul will not even think of it until he must. He will think only that the Galatians will answer: "No, no; it was and is not in vain!"

5) The sufferings were terrible experiences; beside them Paul places the most glorious works. He introduces the new question with οὖν and rests it on the preceding ones, especially on v. 2, since he repeats

some of the terms there used. **He, accordingly, who furnishes you the Spirit and works works of power among you,** (does he do it) **from works of law or from the hearing of faith?**

Instead of using verbs in the sentence: "Does God furnish and work," etc., Paul substitutes participial descriptions of God and thus elides the verbs and makes the question far more effective. Both present participles are qualitative in the durative sense. They refer to any and every furnishing and giving, whether it occurred at the time when the Galatians were converted or since then. Little is gained by saying that these are imperfect participles, i. e., the present doing duty for the imperfect since it has no participles of its own. We may translate: the Furnisher — the Worker and reproduce the exact sense.

It is Paul's habit to round out and to amplify what he begins. He does this here: first, by adding to the idea of receiving the Spirit on the part of the Galatians (v. 2) the correlative idea of bestowing or furnishing the Spirit on the part of God; secondly, by adding to the first essential reception (v. 2) of the Spirit (v. 2), by which spiritual life was kindled in the Galatians, the further idea of working mighty works of power by the Spirit. Like the simplex, the verb ἐπιχορέω means, "to stand the expense of bringing out a chorus" at some public festival and thus in general "to furnish," "to supply," but always with the strong connotation of great, free generosity. The patron paid the entire expenses of the training, the costuming, and the staging of the chorus, which called for a lavish hand. So God bestowed his Spirit upon the Galatians in full measure. But this is said by way of preamble to the manifestation of the Spirit which the Galatians had witnessed, namely the working of works of power. The term occurs regularly as a designation for miracles in which omnipotent power shows itself operative in a special degree.

This δυνάμεις does not signify any and all of the charismata. Paul does not say: "signs, wonders, and works of power." If he had "charismata" in general in mind he would have used that word. With the specific term "works of power" he thinks back of the time when he labored among the Galatians, when the Lord "gave testimony unto the Word of his grace and granted signs and wonders to be done by their hands" (Paul and Barnabas), Acts 14:3. In v. 8, etc., Luke reports one of the works of power, the healing of the lame man at Lystra.

Ἐν ὑμῖν = "among you"; works of power were never wrought in the hearts of men. In the miracles wrought by Paul and by Barnabas in Galatia the Galatians had the overwhelming evidence of the presence of the Spirit. Luke says that these miracles attested "the Word of the Lord's grace." Paul now puts this very point into his question: "Was all that due to, the result of (ἐκ), works of law or was it the result of the hearing of faith?" See v. 2: Was the source "what you were made to hear as belonging to faith"? Who ever knew a Judaizer to whom the Lord granted a single work of power? But wherever the apostles went, these works followed, yea, in abundance, granted lavishly by God (Acts 14:3). The view that such works continued indefinitely, and that any or all Christians wrought them, is untenable. A few works of power were granted by way of addition, but this occurred very seldom. Paul is not referring to these by his question.

These questions are to stir the thoughtless Galatians into doing some mighty necessary thinking. Let them wake up! A few proper questions will make them throw out the Judaizers. The same treatment ought to be accorded the deceivers of our time. Oh, if only all of us would think! Put the Word and true Christian experience with the Word into simple honest questions and answers like a catechism, and you are armed and proof against deceit.

* * *

The all-decisive case of Abraham

6) When Paul introduces the case of Abraham he introduces the greatest Scriptural evidence. When he writes καθώς, "even as," he parallels the Galatians and Abraham and does so regarding the essential point of faith and faith alone. All Judaizers are disowned by Abraham and by the Scriptures which speak of Abraham, and if these Judaizers try to annex Abraham, they can do so only by falsification, which is not annexation.

But the parallel is at once intensified. Those who are like Abraham in the faith of Abraham are sons of Abraham — no less. That means that all who trust in works of law are aliens to Abraham; the Scriptures make them such. More than this. From the very beginning the Scriptures included the ἔθνη, the believing Gentiles, in this Abrahamitic sonship. This includes the Gentile Christians in Galatia. Their faith includes them, their faith alone. This flatly contradicts the Judaizers who demand that all such Gentiles must also become Jews by submitting to circumcision and the Jewish ceremonial works of law. Abraham is the father of believers, Gentile as well as Jewish believers; faith alone makes them his sons. The Scriptures say so. Let the Galatians think of that and rejoice! The moment they do they will cast out all Judaizers.

Even as Abraham believed God, and it was reckoned unto him for righteousness. Realize, then, that they (whose characterization is derived) **from faith, these** (these alone) **are sons of Abraham.**

Verses 6-9 epitomize Romans 4. The conclusion that Galatians and Romans must therefore have been written at about the same time disregards the fact that this exposition of Gen. 15:6 and of the whole Old Testament account of Abraham goes back through the entire ministry of Paul. For him as a former Jew in all his apostolic contact with Jews Abraham and what the Scriptures said about his faith were vital. This was true already in the case of the Baptist (Matt. 3:9).

Paul uses Gen. 15:6 without quoting it: "Abraham believed God," etc. The dative does not mean, "in or on God," but believed what God said, the promise God made to him in Gen. 15:4, 5. He believed the promise about the Heir (Christ) who was to come out of his bowels via Isaac who was as yet unborn; he believed that through this Heir his (spiritual) seed would be in number like the stars of heaven. Abraham believed in Christ (John 8:56), in the gospel. The genuineness of his faith shone out when he held fast to this promise despite God's command to offer Isaac as a burnt offering, accounting in his faith that God was able to raise Isaac (from whom the Heir was to descend) even from the dead, Heb. 11:19. Behold the faith for which Abraham was pronounced righteous!

Moses writes regarding it: "And it was reckoned to him for righteousness," which is only another way of saying: "Through (διά) or as a result of it (ἐκ) God declared him righteous." When did God so reckon? Did he wait until Abraham had proved his faith by proceeding to sacrifice Isaac? Abraham's justification is recorded in Genesis 15 before Isaac's birth and not in Genesis 22. The moment he believed God reckoned him righteous.

Was his believing a good *work* that was of such a value to God as to *make* Abraham righteous, so that God's reckoning was merely computing this value? Moses says the opposite. Λογίζομαί τι εἰς τι = "to reckon something for something": "Something is transferred to the subject (person) in question and reckoned as his which he for himself does not have, . . . it is figured in for the person *per substitutionem;* the object present (faith) takes the place of what it counts for (righteousness), is substituted for it." C.-K. 681. When Abraham believed he was in himself no more righteous than before he believed, but God counted his faith as righteousness for him. God's accounting did not *make* him righteous, it did not change Abraham's *person*, it changed his *status* with God. Although he was not himself righteous, God regarded him as being righteous.

Do you ask how God can do so? Any suspicion of arbitrariness or of lack of strict justice is due only to our own crooked minds. The justice of the act is perfect. We know *a priori* that unjustness and injustice are impossible in the case of God. But we ourselves see it when our dogmaticians point out that this is not an analytic but a synthetic pronouncement of God. There is no virtue or merit either in the believer or in his act of believing, nothing of the kind to the end of his life (analytic).

Here there is something else entirely, more than the believing, namely the object believed, Christ, his expiation ("crucified" v. 1), his merit. The faith that holds to these, for the sake of these and these only (synthetic) is reckoned for righteousness. The substitution is the perfection of justice. Christ's merit and his righteousness are his own, but he wants them to be ours, makes them ours by faith, even himself kindles that faith; and in the instant of faith this faith, because of the object it holds, secures the verdict of righteousness.

The expression used by Moses and by Paul is most exact: faith for righteousness. When God came with his grace and his glorious promise, Abraham trusted that grace and promise and had them as his very own, and they constituted his righteousness, the quality that is due to God's own verdict on all who have his grace and his promise. Abraham did not produce his faith nor any part thereof. "Abraham believed God" is plain as to that. God came to Abraham, and not he to God. God made a glorious promise to Abraham, made that promise shine into Abraham's heart with all its divine power of light, grace, and blessedness. So was he brought to believe. Abraham, indeed, believed, but God's Word and his promise moved him to believe. Nothing else and nothing less could do so.

Nor was there a possibility that Abraham himself might add a little. There was no need to add anything, the promise and the grace were all-sufficient (*gratia sufficiens*). God left nothing to be added for the simple reason that Abraham had nothing he could possibly have added. There is only one preparation for faith, and that, too, God makes and alone can make when, by his law, he brings home to us our utter sin and need of his grace. So Abraham believed, so justifying faith is wrought by God.

7) From the incontestable fact laid down by the Scriptural ἐπίστευσε, "he believed," Paul at once draws an equally incontestable conclusion with the illative ἄρα. He states it imperatively: "Realize, then," etc. The imperative fits the context much better than an indicative would. The tense is the present; the realization is to be enduring and ever renewed. It pertains to the Galatians and to all believers: "these (whose characteristic mark is derived) from faith, these (these alone) are sons of Abraham." Here again ἐκ appears (v. 2, 5), its opposite occurs in 2:12, "they (whose mark is) from circumcision." The demonstrative "these" = these, decidedly these alone, and none who are without faith. Faith makes them like Abraham in his faith, joins them to him inwardly, spiritually for-

ever. Thus they are "sons of Abraham." A great gulf lies between them and all who are marked by "works of law." Can the Galatians help seeing that gulf and remain on the right side of it?

Abraham's "sons" is the proper terms (not, "children," A. V.). Τέκνα suggests the idea of descent, υἱοί that of *Zugehoerigkeit,* belonging to, as in "sons of the prophets." C.-K. 1082. So also "sons" marks their standing: they stand with Abraham. Again, "sons" is used to mark the fact that they stand with a father, stand for what their father stands. In all these senses also all Gentile believers are allied with Abraham as his true "sons."

8) Continuative δέ adds another vital statement in regard to Abraham and his real sons and brings the matter down to the time of Paul and the Galatians. **Now the Scripture, having foreseen that God declares the Gentiles righteous in consequence of faith, proclaimed as good news in advance to Abraham: There shall be blessed in connection with thee all the Gentiles.**

What God did with Abraham by declaring him righteous in consequence of faith alone is in the most vital way connected with what he is now doing as Paul writes; it is all of one piece. It is shown to be so, not by a deduction that Paul now makes, but by what God himself declared to Abraham ages ago.

"Having foreseen, the Scripture proclaims," etc., reverses participle and subject and thereby emphasizes both. To say that the Scripture foresaw is not a mere personification. That would be only a rhetorical figure, but the Scripture is actually the Word of God as it was expressed by himself in permanent form by means of inspiration. It is thus that "the Scripture" and "God" are identified; in fact, the two cannot be separated as is done by those who deny or reduce inspiration. God is in the Scripture, and thus the Scripture foresaw.

The aorist refers to the time of Abraham. The word that God spoke to him at that time was put into writing by Moses at a much later time. The foresight is found in the Scripture because the Writer who used Moses spoke with that foresight when he addressed Abraham. Paul is content to speak of the periods of time involved, the age of Abraham and the time in which Paul was living. In reality, all God's works are known to him from all eternity, timelessly, and all his counsels and his plans go back before the founding of the world.

Paul says that the Scripture foresaw "that God declares the Gentiles righteous in consequence of faith," ἐκ, as a result of faith. This is usually regarded as indirect discourse; hence our versions translate, "would justify." But Paul states the simple fact in his own language as he sees it day by day with his own eyes: "God justifies the Gentiles out of faith." That is why he writes "God" does this, i. e., does it now; and thereby he in no way makes "the Scripture" one who looks at "God" as being another. But this he does say, that what God is now doing is not a thing that is new, novel, at all strange for the Scripture. The very first book of Scripture saw it many centuries ago, saw it with all the clarity with which Paul and the Galatians now see it, in the same actuality.

Subject and verb are reversed in order to obtain emphasis on each, and the phrase is placed forward in order to secure the chief emphasis for it. "From faith," from faith God's verdict flows. Nor is it at all marvelous that God now does this with the Gentiles; it is the same thing God did with Abraham before the first Scripture was ever written. There was ever even as there is now but one way in which God pronounces a sinner righteous.

Hence the first book of Scripture proclaimed in advance as good news to Abraham: "There shall be blessed in connection with thee all the Gentiles." But how can Paul say that the Scripture proclaimed to Abraham when the Scripture was not written until long after Abraham's time? Here the identification of the Scripture with God is still stronger than it was in the participle. But the real point to be noted is that what God spoke directly and in person to Abraham, that is what all nations were to read as good news, the same good news that it was to Abraham. Abraham did not receive it in the form of writing, he received the substance without which there would never have been inspired writing. Abraham heard it πρό, "in advance" of the time when the Gentiles were to be so blessed. On the augment in the verb see B.-D. 69, 4. "In advance" is to be construed with the future "shall be blessed."

He heard it as good news. We are told by some interpreters that this was not "the gospel," and that our versions should not translate thus. That is an incorrect contention; it is the very sum and substance of the gospel. On this statement made to Abraham rested Abraham's faith, the faith by which he was declared righteous, the faith that was reckoned to him for righteousness. That is the same gospel we have today, save that now the promise has become fulfillment.

Another incorrect view is that "shall be blessed" does not include justification. The term is wider than "shall be justified," but justification is the central blessing without which no spiritual blessings other than this come to anybody. In this very sentence we have the statement "that God *justifies* the Gentiles from faith" as the thing the Scriptures foresaw and by God's own mouth told Abraham in advance in the words: "There shall be blessed," etc. See Gen. 12:3 and 18:18; also 22:18. Subject and verb are again transposed, each is thus made emphatic. In v. 2 the reception of the Spirit, the greatest and the most comprehensive blessing, includes justification as its chief factor. Note that the future tense "shall be blessed" is the assured fact, the yea and amen of God. That is why Paul writes: "God (now) justifies the Gentiles." The agent in the passive is God; "shall be blessed" = "I myself will bless."

Ἐν σοί is "in thee" in the sense of "in union or connection with thee." The circle drawn by the preposition has within it, first of all, Abraham himself, and as it is drawn around him by God it is drawn also around all the Gentiles. It is one and the same circle of blessing. The neuter plural subject here has the plural verb in the Greek as it may have when persons are referred to. While Abraham is the forefather of the Jews, when he received this promise he was as much a Gentile as the Gentile Galatians themselves. He was still uncircumcised, a point which Paul drives home so forcibly in Rom. 4:10-12. The astonishing thing to him was not "Gentiles" but the vast number, "all the Gentiles."

But "in thee" contains vastly more. This means Isaac over against Ishmael. This does not imply that Ishmael could not share in the blessing but that Isaac would be the progenitor of the Messiah, and that the line would continue through Jacob (not Esau), Judah, David, etc. "In thee" speaks of the Messiah, of the Messianic blessing. This world-wide blessing in the Seed of Abraham (v. 16), in Christ, was put in the form of promise for Abraham, for him to believe it. Every promise aims at faith, intends to produce faith. It can be received in no other way. This promise set Christ before Abraham. Abraham "believed" (v. 6). "Abraham rejoiced to see my day: and he saw it, and was glad" (John 8:56). Thus was Abraham justified.

"In thee — all the nations" = first, that Christ would be the fount of blessing for all the Gentiles the world over; secondly, that they would appropriate this blessing as Abraham appropriated it, by faith alone. The Hebrew has "all families of the earth"; LXX, "all the tribes of the earth"; Paul, "all the Gentiles," or as we may render, "all the nations." After a fashion the latter is better, for when the promise was spoken, no Jewish nation existed, and this nation was to be included in the circle as were the rest. Still here the whole point rests on non-Jews, on Gentiles. By faith alone they enter the Abrahamic circle as "sons of Abraham" (v. 7).

9) This is stated directly. **Consequently those** (whose characteristic mark is derived) **from faith are blessed with believing Abraham.** The blessing is for all, but to each one it comes ἐκ πίστεως, out of faith as the fount and source. In v. 7 οἱ ἐκ πίστεως are the "sons of Abraham"; here they are blessed σύν, in association with, Abraham. And Abraham himself is called πιστός, which cannot mean "faithful" (our versions), reliable, trustworthy (in the passive sense), but must have the same meaning as ὁ ἐκ πίστεως, "believing" (active), C.-K. 869. Note the plural used in Eph. 1:1: "to the saints and believers." C.-K. calls this the standard Jewish designation for Abraham. Paul, however, uses it in a pointed way, where the decisive thing is that Abraham "believed" (v. 6), that his "faith" was reckoned for righteousness, that "faith" makes sons of Abraham. The clinching statement is that "those of faith" are with Abraham as πιστός, a man marked by faith.

"They are blessed." This changes the future tense used in the promise into the constant present: ever and ever blessed; the passive again makes God the agent. The essential blessing for all these believers is the fact that, like Abraham, their faith is reckoned for righteousness or, as Paul puts it in his own words: "God declares them righteous." With justification there go all the other spiritual blessings that are described at length in Romans 5 to 8. Note that ὥστε is paratactic, it occurs in a sentence by itself and for this reason has the indicative (R. 999).

The case of Abraham is all-decisive. Faith alone obtains justification and all resultant blessings. The Scriptures so declare not only regarding Abraham himself but regarding all other men who believe as Abraham did and are thus joined to him as his sons. This is the positive side; now the negative is stated which is equally decisive as, of course, it must be.

The all-decisive exclusion of works of law

10) **For as many as are** (people whose characteristic mark is derived) **from works of law are under a curse.**

This is the simple fact concerning the entire class of workers with law and γάρ offers it as the negative proof for justification by faith alone. Two classes of men stand in absolute opposition: οἱ ἐκ πίστεως — ὅσοι ἐξ ἔργων νόμου, those marked by faith — those marked by works of law. All of the former are of the same type; the latter, "as many as," are of various types; but despite their variety they are one, alike in "works of law" (see 2:16). The Scriptures declare the one class blessed, the other cursed. "Under a curse" means first, under a divine verdict of curse; secondly, under the power which works out and finally completes the curse.

As he did in the case of the blessing, so Paul now does in that of the curse: he offers the Galatians no assertion of his own, apostle though he was, but, as Jesus so often did, brings the clearest passages of Scripture as proof. **For it has been written: Accursed everyone who does not abide in all the things that have been written in the Book of the Law to do them!**

This is the sword of Damocles which hangs over the head of all workers with law. Paul quotes the LXX of Deut. 27:26 with a slight change. The Hebrew is: "Cursed he that confirmeth not the words of this law to do them," i. e., confirms them by doing them without fail. This curse is, indeed, conditional. One may escape it by abiding in all the things written in the Book of the Law (Torah) by doing them. The aorist infinitive denotes complete doing, and "all the things" excludes exceptions. Paul does not prove that no man can possibly keep the law; how self-evident that is he shows in the next verses. Besides, who among the Galatians would claim that *he* had kept the entire law? Most of them had been Gentiles, pagans, who were guilty of the most frightful transgressions of the law.

In the expressions, "it has been written," "all the things that have been written," the perfect tenses have the force: once written and thus now on record, permanently so for all time. The former is the regular formula for introducing Scripture passages and contains the very idea of ἡ γραφή, the Scripture, with its divine and thus final authority. The point of note in *biblion* is this, that the very roll or scroll (βίβλος = papyrus plant from which papyrus sheets or "paper" were made) on which the divine law is written bears this curse for all workers with law. Let all the Galatians who are listening to the Judaizers mark it well. Every one of these Judaizers is under this curse. Will the Galatians, too, allow themselves to be drawn under it? "Accursed" means to be under the divine ὀργή or wrath, awaiting the final ἀπώλεια or destruction. The infinitive with τοῦ is epexegetical (R. 1086) and not final.

11) To make the matter perfectly clear Paul adds (δέ) that the law was never designed by God to produce the verdict of justification, that God designed faith (the gospel) for this purpose. He has already pointed to Abraham and to all the sons of Abraham who are justified by faith alone. Here is

the inner, the basic reason for that fact. **Now that in connection with law** (no article, any kind of law) **no one is declared righteous with God is plain because, The righteous — from faith shall he live.**

It is a fact, in connection with law no one is ever declared righteous with God (παρά in the sense of "in God's judgment," B.-P. 973). This is so plain "because" God has said in most simple words how a man receives the verdict of righteousness, namely "in consequence of faith."

Paul might have said that no one is justified in connection with law because no one is able to meet the demands of the law and have brought proof for that fact. This would limit the whole elucidation to law alone, i. e., to negation. It is simpler and better at once to advance to the opposite affirmation, to God's own declaration as to how a person *is* declared righteous with God. For this is the main thing: How am I justified? The other: How am I *not* justified? is only corollary. When I know the one right way I will discard any proposed wrong way.

Ἐν, "in connection with" law, of course, means the connection indicated by "law" itself: law *demands*, demands constant, flawless, complete doing on my part, i. e., works, "works of law." But every connection which any sinner is able to make with law, or the law itself makes with him, damns him from the very start. He goes down before every single demand of the law.

Not the connection with law and any attempt to meet its demands by our doing does God declare to be the way to obtain his verdict of righteousness and consequent life. In Hab. 2:4, which Paul simply repeats as being well known to all his readers, the prophet says: "The righteous — from faith shall he live." Some would construe together "the one righteous from (out of, due to) faith" and leave as the predicate only the verb "shall live." But in the Hebrew the phrase "from faith" is marked by the tiphcha to indicate that it bears the emphasis and is thus to be construed with the verb. In English we should underscore the phrase: "The righteous — *from faith* he shall live." "From faith" is exactly what Paul means.

Nor is it correct to say that we have two thoughts: 1) the righteous shall live; 2) his living shall be due to faith. The thought is a unit: By faith alone shall the righteous live. Again it is not the thought of the prophet that a man is pronounced righteous by God, and that he *then* gets faith, and that he *then* lives. All three occur simultaneously: the pronouncement — faith — life. No man is righteous for even a second before he has faith, or has faith even a second before God declares him righteous; the same is true with regard to his being alive. The prophet and Paul with him emphasize faith. Righteousness and life are inseparable from it. Nor is the gospel omitted; faith is ever the product only of the gospel, and the gospel is ever the contents of faith.

Here, as in Rom. 1:17, Paul corrects the LXX who translate, "out of *my* faith," i. e., God's faith or faithfulness. The Hebrew has *"his* faith," i. e., the righteous one's faith. Paul does not restore "his" because he wants to make the statement entirely general by stressing the function of faith as such. On the context in Hab. 2:4 see Rom. 1:17. The great point is that "the righteous one" has "faith," something that he could not possibly get from any connection with law. Righteousness and faith go together and are never separated.

There is no need to explain, for this has been done already in v. 6 and again in v. 8. So there is also no need to explain the predicate that the righteous "shall live" out of the faith by which he is righteous. We have been told in v. 7 that spiritual sonship with Abraham is due to faith, and in v. 9 that all spiritual blessings come from faith. Both statements include what the prophet says: spiritual life is due to faith. This future tense does not refer to some distant time: "shall live" when he reaches heaven or at the final judgment. The righteous man is not dead until that time. John 3:15, 16: "Everyone believing *has* ($\v{ε}χη$) life eternal," has it as believing and while believing. This is the so-called logical future: right out of faith, in the instant of its coming into existence, life springs. Yea, faith is the new birth.

Von Hofmann and Zahn advance the view that we should combine into one word $δηλονότι$ = *videlicet, scilicet*: "Now that in connection with law no one is justified, *namely that* the righteous shall live due to faith while the law is not of faith, but, etc., therefore Christ," etc. (v. 11). Glance at this *videlicet* in Liddell and Scott and note that it cannot be used as proposed. See how three parenthetical statements are thus added one on top of the other — a curious proceeding; nor has Paul the "therefore" that is supplied in v. 13. It is true that $δῆλον$ is often placed first, but that does not prevent its being placed last when this is desired. Regarding the absence of the copula, this is most common in the Greek.

12) The one who is justified will ever live as a result of the faith by which he is justified. **But the law does not belong to faith; on the contrary, He who has done the things shall live in connection with them.** That is why no connection with law justifies with God (v. 11). That is why Habakkuk wrote concerning the justified man that faith alone will give him life (v. 12). The law is a stranger to faith; it knows nothing of a faith that justifies a sinner; it only curses sinners (v. 10); it knows of only one way to get life, and that is that the man must do, do completely, the things the law lays down, failure to have done so is absolutely fatal.

It is important to note that in the term "the law" the article is generic: everything that definitely deserves the name "law." We should not restrict this word to the Mosaic law; this is included, and the Judaizers in Galatia operated with this law, namely with its ceremonial requirements but not with its moral section (the Ten Commandments). Paul includes the latter as well as all that can rightly be called law.

We should also note what constitutes "law" and "the law." This is not the statutory formulation in a code but the *Rechtskraft*, the power of right involved in the law. C.-K. 758 defines: *die mit Rechtskraft ausgeruestete Forderung, die sich immer aufs neue durch die Rechtsfolgen zum Bewusstsein bringt, die daran geknuepft sind* (also p. 753), the demand endowed with the power of right, ever forcing itself into the consciousness by the consequences of the justice thereto attached. Thus an integral part of law in the Biblical sense of the word is the promise and the curse operating in the law. Paul speaks of the former here, of the latter in v. 10.

Here ἐκ πίστεως is construed with ἐστίν in the partitive sense of ἐκ (B.-P. 366, 4 δ): to belong to something (R. 599 does not list εἶναι ἐκ). Because of its very nature the law has nothing to do with faith. It always *demands* with the power of right and justice; faith always *receives* gratuitously. The two do not match in any way. The fact that they are entirely opposite Paul again establishes by appropriating the well-known Scripture passage, Lev. 18:5: "He who has done the things shall live in connection with them," the connection being that he has done them. The substantivized participle is an aorist and thus denotes complete doing. Our versions lose this important point by translating, "he that doeth." The two are opposites even in this regard: faith has justification and life the instant it begins; doing works of law would get life only when the doing is ended and complete. But the point Paul makes is that faith and doing are opposites. Doing furnishes what is legally and of right *demanded;* faith receives what is gratuitously *bestowed.*

What makes the two quotations so striking is the fact that ζήσεται, "shall live," occurs in both. There *are* two ways to get eternal life: in one instance life is *earned* by complete doing; again life is *given* to us. The trouble with the former is that it is closed to the sinner. Before he can begin any doing, his sin bars the way to life by any use of law. Ἐκ πίστεως, life flows as a pure gift "out of faith"; ἐν αὐτοῖς, life lies as an earned merit "in them," i. e., in all the deeds of law when these are complete.

Now we may note that Paul has built a regular negative syllogism. The conclusion is put first: By the law no one is justified. The major premise is: The righteous one shall live by faith alone; the minor: the law does not belong to faith. Hence, it is true beyond a doubt that by the law no one will live, no one is justified. Thus the line of thought begun with Abraham's justification by faith is duly unfolded.

13) One thought remains to be mentioned, to show how God set aside the law and opened the way of faith. This showing forth is done in typically Pauline fashion. He never lets his explanation run out into a duality, he always brings it to rest in a unit point. This exemplifies the penetration with which his mind works. Here he has two divergent lines of thought, the one a positive thought regarding faith, the other a negative thought regarding law, the one ending in a blessing, the other in a curse. He now ties them together into a knot. He does it in Christ. Christ took the curse upon himself and so made the blessing possible to faith. Thus also — and this is another feature of his masterful mind — Paul brings us back to Christ crucified who was mentioned in v. 1, yea, also to Abraham and

to the Spirit. What a joy to follow a mind such as that!

The absence of a connective in the Greek arrests attention. That is the plain intent regarding the following great statement about Christ. **Christ bought us free from the curse of the law when he became a curse in our stead, because it has been written: Accursed everyone who hangs on wood! in order that for the Gentiles the blessing of Abraham might come in connection with Christ Jesus, in order that we might receive the promise of the Spirit by means of the faith.**

This letter is addressed to the Galatians. When Paul says "us" and in v. 14 that "we" receive he refers to himself, to all the brethren who were with him at the time of this writing (1:2), and to all the Galatian readers, the great majority of whom were former Gentiles. "Us" and "we" are not the Jews. The argument that these pronouns are in contrast with the phrase "for the Gentiles" (v. 14) is untenable. How does Christ's purchase of the Jews bring the blessing of Abraham "for the Gentiles"? This can be done only by his purchase of the Gentiles as well as of the Jews. And how can Paul add that "we" Jews get to receive the Spirit? Do Gentiles not receive the Spirit? Did Paul not say that the Gentile Galatians had received the Spirit (v. 2)?

The argument that the Jews alone were under the law is unconvincing. This view misunderstands the force of "the law" by thinking that it refers to the Mosaic law code, and that the Gentiles were not under this code since it had not been given to them. Paul does not use the phrase "under the law" in this section. When he refers to the law in v. 23; 4:4, 5; 5:18 (Rom. 6:14, 15), the phrase he uses is "under law" (without the article). See v. 12 on "law." Men can be in only one of two conditions, under law or under grace (Rom.

6:14, 15), *tertium non datur*. This refers to Gentiles as well as to Jews. Rom. 2:12-16 is Paul's own exposition regarding Gentiles and law. All who are under law, no matter of what kind, be they Jews or Gentiles, are "under a curse" (v. 10), most of all those who seek to get salvation "out of works of law." The great thing proclaimed in the gospel is the fact that Christ bought them all free from the curse of the law.

When Paul writes: bought *us* free, us believers, he does not have in mind a limited atonement. In II Pet. 2:1 those who bring swift destruction on themselves (damnation) are said to be bought by the Lord. Christ redeemed the world and not only the elect. When we believers are mentioned as those who were ransomed and bought by Christ, this is said because we are the ones who appropriate this redemption. In fact, our ransoming is certain only because Christ ransomed the world. It has been well said that, if Christ had left out one person, I, who know my own unworthiness and sin so fully, must conclude that I am that person.

Furthermore, the law itself declares that only he who keeps its precepts completely shall live (v. 12), all others shall perish. Does this exempt the Gentiles? Rom. 2:12-16 is the answer. Had the Galatians been exempt who had at one time been pagans? Finally, if "he bought us" refers only to the Jews and not equally to the Gentiles, the appended ἵνα clause cannot be properly understood, then the blessing of Abraham was to come for the Gentiles by some other act than this purchase. Such an idea is unthinkable. The Bible knows of no partial redemption, one of Jews only.

Ἐξαγοράζειν is stronger than ἀγοράζειν, but both are used with reference to the purchasing act of Christ, the former again in 4:5, the latter repeatedly in I Cor. 6:20; 7:23; II Pet. 2:1; Rev. 5:9; 14:3, etc., although it is variously translated in our versions as buy, purchase, redeem. The compound verb with the following ἐκ phrase means, "to buy out of" i. e., "free from." We have a close synonym in the noun ἀπολύτρωσις, "ransoming" by the payment of a λύτρον or ransom. The idea of ransom cannot be eliminated from this noun, so that it means only "deliverance." The two verbs mean literally "to buy," and that means to pay a price for something. That price is the life of Christ laid down in death, cf., v. 1, Christ crucified. His life, blood, death are the price, the λύτρον. This entire imagery goes back to the Old Testament, to its idea of substitutionary blood sacrifice.

Yet, as is the case with regard to a number of concepts and expressions, many modern interpreters search in paganism instead of in the Old Testament for an understanding of the idea of ransom. Thus Deissmann refers to the pagan way of freeing slaves. The slave's earnings were deposited in a temple; finally the master brought his slave to the temple and took the price. Henceforth the slave was under the god's protection and thus free from human masters. C.-K. 63 accepts this and says that Paul deepened the idea while he retained the outward features connected with it. C.-K. disregards Zahn's views on this matter. This pagan transaction is misunderstood. Neither master nor pagan god *buy* anything, the slave *buys himself*. The price is paid in cash; yet I Pet. 1:18 specifically denies that we were ransomed "with corruptible things as silver and gold" and in contrast affirms that our ransom was "the precious blood of Christ, of a lamb without blemish or spot." Neither master nor god died in order to buy the slave's freedom. All the essentials are different; there is not even an outward resemblance.

Meyer states the facts with precision: "Christ bought them free; and he did it by this that he gave

Galatians 3:13 151

away his life on the cross as the *lutron* (ransom) that was paid to God, the *dator et vindex legis;* thereby he obtained for them the forgiveness of sins by his *mors satisfactoria* which was suffered according to God's gracious counsel in obedience thereto, so that now the curse of the law, which should have struck them, had no more application to them." Here there is no slave who buys his own release. Here there is the curse of which v. 10 speaks. From this curse Christ "bought us free by having become (aorist) a curse in our stead" (or: "when he became"). The two κατάρα, "curse," are the same. That means substitution: Christ took the curse of the law upon himself. "Became" is the completed act. We were not freed from our peculiar curse by Christ's taking some other kind of curse upon himself but by assuming ours.

The expression is powerful; it is not "became accursed" but "became a curse." Not some part of our curse affected him through his contact with us, but our whole curse was on him so that he was all curse. The expression used in II Cor. 5:21 is still stronger: God himself made the Sinless One "sin in our stead" (see this passage). Isa. 53:6; I Pet. 2:24. It is said truly, "Christ became the embodiment of our curse." He became this voluntarily; he gave himself (1:4; 2:20).

This fixes the meaning of ὑπὲρ ἡμῶν. R. 631: "There are a few other passages where ὑπέρ has the resultant notion of 'instead,' and only violence to the context can get rid of it. One of them is Gal. 3:13. In v. 10 Paul has said that those under the law were under a curse, ὑπὸ κατάραν. In v. 13 he carries on the same image. Christ bought us 'out from under' the curse of the law by becoming a curse 'over' us, γενόμενος ὑπὲρ ἡμῶν κατάρα. In a word, we were *under* the curse; Christ took the curse on himself and thus *over* us (between the suspended curse and us), and thus rescued us *out from under* the curse. We went free while he was considered accursed. It is not a point here as to whether one agrees with Paul's theology or not, but what is his meaning. In this passage ὑπέρ has the resultant meaning of 'instead.' The matter calls for this much discussion because of the central nature of the teaching involved." The curse would have crushed us forever; it crushed Christ in death, but his death satisfied the law and thus ended the curse, Christ arose from death. On the preposition see also 2:20.

The fact that a curse is involved in Christ's death is substantiated by Deut. 21:23, which Paul quotes in brief but does not follow the LXX with its participle "having been (and thus still being) cursed." He uses the adjective: "because it has been written (3:10): 'Accursed everyone who hangs on wood'." The Hebrew has the noun: "A curse of God the one suspended," curse in the metonymic sense of "an accursed object" (Ed. Koenig, *Woerterbuch*). Paul's translation by means of the adjective is very accurate. The fact that he omits the word "God" causes no change in meaning, for it is God's law and thus God who renders "accursed."

Let us note what is implied. After the execution and as an added disgrace the body of a criminal was suspended on a post and became an accursed object, one whom God's curse had struck down. That is why the LXX could use κεκατηραμένος, the perfect participle which conveys the idea that the object remained accursed. But that is why Paul declined to use this participle: Christ did not remain so. The passage applies to Christ when he hung on the timber of the cross. The Jewish eye regarded that dead body as an accursed object. It saw correctly: that body had suffered God's curse. In Paul's own words: Christ became a curse (a cursed object) in our stead. Paul intends to say that this fact was visible even to the eye.

If Christ had been treated as Stephen was, this would not have been apparent. Stephen's dead body was not hung up as an accursed object. We now see why Jesus said that it was necessary for him to be delivered into the hands of the Gentiles and to be crucified. We see why Paul emphasizes Christ crucified, crucified. God wanted Christ to be seen as what he actually became: a curse. Read Acts 5:30; 10:39; 13:29; I Pet. 2:24 in this light. Note that in the first two passages Christ's being hung on timber is appended to his being slain. It was the cross that said to all Jews that Jesus was accursed. Yet this very cross brought the infinite blessing of Abraham for the Gentiles. The symbol of the curse was the symbol of this blessing for all the world.

14) That is what the two ἵνα clauses state. Christ became *an object* accursed "in order that for the Gentiles *the blessing* of Abraham might come (aorist to express actuality) in connection with Christ Jesus." This was God's purpose, the aorist implying that it was attained. The Galatians are evidence of the attainment. The thought is paradoxical in the highest degree: a curse of God gets to be the greatest blessing of God. And yet it is not at all paradoxical. The curse that struck Christ like a fiery flame was quenched in his blood and death, and so the blessing of that quenched curse flowed out to all the world in life and salvation.

"The blessing of Abraham" is the one promised to him, cf., v. 8. It blessed Abraham as a believer; it blesses all other believers (v. 9) together with Abraham. It is εἰς, "for," all Gentiles, not in connection with law and works of law, but "in connection with Christ Jesus," this man "Jesus" who was anointed as our Redeemer (Purchaser). The connection is faith. The fact that it is intended for the Jews as well as for the Gentiles need not be stated, for Jesus himself was a Jew. The other does need to be stated because the Gentiles do not need to become Jews in order to share this blessing.

The blessing of Abraham is one that is intended for the whole world in Christ Jesus. Its chief content is justification by faith in Christ, our Substitute under the curse. We do not understand the commentators who make the blessing to Abraham and to the Jews one thing, and from this blessing send another thing upon the Gentiles.

The first ἵνα clause is objective although "in connection with Christ Jesus" points to the subjective side, namely faith by which alone the connection is made. The parallel purpose clause brings out the subjective side: "in order that we might receive the promise of the Spirit by means of the faith," aorist, actually receive. A glance shows how this harks back to v. 2, the Galatians had so received the Spirit. As in v. 2, so now again "faith" is combined with the Spirit. Since it is placed last, this phrase has the emphasis.

"The promise of the Spirit" has the appositional genitive just as in Acts 2:33 (R. 498). Jesus calls the Spirit "the promise of my Father," whom he will send (Luke 24:49); in Acts 1:4 the apostles are to wait for this promise. Faith is the means for the Spirit's reception (διά), the means which he himself works. To receive and to have the Spirit is to be declared righteous, to have life, and thus all the other spiritual blessings of Abraham, grace upon grace (John 1:16).

"We" in the verb is identical with ἡμᾶς and ἡμῶν in v. 13. Therefore "us" in v. 13 cannot refer to Jews only, and "we" in v. 14 to both Jews and Gentiles. "We" and "us" are Paul, the brethren with him (1:2), and the Galatians. In the case of these the reception has taken place, and that by means of faith only. Paul has the Galatians themselves say so in v. 2; has them deny that the source was works of law. That is the sense of the phrase here at the end.

Thus everything, everything excludes works of law. Every pertinent Scripture statement on both law and faith. Christ himself is in harmony with these. Faith opens righteousness to all the world. No man is saved except by faith; any man may be saved by faith.

Paul's exposition is like an arrow hitting its mark. From beginning to end there is not a single weak statement. Not one that deviates from the other by a hair. Here there is compactness, every sentence is freighted to the last word. Try and write a paragraph like this! Inspiration guided Paul's pen. Here is convincing light and power for the Galatians. In fact, here is conviction even for Paul's opponents in Galatia, the Judaizers, which should take hold of them mightily in order to draw them away from seeking justification in works of law and to bring them, too, to faith, to the blessing of their ancestor Abraham.

2. *The Galatians must Know the Limitations of the Law, 3:15-4:11*

It certainly cannot upset or alter God's own testament.

15) All Judaistic errors rest on misconceptions regarding law. Too much is then naturally expected of law. Paul has already shown that it leaves all who trust in works of law under the curse, that it cannot possibly justify, that this is done only in connection with Jesus Christ who has borne that curse in our stead. All this will become still clearer when the limitations of law become known. These are indeed great. In the first place, the law on which the Judaizers rely came all of 430 years *after* God put his testamentary promise into force. It ought to be as plain as day that no testament, not even a merely human one, can be

annulled or even altered *after* it is in force. It is preposterous to think that the Mosaic law altered God's testament. This is the first great point.

Again Paul cites history. He has already stated what the testament is and also presented what it conveys by means of its immense promise and the first heir and beneficiary under that testament (v. 8) plus those who are excluded by the testament (v. 10). Now he takes up the Mosaic law in its relation to this testament as to the point of time.

Brethren, I speak in human fashion. Though (only) a man's, having (once) been confirmed, no one voids a testament or adds thereto.

The thought as well as the address indicate the beginning of a new section. "Brethren" is significant for the Galatians, see 1:11. Here the touch of affection is added which reaches out to win the readers. "In human fashion" means in a way so simple that anyone can understand. Paul will in particular use an ordinary illustration, the inviolability of a confirmed human will and testament. That illustration will help to make the main thought clear. By drawing attention to the fact that this is a human illustration Paul does not excuse his use of it but rather states in advance just what it is so that his readers may at once catch the point he presents.

Ὅμως, here and in I Cor. 14:7 = "although" and is purely concessive. True, this is not ὁμῶς, "likewise," (R. 233 on I Cor. 14:7). When R. 1154 makes it adversative, its position an instance of hyperbaton (423), and has it modifying the participle (1155), we cannot agree. Our versions are correct; B.-P. 903 and B.-D. 450, 2 leave us uncertain; the classics do not help us. In both passages the concessive adverb is in the most natural way to be construed with the very next word: "though (only) a man's," though only a mere human covenant; I Cor. 14:7: "though (but) soulless" instruments. This is concession although we may continue with "yet."

The word διαθήκη is evidently to be understood in the sense of "testament" and not "covenant" although our versions leave us in doubt, and some writers prefer the latter. Regarding the meaning of the word in the LXX who used it to translate b^{e}rith, regarding the reason for this, and then regarding the New Testament use see the summary given in Matt. 26:18 or I Cor. 11:25. "Testament" is beyond question the meaning here where it is used with the singular "a man's," a human testament being referred to. If a human covenant were referred to, we should have the plural. Human covenants are made between at least two persons or parties and are mutual. A human testament is always made by an individual, is always one-sided, the testator alone makes disposition of his property. That is why this illustration fits the promises of God to Abraham, which constituted the old covenant. They and it were absolutely one-sided, from God to Abraham, and not mutual, not between the two. The imagery is here that of a testament with an heir and with an inheritance.

It is a confirmed, ratified, we should say probated testament that is the basis of the illustration, the perfect participle stating that it is still in force. This belongs to the *tertium comparationis*. Paul's illustration should not be regarded as an allegory, and the making of the testament and the details of ratifying it should not be introduced, plus the death of the testator, etc. Then counterparts are sought in God's testament, and none are found. No; this is a testament that has been probated and has been in force, and the point of comparison is the inviolability, the fixedness of such a testament. Nobody can void, annul it, and put something else in its place. Nobody can "add anything thereto," affix a codicil to it and thus alter the original testamentary provisions. Of course, the testator can tear it up and write a new will or can add codicils to the one he has written. But this is not a will that is still in the testator's hands but one that is already in operation.

No ancient or no modern legal practice allows a will that is duly in force to be set aside by a substitute that is offered by somebody else, or allows the additions of codicils by any person. Once in force, the will stands exactly as it is. There is no need to inquire to what law Paul refers, to Roman, Jewish, or that of some nation or province. The Galatians were a mixed people. Paul's illustration is one of universal applicability, not for quibbling lawyers, but for common people. In fact, the illustration is true everywhere today.

16) After the chief point of the illustration has been fixed, Paul states the fact he is illustrating. **Now to Abraham were spoken the promises and to his Seed. Not does he say, And to the seeds, as for many, but as for One, And to thy Seed, who is Christ.**

These promises resemble a human testament that is duly in force and in process of administration. Although they were repeated at intervals, they are one confirmed testament that became operative the moment it was spoken. Although they were spoken by God himself and were not at once written, they stand like a man's testament that is administered after his death.

In these testamentary promises two beneficiaries are named: Abraham — his Seed. One is placed first in the sentence, the other last, both are thus strongly emphasized. Since Paul specifies that "his Seed" refers to Christ, comment so often neglects Abraham and expands on this Seed. We should not neglect Abraham. He is here not named as a mere individual, as one of many beneficiaries of the testament. Even

Isaac, Jacob, and the patriarchs could not be named here as Abraham is. Whatever promises God spoke to them were entirely Abraham's. *He* was the heir. All others only share in his inheritance. They inherit only as spiritual "sons of Abraham" (v. 7).

But God named two heirs. These were, indeed, two individual persons, for the second heir is called "his Seed." This very word connects the two. There would be no Abraham, the father of believers, who has multitudes of spiritual sons, without this Seed. The whole blessing of the testamentary promises were Abraham's and made him the father of these sons, but only through this Seed. As the Seed of Abraham he was himself promised to Abraham when no hope of fulfillment seemed possible. That promise Abraham believed (v. 6) and is thus named the heir together with the Seed. Here Paul writes that the promises were spoken to Abraham's Seed; in v. 19 we have the coming of the Seed. When they were spoken to Abraham for him to believe and to become the earthly ancestor of Christ, these promises were at the same time spoken to Christ who was himself both the fulfillment and the one to fulfill the promises. "To Abraham — and to his Seed" thus differ according to the nature and the relation of the two persons. They, indeed, belong together as do no other two, as already stated, but the Seed is supreme.

When Paul writes that God does not say: "And to seeds," as placing the promises upon (ἐπί) many (plural), but as placing it upon One: "And to thy Seed" (singular), and with the demonstrative ὅς adds "he who is Christ," the repetition of καί in the cited words points to Gen. 13:15 and 17:8, where this "and" appears with the dative. Some consider only these two passages and overlook Gen. 22:18 and thus get into difficulties. For is *zera'* as it is used in those two passages not a collective? How can Paul then say: "Who is Christ"? Some think that the way out of the difficulty is to make "Christ" a collective; the reference given in the A. V. is to I Cor. 12:12, i. e., to the mystical Christ, he plus all believers. Then "Christ" would include Abraham, and "thy Seed" becomes unintelligible. Then v. 19, "up to when the Seed comes," is contradicted, for here "the Seed" is decidedly an individual and not a collective group. The mystical Christ is not the solution.

In its place we are told that Paul reverts to the rabbinical type of exegesis which he learned under Gamaliel in the days when he was a rabid Jew. Zahn answers this supposed use of *midrash* in Paul: "Paul knew his Old Testament and his Hebrew rather better than his commentators; it is ridiculous to defend him against the charge that he misreads the collective *zera'* and imagines it to be the individual person Christ." We add that this is the more unwarranted when we read Gen. 13:15 and 17:8, both of which promise the land of Canaan to Abraham's Seed. In various passages of his epistles Paul himself uses "seed" as a collective. The Hebrew plural is used only once in the Old Testament, in I Sam. 8:15.

Paul considers the collective singular in the light of Gen. 22:18 and of the other promises made to Abraham. That is why, to begin with, he says that the promises were spoken to these two. They applied to others only because they applied to these two in a peculiar way, yea, because they applied to Christ in a most particular way as "Abraham's Seed," as we have already shown. This appears so clearly in v. 19 where "the Seed" is individual and not collective. What Paul says is that a plural like "seeds" would not do even in Gen. 13:15 and 17:8; it had to be a singular "as for one," it had to be this collective: "and to thy Seed." The plural would lose, would at least render uncertain, the reference to Christ; the collective singular conserves this vital reference.

Paul is not writing for scholarly but for common readers. These will see that he is not confusing a collective with an individual, and that "Christ" is not a collective. They will see that the collective is the collective it is because it focuses in Christ. In all the spiritual seed of Abraham (collective) there appears "Christ," the individual. Hence he also writes "who," not "which" is Christ. The gender of the relative is attracted to the gender of the predicate "Christ," but here this is done for more than a grammatical reason. Some have called this attraction harsh, but they overlook the inner reason for this. Paul expects his readers to read the prophecies as he reads them, at least to follow him in getting what those prophecies contain. As all of them start with Abraham, no matter how great a collective group they include ("sons of Abraham," v. 7, "thy seed"), so all of them focus and center in "Christ"; for Abraham and Christ, these two, in the way already explained, produce the collective.

A word needs to be said regarding Ishmael, the descendants of Keturah, Esau, etc., since all of them are so often excluded from "thy seed." Please remember how many Jews were also excluded (Rom. 9:6b). "Thy seed" is spiritual. Both Rahab and Ruth (born of pagans) belong to "thy seed." If Ishmael, if any of the children and the descendants of Keturah believed, they, too, belonged to this spiritual collective. It is only an assumption that all of them disbelieved the promises made to Abraham. Note, too, that the assumption is incorrect that Paul here traces the line of descent for Christ: Abraham, Isaac, Jacob, Juda, David. This assumption leads to wrong deductions about Ishmael, the children of Keturah, etc., and overlooks the exclusion of so many Jews from the seed.

17) Now Paul makes the application of the illustration used in v. 15, that even a human testament, after it has been confirmed, cannot be voided or altered. **Now this I mean: a testament that has been confirmed in advance by God, the law that has come four hundred and thirty years later does not unconfirm so as to put the promise out of effect. For if the inheritance** (is derived) **from law, no longer** (is it) **from promise; but to Abraham God has graciously granted it by means of promise.**

Here we have the stunning confutation of all Judaizers and of all those who are Judaistically or legalistically inclined. A confirmed human testament stands. God's testament, duly confirmed, stood for hundreds of years before the Mosaic law was even given, before anybody could even conceive the idea that this law in any way altered the testament or its divine confirmation. These hundreds of years confound all Judaizers.

When Paul places the divine reality beside the human example that he used he advances the argument from the less to the greater.

Paul uses direct discourse in apposition to τοῦτο. He simply states the fact: the law does not unconfirm God's confirmed testament for the simple reason that the law came so much later. The perfect participle (see v. 15) = "still standing confirmed." It is not stated how God made the confirmation but compare Heb. 6:13-18. Do not ask why any testament of God's still needed confirmation. It needed none for its own validity; the confirmation was made wholly for the sake of men in order to give them the strongest possible assurance for faith. This reveals the enormous sinfulness of unbelief which calls the very oath of God perjury.

The participial phrase introduced by μετά is attributive and is thus a compact unit with the noun it modifies. The time, 430 years, is an understatement.

When men are eager to prove something they are inclined to exaggerate their arguments and thereby defeat themselves. The opponents note the exaggeration, discount or reject the argument, and even question the person's veracity. But an understatement acts in the opposite way; the opponents see that the statement spoken against them could be made much stronger. The effect is according. In I Cor. 10:8 Paul writes 23,000 although Num. 25:9 reads 24,000. The latter is a round number, so also is the former; Paul purposely does not make it as large as possible; he lets his readers say: "There were even more slain!"

He does so here. Instead of making his own discount, Paul takes one from Exod. 12:40, etc.; 430 years (Acts 7:6 has the round number 400 which is used also in Gen. 15:13). Paul's readers see that he uses Exod. 12:40, that this covers only the stay in Egypt, that Paul might add the years the patriarchs remained in Canaan before Jacob migrated to Egypt. No one knows how long a period this was; the estimate is about 200 years. Paul excludes all dispute about an estimate regarding this time spent in Canaan, he ignores it. The Scriptures have this 430. Any testament that has been confirmed and has been in force for over four centuries certainly cannot have its confirmation upset or modified by something that comes into existence at so long a time afterward.

We have the same verb in the participle "having been confirmed" and in its opposite ἀκυροῖ, "does not unconfirm," i. e., deprive of confirmation. They are purposely chosen so as to match. "Disannul" in our versions is too narrow, for the verb intends to include both verbs that were used in v. 15: complete annulment (voiding) and also modification (adding codicils which change the original will). Neither in whole nor in part is God's testament deprived of confirmation by the law which was given 430 (to name only this figure) years later.

Paul names the feature of the testament here in question which is no less than its very heart: "so as to put the promise out of effect." "The promise" is properly singular, for it refers to Christ, the Heir, the full inheritance in him. Nothing that came 430 and more years later cancels or puts out of effect this promise by voiding the whole testament or by changing it in part with a codicil. The will would be wrecked in either case, for "the promise" is really the whole will. Εἰς τό denotes result; when it is called contemplated result, this is done only because it is negative and denied (understand R. 1003, 1072, 1090 in this sense).

18) "For" makes still clearer the fact that the law, which came into being hundreds of years later than the testament, does not alter its confirmation, does not put its promise out of effect. Paul states it conditionally: "If the inheritance (is derived) from law, no longer (is it derived) from promise." If, since the days of Moses and Sinai, the source of the inheritance lies in law, then a mighty reversal has certainly taken place, then the source is no longer what it was before, in Abraham's time and in the centuries following, namely promise. Then no one is able to get this inheritance by simply believing the promise as Abraham, the patriarchs, their families and descendants did during those centuries; then one is now able to get it only by doing works of law as the Judaizers claim by meeting all the legal requirements. Then God's own confirmation, the oath he made when sealing the testament promise, is canceled and no longer confirms as it did confirm prior to the coming of the law. With such a confirmation the testament promise, the promised inheritance, falls to the ground; it is put out of effect, abolished.

Paul does not reason about it. He does not ask whether it is thinkable or possible that God's oath-bound confirmation and the promise which it sealed can be thus abolished. The only possible answer is "no." Paul does something that is still stronger. He is a theologian of fact. Facts are invincible. He sets down the cold fact: "but to Abraham God has graciously granted it by means of promise," i. e., by means of promise alone without law or works of law of any kind. He uses the perfect tense "has granted it," so that after it was thus granted it stands. Here is the staggering fact that stands forth as plain as day. Paul lets it confront the Judaizers and the Galatians who are inclined to follow them. Abraham had the inheritance of the confirmed testament by faith in the testamentary promise alone without any law or works of law, and these Judaizers are now telling the Galatians that they can have it only by obeying the Mosaic law that was given hundreds of years later. This is not even modification, it is utter cancellation of God's testament.

The Greek is able to emphasize all the terms by a proper placement in the sentence. "To Abraham" is placed forward; the Judaizers say, "*not* so to the Galatians." The phrase "by means of promise" is placed before the verb and the subject, and verb and the subject are reversed, all three are emphatic, especially "God." This is what *God* has done; this is the *means* he used, the only one; this is his *act*, a gracious granting. We cannot reproduce all this in English but must see it in the Greek in order to get the full meaning of what Paul writes. Note, too, that God's testament is entirely promise without a single legal stipulation; testaments convey an inheritance, the one term connotes the other. Some human testaments may require something on the part of an heir as a condition of receiving the inheritance; God's testament does not, it is pure promise.

19) Paul has completely refuted the idea that the law affected the testament in any way. But this leaves the positive question, in fact, raises it: **Why, then, the law?** Indeclinable τί = "why" (B.-P. 1310: *Wozu in aller Welt das Gesetz?*); B.-D. 480, 5: *Was soll also das Gesetz?* If what Paul states are historical facts regarding the testament and the Mosaic regulation, there seems to be no reason for God's giving the law although he did this so much later. Those who have the question read: *"What,* then, is the law?" (R. V.; the A. V. is correct) think that the answer is delayed until v. 24; that Paul had to delay it until he had disposed of other pertinent questions. But the question is "why," and the answer follows at once. It is

The temporary nature of the Mosaic law.

Not only did this law come in 430 years later, it remained in force only for the Jews, only until their historic mission was accomplished, only until Christ came, and then it was abolished even for the Jews.

For the sake of the transgressions it was added until (the time) when the Seed came, to whom the promise had been made — (this law) **put into force as an ordinance by means of angels in connection with a mediator's hand.**

The question that is here answered is not one that is raised by some Judaizing objector. The Judaizers had probably never faced the fact that the law, which they made so essential to Christianity, came in centuries after Abraham; had never asked why it came in then. It is Paul who sees all these facts and God's intent in so arranging them. There is, of course, no question that God gave the law although the fact is added that it was given in a way that was much inferior to the giving of the testament.

"For the sake of the transgressions" has the word χάριν which is merely a preposition: *wegen*, B.-D. 160, and may denote the reason or the aim (B.-P. 1398). Here the latter is the case. When Paul says that the law "was added," this cannot mean as a codicil to the testament, an idea that has already been completely excluded. It was not added to the testament as a part of it or for testamentary purposes. It did not have to do with the testament and its provisions but with "the transgressions." These were its aim and purpose. But not: "in order to check or to stop the transgressions"; the very contrary, "in order to bring them out fully as what they were, namely transgressions." The idea is not that there were a lot of transgressions, and that these needed a check in order to prevent undue spreading, and that the law was introducced to do the checking. Rom. 4:15 shows that without law there is no transgression. The very word παράβασις implies a law or norm which is overstepped. The Greek has the image of walking "beside" the law or norm and thus spurning it while our word "transgression" suggests the picture of a boundary that is illegally crossed into forbidden territory.

It is astonishing yet altogether true, the purpose of the law is transgressions. It is for sinners only; sinless persons need no law. But the moment the law meets a sinner, he reacts by transgression because of the sin in him. The law brings it out so that he and all men may see it. Compare Rom. 5:20 and 7:13. Let us make it drastic. While it is latent, sin stirs but slightly. It is like a lion who is asleep or is moving about quietly. Apply the stick of the law to it, prod it a little, and its fangs flash, its rages and roars, it tries to rend and tear, it displays what a wild beast it really is. That stick does not make the beast a beast; it cannot kill or change the beast; all it can do is to make it show what it is. That is true even when the stick is heavy enough to subdue the beast for the time being; the very subdual is brought about by overpowering force alone.

Again Paul speaks historically: "up to (the time) when the Seed came." He refers to the law of Moses with its many regulations which was given for the period from Sinai until Christ and Calvary. This is the law with which the Judaizers were operating on the thoughtless Galatians. It was abrogated in Christ, "to whom the promise has been given." The Greek has the perfect for which the English would use the past perfect "had been given." The historical mission of the Mosaic law ended when the promise to Abraham (v. 18) was fulfilled in Christ who is here called "the Seed" as explained in v. 16.

Paul carefully keeps the connection. We may say that the Mosaic law was given when the Jewish nation began to be a nation after leaving the Egyptian bondage, and that the law ended when this nation lost its national existence by rejecting Christ. This law, of course, also segregated the nation, was a strong hedge about it, kept it from mixing with other nations; but Paul is not speaking of this function of the law.

We may add still more. The Mosaic law also contained elaborate regulations for removing the guilt of the transgressions of the Jews. This law established the priesthood of the Jews, the sacrifices, the cleansings. They were entirely law since they had been ordered by God, and yet in all of them there was gospel, the adumbration of Christ, whose blood cleanses us from all sin. This shows that when Christ, the substance, came, the adumbration, having served its purpose, vanished. The letter to the Hebrews has much to say on this phase of the subject.

This still leaves the larger question about the time from Adam until Moses and Sinai and about the time since Christ and Calvary. Rom. 5:14 refers to the former period and shows how men died because of sin. Rom. 2:12-16 adds that even the Gentiles, who never had the Mosaic law, have God's law, although it is blurred, written in their hearts, their own conscience condemning them. This is the moral law which Moses formulated in full clarity for the Jews. Rom. 7:7-13 shows how this law smote Paul and revealed his sin and his subjection to death. This is the law that still operates in sinners. Romans 2 shows that moralism, the effort to keep this law, is *not* the way in which to escape condemnation, is only the surest way of sinking into greater condemnation. It is this to the present day. The only escape lies in justification by faith, Rom. 3:20, etc. This escape delivers us from all condemnation of law.

This clears up what Paul says to the Galatians regarding the whole Mosaic law, its ceremonial as well as its moral content. The Judaizers laid great stress on the ceremonial phase of the law and demanded that the Galatian Christians keep this in order to be saved. Not only a part of the Mosaic law is abrogated in Christ, but all law with all its condemnation is ended for the believer in Christ; Rom. 8:1: There is no more κατάκριμα, verdict of condemnation from any law, for those who are in Christ Jesus by faith.

Christ is "the Seed" of Abraham, to him the promise has been made, i. e., in God's testament. He is the Heir who has the whole inheritance; and all of us who are joined to him in faith, all of us who are "in Christ Jesus" (Rom. 8:1) are joint heirs with him (Rom. 8:17), who have escaped from all condemnation of law.

The temporary nature of the Mosaic code, as far as it was intended only for the Jewish nation, is evidenced also by the way in which this code was given to the Jews. Paul uses the same word which Stephen employed, but he has the aorist passive participle διαταγείς, "put into force as an ordinance," while Stephen uses the plural noun διαταγάς (see Acts 7:53). The agent in the passive is God; the aorist records the historical fact. God used the angels in his communication of the ordinances to Moses. We must include far more than the two tables of stone, namely also the whole Tabernacle and many other features. Paul and Stephen refer to Deut. 33:2, compare Heb. 2:2.

Just how the angels functioned in the giving of the law to Moses we do not know. Deut. 33:2 speaks of the thunder, lightning, earthquake, trumpet on Sinai. Over against the Gentiles, who had no law that was given in such a glorious way, this mode of giving exalted the law of Moses; the Jews were proud of having such a law. Here, however, the reverse is stressed. The glory remains, it was given "through angels," but Christ, the Seed, who received the promise is vastly greater than all angels. So also the testament promise is far greater than the ordained law.

Ἐν differs from διά; the angels were God's servants, his means, but Moses was not Israel's servant and means but Israel's representative. Exod. 20:19. This shows us the sense of μεσίτης, which does not here mean *Friedenstifter* but *Uebermittler*, not a mediator or an intermediary between two estranged parties who brings them together again but one who merely transmits. In the matter of the law God functioned through angels, yet not with Israel itself but with Israel's representative who bore all the ordinances to the people.

"Hand" = service. Moses is not mentioned by name. The anarthrous nouns say that he belongs to the class of men who represent others; there is a class of them. In the case of "the Seed," Christ, this was far different. He inherited the promise of the testament; he was the Mediator in the highest sense of the term, himself the God-man who reconciled the world to God.

20) This helps us to understand the statement which, despite its simplicity, is said to have received about 250 different and divergent interpretations. **Now the mediator does not belong to one person; but God is one person.** One person acts for himself; it is a multitude such as Israel that needs a mediator in the sense of a representative to receive what the one (God) transmits to all of them. Let us keep to the context; this is said with reference to the transmission of the law to the whole people of Israel by Moses. It is also said in contrast to the way in which the testament and its promise were given. Being one person, God acted for himself and needed no representative when he was giving the law; being a young nation, Israel had a representative when it was *receiving* the law from God. God did not give the law to each Israelite separately; Moses received it for all of them.

The article in the expression "the mediator" is generic, it generalizes from what is said about "a mediator's hand" in v. 19. "Is not of one" is the Greek idiom for "does not belong to one." God is one person and can act for himself. The διά used in v. 19 shows that the angels were not regarded as God's representatives even also as there was a number of them. The observation is correct that, if Paul had intended to say that a mediator does not belong to one party only but always to two parties, he would have said "two." But then "mediator" would signify a go-between who brings two separated parties together. The giving of the Mosaic law was not at all a transaction of this kind.

The point is that Paul brushes away the idea that the law is in some way an addition to or an alteration of God's will and testament to Abraham which was already in full force for hundreds of years. It is only a temporary and a subordinate set of regulations that were intended for the Jewish nation. Hence the great difference in the mode of procedure. When God established his testament with Abraham, God appeared to Abraham (Gen. 17:1-21) in person, and when the testament was executed, God was in Christ (II Cor. 5:19). The testament was given in person to the one Abraham; correspondingly, the inheritance was paid out to the one Heir, Christ. But the law was intended for the whole nation of Jews, their representative Moses brought it to them. The difference is so great that without perversion of the facts nobody can possibly make this law anything that is even remotely like a late codicil to the testament, to say nothing of substituting the law for the testament and thereby making it void.

The great lack in the law: its inability to produce life.

21) In v. 15-18 Paul stresses the late date of the law and the fact that this excluded any modification of the testament by means of the law. In v. 19, 20 he shows the temporary nature of the law which was evidenced also by the way in which it was given. Now he adds the fact of the inability of the law to give life, which means that it could not possibly produce righteousness.

The further question is raised. If the law is so distinct and different from the testament, is only temporary in its function, etc: **Is the law, then, contrary to the promises of God?** Paul repudiates the idea as being altogether wrong: **Perish the thought!** This expression is explained in 2:17. To have the law alter the testament, to attach it to the testament (gospel) as a vital part, or to substitute it for the testament, is the one extreme; to make the law a contradiction of the testament (gospel) and thus to cast aside the law (antinomism), is the other extreme.

Galatians 3:21

By rejecting the first of these alternatives we are not forced to accept the second; and, of course, vice versa. Both are false, contrary to the facts. We do not have to decide between extremes.

Since the Judaizers would not think of rejecting the law of Moses as being contrary to the testament, since they would point to this extreme alternative only in order to force acceptance of the opposite extreme, Paul does not at once show that the law is not contrary to the gospel but points to the lack and the inability of all law. It is not κατά, "against or contrary to," the testament (gospel) but differs from it in that vital point which the Judaizers fail to see.

For if there had been given a law, one able to make alive, actually the righteousness would have been (derived) **from the law.** "Law" in general (no article), thus also the Mosaic law but equally all other law lacks the ability "to make alive" (aorist, punctiliar), to produce spiritual life. That is why it cannot produce "the righteousness" we need to attain salvation. For one must have life in order to live in righteousness even to the slightest degree. That is why Paul points to this inability to bring forth life.

With regard to the testament of promise matters are different; it produces faith which is life. It grasps God's righteousness in Christ (Rom. 3:21,22), (the imputed righteousness), which means salvation, and it brings forth a life of righteousness (acquired righteousness). See the vast and the essential difference between the testament (gospel) and all law!

Yes, the law "was given," John 1:17. The Mosaic law was, indeed, a great gift of which the Jews were rightfully proud — if they had only used it aright (Rom. 3:20). The implication of the statement is the fact that law is always given, it is never produced by man himself. All evolutionary origin of law is denied. The passive includes the agent: there must always be the divine Lawgiver. This is true also of the law written in the hearts of Gentiles which is greatly blurred by the darkening effect of sin.

We may find a condition of past unreality in the apodosis as well as in the protasis. For ἦν with ἄν may be either present or past unreality, the imperfect of "to be" doing duty for the aorist of this verb (R. 1015). Only the context decides. Here past unreality is more in place than present: "would have been" and not "would be." For Abraham must be included, he who certainly obtained righteousness without law (v. 6), he who received the testament of the promises (gospel), v. 16. On "righteousness," the quality due to God's verdict, see v. 6. "A law, one able," etc., leaves "law" (without the article) general, while the articulated participle makes a particular application (R. 777).

If a law had ever been given by God that was able to produce life, then and then alone the righteousness would have been ἐκ νόμου, have its source in this law. But the world has never received a law of this kind. If a law were of this kind, it would not be law; if it were law, it would not be of this kind. The very idea of a law producing life is a contradiction. That means an equal contradiction in the idea of law furnishing righteousness. When the Judaizers and the Pharisees in general sought to do "works of law," these were not righteousness but filthy rags (Isa. 64:6), a pretense, a spurious imitation; God did not declare these workers of law righteous, they declared themselves righteous (Luke 16:15) as the criminal always likes to acquit himself.

22) How the matter really stood since there was no law that was able to make alive and afford the needed righteousness, is now stated in a striking way. **But the Scripture locked up everything together under sin in order that the promise might be**

Galatians 3:22   175

given as a result of faith in Jesus Christ to those believing.

'Αλλά is placed in contrast with the question Paul has emphatically denied in v. 21. No, the Mosaic law is not contrary to the promises made to Abraham; no law can compete with the promises since it is unable, as the promises are, to produce life and thus righteousness. "But" this was the situation: God locked up everything together under sin in order to achieve his great purpose, the gift of the promise to all believers. It could not come out of law which because of its very nature cannot produce life and righteousness. The gift was pure promise, and faith, faith alone was to receive it as a possession.

Paul does not say that "the law" locked up everything together under sin but that "the Scripture" did so. He again identifies the Scripture with God (v. 8). "The Scripture" is God's recorded will. The supposition that this refers to one particular passage such as Deut. 27:26 (see v. 10) is too narrow. When "the Scripture" is named, there is a reference to many passages; we have a sample in the list Paul uses in Rom. 3:9-18. Many more may be cited. They all express God's judgment on sinners. Rom. 3:9 states that this includes Jews as well as Gentiles.

"The Scripture locked up everything together under sin." The verb is placed forward for the sake of emphasis: no less did the Scripture do than lock up everything together in one mass, allowed no difference (Rom. 3:22), made no exception. It is striking to note that Paul does not say "all men" but uses the neuter "all the things," i. e., "everything." Yet τὰ πάντα is not the indefinite πάντα; "everything" refers definitely to all that pertains to men, all of whom were sinners. We may think of their thoughts, words, and deeds, of their whole character and life. The view that this neuter plural means σπέρματα, "all the seed," i. e., all Jews, is strange. Everything without exception was locked and sealed and thus doomed "under sin" by the recorded judgment of God. "Under sin" = under the curse and the power of sin. Nothing pertaining to men could possibly escape the divine judgment which condemned all of it as sin.

The law extended back only to Moses. While it was recorded later than the giving of the law on Sinai, the Scripture reaches back to Adam by whom sin came into the world (Rom. 5:12). This is the reason that Paul writes "the Scripture" and not "the law." The other reason is this, because the Jews had the Scripture they could thus see what this Scripture did with "everything," namely lock it all up together under sin. What hope was there, then, that those who had all of this Scripture before their eyes might escape this locking up by means of works of law? Absolutely none.

For the purpose which God had in mind in this Scriptural judgment of his was by no means to leave men with "everything" they had, thus locked up and doomed to damnation. The Scripture itself recorded his ultimate purpose which was man's salvation: "in order that the promise might be given as a result of faith to those believing." This was the one way of escape. This promise is the one Abraham received, by which he received righteousness through faith (v. 8, 16), the promise to be fulfilled in Abraham's Seed who is Christ. It was God's purpose to convey this promise to men, to bestow it upon them as a gift with all that it contained. How the gift was to be bestowed is stated most clearly: "as a result of faith in Jesus Christ to all those who believe." Faith is doubly emphasized, both as a source ($\dot{\epsilon}\kappa$) and as a mark of all who have the gift (the characterizing participle). The Scripture placed Abraham before all the Jews who had the Old Testament by pointing to his faith and by calling attention to the fact that he believed the promise even long before the Mosaic law was given.

How, then, can Judaizers say, or the Galatians for a moment believe, that the substance of the promise (gospel) is received by means of law and works of law? A promise is received only by faith. Promise and faith are correlatives. See this in v. 6-9; also that works of law leave one under the curse in v. 10. Faith and believing are the subjective means as the promise (gospel) is the objective means of righteousness. "Faith" always has its contents, is never empty; it is "faith in Jesus Christ" (objective genitive), he in whom as Abraham's Seed the promise given to Abraham is fulfilled.

It is all so plain in Scripture. But the Jews found only law and then misused this law for works of law. And now the Judaizers were trying to draw the Galatians back under law where righteousness could never be obtained, where they would again be locked up under sin. "Locked up together" is a characteristic term of this epistle which proclaims the gospel of Christian liberty.

The law was only a guardsman and a paidagogos.

23) The Scripture locked up everything under sin. The Scripture record goes back to Adam, the first sinner. What, then, had the Mosaic law to do which came in so late after Abraham's time (v. 17)? Its function was very secondary and also ended with Christ (v. 19). **Moreover, before the faith came, we were being kept under guard by law, being locked up together for the faith about to be revealed.**

During the period when the Mosaic law was in force it functioned as a legal guardsman — that is all.

It stood as a guard over those who were locked up together under sin. Call the law a warden for that period. In v. 17 Paul states when the Mosaic law arrived; in v. 19 until what time it functioned, "until the Seed (Christ) came." "Before the faith came" covers the period thus already marked out: from Moses to Christ.

"Before the faith came" thus = "until the Seed (Christ) came." What the coming of the faith means we see from the phrase "for the faith about to be revealed." The coming refers to this revelation. It occurred with the coming of Christ, with his bringing the great fulfillment of the testamentary promise. This fulfillment stood forth in complete revelation for Jews and for Gentiles alike (v. 8, 9). Paul uses a striking term when he speaks of this as "the faith" arriving and being revealed. Note the article, it is not "faith" in general but *the* faith" in a specific sense. Abraham certainly had faith (v. 6), so did all the Old Testament saints, namely subjective faith.

"The faith" is to be taken objectively yet not as designating a period. It designates the substance of all justifying and saving faith in the hearts of believers. Before this substance came in Christ it existed only in promise and was embraced by faith as the sure promise of God (Abraham is the example). Then Christ brought the fulfillment, and in him this stood fully revealed; from then on believers embraced the fulfilled and revealed promise, i. e., the Christ who had actually come as promised, "the faith" in this sense.

Δέ is not adversative; it = "moreover" and adds the new point as to how the Mosaic law functioned during this period with reference to Christ, "the faith" in the sense of substance. This law could do nothing toward bringing the faith. Christ's coming was completely assured by the promise. Only this much is true, the Mosaic law would have had no object and would never have been given save for the promise and its fulfillment in Christ.

What, then, did this law do during this entire period of waiting since it came in on Sinai? It was posted as a guard or sentry over us, Paul says, who were locked in together under sin by the Scripture as stated in v. 22: "By law we were being kept under guard as being locked up together for the faith (Christ)," etc. "By law" (no article) means that the Mosaic law acted as law. The Mosaic law was, of course, "law" and therefore acted in the capacity of law. One of its functions was to stand guard. So the Mosaic law stood guard as law, like a sentry, until it was relieved of its duty by the arrival of Christ, "the faith."

When Paul says "we were guarded" he, of course, means "we Jews." But this is to be understood in the sense of Rom. 3:19; the law speaks to those who are under it, to whom it was given, and these were the Jews and not the Gentiles; but when the Mosaic law held all the Jews under guard as it did, it thereby stopped every mouth and declared the whole world guilty and subject to God's judgment. What this law did for the Jews had its bearing on the whole world, also on all the Gentiles who did not have the Mosaic law. If God dealt so with the descendants of Abraham, how would he deal with those who were nothing but pagans? In v. 22 the Scriptures locked up "everything" under sin. Paul now adds that the law stood sentry even over the Jews as those who were locked up.

The imperfect "we were being guarded" reaches back to Sinai and covers that entire period; it is matched by the durative present participle "as being locked up together"; but both tenses imply that this condition was to be followed by another, for both are open tenses, their action is not final. The idea of the verb is not that of being guarded against hostile attack but that of being in a prison and prevented from any possible escape; yea, there stood this mighty sentry all the time so that all Jews might see that they could not escape.

Yet he stood there because they were to escape. We have this stated already in v. 22. From Adam onward the Scripture confined everything under sin only in order that men might accept the promise by faith in Christ and thus escape from sin. Now Paul adds (δέ) that even then the Mosaic law kept its guard over the Jews, including those who believed, as locked up together for the fulfillment that was to be revealed in Christ. During the period from Sinai until Christ the sentry stood guarding even the believers. All the old Jewish believers had to observe the Mosaic law. The idea is not that they were still held under the damnation of sin like the unbelieving Jews but that they were held by this sentry "for the faith about to be revealed," for the Christ about to come. With their faith in the promise they were not to stray off from the fulfillment of that promise. The fulfillment would come from the Jews and from no other source (John 4:22); the Samaritans, for instance, worshipped they knew not what. It was the Mosaic law which kept the Jews for the fulfillment.

"About to be revealed" is a periphrastic substitute for the future tense and is not often found with the aorist infinitive (R. 857), but is punctiliar in the case of this aorist infinitive (R. 878). The revelation was to occur at a definite future time, namely when Christ came (v. 19). That would be the complete revelation for the Jews and for the whole world. Then the sentry duty of the Mosaic law would no longer be needed, it would end.

That time was now past. The guard had been recalled. What folly for the Judaizers to claim that he was still on duty and to invent for him an outrageous duty, one that he had never had, namely to hold believers to works of law by which nothing could be attained except the curse (v. 10)!

24) **And so** (ὥστε, R. 999) **the law has been our slave-guardian for Christ in order that as a result of faith we might get to be declared righteous. But the faith having come, no longer are we under a slave-guardian.**

With a closely allied figure Paul restates what he has just said about our being kept under guard by law. The sentry has been a παιδαγωγός for the Jews until Christ came. This term is literally, "boy's leader" and refers to the attendant, generally a slave, whom a wealthy Greek or Roman father provided for his son during the years between seven and seventeen, whose duty it was to attend and to watch over the lad. He took the boy to school and to gymnastic exercises, watched and corrected his deportment so that it might befit his station, and kept him from hurtful associations and influences, from foolish and hurtful actions. The lad was thus trained early and long ever to be a gentleman. The forbidding *vultus paedagogi* came to be proverbial. This "boy's guide" was not the boy's teacher except as indicated; nor was he appointed to administer punishment, for the father attended to the latter.

"And so," Paul says, "the law has been our boy's guardian for Christ," γέγονεν, "hath been" (R. V.), "was" (A. V.), but not "is become" (R. V., American Committee); for this function of the Mosaic law as also this law itself with all its ceremonialism ended with Christ. This perfect does not reach from the past to the present (Paul's time, our own time), it stopped when Christ came; the graph is not ●————→ but ▶————→● (R. 895).

Paul's statement is historical and not general or doctrinal. The American Committee seems to have confused the past historical fact which Paul presents to the Galatians, that during the period from Sinai to Christ the Mosaic law functioned as a *paidagogos* for the Jews, with the doctrinal statement which we formulate when we now adopt Paul's language about a *paidagogos* and call the moral law, no matter in what formulation, in that of the Ten Commandments or in any other, a means for directing or driving us to Christ. Paul is speaking of the ceremonial contents of the Mosaic law which were completely abrogated when Christ came, which had fulfilled the purpose for which they had been given when the faith was revealed (v. 23).

Yes, all the ceremonial regulations served just as a slave-guardian did for the boy in his charge. These regulations kept the Jews from mingling with the Gentiles, the bad boys who had no guardian, whose influence and association would bring pagan contamination. All these regulations focused on Christ; they were full of types of Christ. Think of the high priesthood, the sacrifices, the Temple itself (John 2:19-21). All these were "for or towards Christ." None of them had any meaning apart from Christ who was about to be revealed; all of them had served their historic purpose when Christ was revealed.

"For Christ" is elucidated by the purpose clause even as εἰς denotes purpose or aim: "in order that we might get to be declared righteous." This does not mean to get this declaration when Christ came. Millions of Jews died during the period between Sinai and Calvary. But this entire law ever pointed them to Christ, their Messiah, so that these Jews might believe in him as Abraham had believed and had been declared righteous as a result of faith. So the Jews were to believe and to be declared righteous (see v. 6, "righteousness"). The Old Testament believers were justified just as we are by faith in Christ, but they had the Christ who was to come while we have the Christ who has come.

This does not mean that the law worked faith and justification. The law never does that (v. 21b). But this we may say: as regulations all these were law; but all the types and figures in these regulations that referred to Christ were gospel. And this gospel content of the legal regulations helped to work faith, for this content went with the promise made to Abraham.

It is a misunderstanding of Paul's figure of the boy's guardian when the figure is made an allegory. This loses the *tertium comparationis*. Compare R., W. P., who regards Christ as "the Schoolmaster" and says that the guardian is dismissed, and that we are now "in the school of Christ." But the guardian sat in the school (and in the gymnasium), watched the boy there, and then took him home. The guardian went everywhere with the boy. He was not only his teacher. The point of this figure is the immaturity of the boy (4:1-3). He was rid of the guardian only after reaching maturity. As far as school was concerned, the school ended for him even before he was seventeen and was considered mature enough to dispense with a guardian slave.

It is startling in a way that Paul says: ἐκ πίστεως δικαιωθῶμεν, for with ἐκ he makes faith *the source* of God's act of justification. But Paul does this already in v. 12, and twice in Rom. 1:17, and in Rom. 4:16. How can faith be the source of justification? If we conceive the essence of faith to be an activity, *ein Holen Christi*, as it has been called, we must say that Paul is wrong, for in this sense faith could not be the source of God's justifying (and we may add his elective) act. But Paul presented faith as a passivity, *ein sich geben lassen*. In the instant of its creation by the gospel

Christ *is given* to faith. When I lie unconscious, say as I drift into death, and am capable of not the least activity, Christ is mine by this divine gift. Faith, so defined, is, indeed, the source of justification. Thus our fathers speak of election "in view of faith" and most carefully explain this phrase as signifying "in view of *the saving merits of Christ* perseveringly apprehended by faith." The power in the source lies in this content of faith and not in an activity. When faith is correctly defined, like Paul, we need not fear to attribute too much to it.

25) Paul continues: "But the faith having come," the faith in the sense of v. 23 (Christ), "no longer are we under a slave-guardian" (no article). With the arrival of "the faith" all mentorship, whether of the Mosaic law or of any other kind, ended automatically. The aorist participle is again historical. With the arrival of Christ everything changed for all believers whether they were native Jews, foreign proselyte believers, or pagans who were converted by the apostles. "No longer are we" refers to the "we" of the previous verses, namely Jews. Everything resembling a *paidagogos* was abolished, not only for believing Jews, but for all Jews; and if for them, then naturally also for all others. Since Christ came there has never been a *paidagogos* such as the Jews had by God's appointment. The apostles were not sent out into the world by Christ to offer the Gentiles the old Jewish legal system but to offer "the faith" alone.

26) The "we" forms occurring in v. 23-25 speak of Jews, the aorists of the time before Christ. In v. 25 Paul comes down to the arrival of Christ and thus says of the Jews that "we (Jews) are no longer under a guardian." He now turns to the Galatians and tells them what this abrogation of the Mosaic law, this abolition of the *paidagogos* means for them.

"For" = that you may understand what this means for you, note what you are. **For you all are God's sons through this faith in Christ Jesus.** All of you Galatians, whether former Jews or former Gentiles, are now "God's sons," nothing less. The predicate, which is placed before the copula, is emphatic. "Sons" is the significant term, mature, full-grown sons, who are in possession of the inheritance, the fulfillment of the promise (v. 18). The A. V. translates "children of God"; but τέκνα could not be used here. Its connotation is dearness; but the believers of the Old Testament time were as dear to God as those of the New Testament. "Children" may also connote immaturity, and it would do that here. Υἱοί, as the context requires, suggests the idea of standing, independent standing, that is free from any mentor such as children would have (a nurse, a slave-guardian).

The point is that the Galatians are not in a position that resembles that of the Old Testament believers. Theirs is full Christian liberty. More than this. The Judaizers were trying to put the Galatians back under the Mosaic regulations, and that not as the Old Testament believers were once under them but in a monstrous way such as God never thought of during the Old Testament period, namely that the Galatians should seek to be saved by observing these regulations. God had appointed the law as a mentor for his children, the Judaizers wanted this mentor turned into a tyrant slave driver for his sons. Paul tells the Galatians that even the mentor is gone, that they are now free sons.

"God's sons through the faith in connection with Christ Jesus" speaks of "the faith" exactly as was done in v. 23-25 where the article appears three times as it now does a fourth time. "The faith" is again objective. This objective substance of the faith is, of course, retained in the heart by subjective faith, by believing;

but Paul stresses the objective means (διά) of the sonship of the Galatians. When this is noted, the debate about the phrase "in Christ Jesus" becomes superfluous. The A. V. does not separate by a comma; the R. V. does and thereby has two separate modifiers of "you are." The A. V. is correct: "the (objective) faith" is ever connected with (ἐν) Christ Jesus. All that we believe centers in Christ, the Messiah who is Jesus. Paul's thought is not clearly apprehended when we take the sense to be: by believing (subjectively) in Christ (as the object). When Paul has this in mind he writes: "faith (no article) of Jesus Christ (genitive) as in v. 22. C.-K. 1083 is misleading when he speaks of *Gotteskindschaft* (it should be *Sohnschaft*) as though a corresponding conduct is implied. The context makes no reference to conduct.

27) With an explanatory "for" Paul adds: **For as many of you as were baptized in connection with Christ did put on Christ.** "As many as" takes up the "all you" of v. 26 and is to be understood in the same sense: whether formerly Jews or formerly pagans. Paul points the Galatians to their baptism as the date when they received "the faith" into their hearts. Baptism is an essential part of "the faith" (substance). By receiving the one the other is received. Both are objective to be, of course, received subjectively.

Robertson's grammar (592) is most convincing regarding static εἰς in Rom. 6:3, etc.: ὅσοι ἐβαπτίσθημεν εἰς Χριστὸν εἰς τὸν θάνατον αὐτοῦ ἐβαπτίσθημεν, and declares, "The notion of sphere is the true one." It is most decidedly. Rom. 6:3 must thus be translated: "As many of us as were baptized *in* Christ (not *into*) were baptized *in* his death (not *into*)." And in Matt. 28:19 the sense is, "*in* the name (not *into*)." This the papyri have taught us. All the former labored explanations of this εἰς are thus permanently corrected. The New

Testament was written when εἰς was being used with verbs of condition and even verbs of being which formerly had been using ἐν so that we meet εἶναι εἰς. This usage continued until in the Greek of the present time ἐν has disappeared. Here Paul writes just as he did in Rom. 6:3: "as many as were baptized εἰς Christ," *in* Christ.

Have no fear in regard to mysticism in the preposition, for the sense of εἰς is ἐν, and the sense of this latter is connection, location in the same sphere: "in connection with Christ." Baptism is ever in connection with Christ, in connection with his death (Rom. 6), in connection with the Name of the Father, etc., (Matt. 28:19), in connection with the remission of sins (Acts 2:38), the sphere and connection being indicated by the noun or the nouns that follow the preposition. Here the idea is not *auf Christum* (Zahn), which would require the Greek ἐπί, or *in Beziehung auf*. The whole action of baptism, the command, all the promises included in the sacrament as well as all else are wholly and completely *connected with* Christ, in one blessed sphere with him.

Paul says: By being baptized in Christ all you baptized Galatians "did put on Christ," or, as the middle may be rendered, "did allow yourselves to be clothed with Christ." On the permissive middle see R. 808, etc.; B.-D. 317. This verb does not mean "to play a role," the Galatians, like actors, being dressed up as Christ (Zahn). Nor does the idea of putting on Christ mean to acquire the same relation to God that Christ had, the relation of sonship. Nor is baptism "a badge or uniform of service like that of the soldier," his *sacramentum*, oath of fealty, a "symbolic picture" (R., W. P.). He who puts on Christ becomes partaker of his salvation. The imagery is not pagan but that of the Old Testament.

To put on Christ is to receive justification: "I will greatly rejoice in the Lord, my soul shall be joyful in my God; for he hath clothed me in the garments of salvation, he hath covered me with the robe of righteousness, as a bridegroom decketh himself with ornaments, and as a bride adorneth herself with her jewels," Isa. 61:10. Compare Luke 15:22; Matt. 22:11; Ps. 132:9, 16. The objection that this is not a wedding is unwarranted. Why must allowing oneself to be clothed refer especially to a wedding? Were the grown sons of Greeks and Romans not invested with garments that marked them as sons?

We should not lose ourselves in these details. The stress is on the name "Christ" which repeats "Christ Jesus" of v. 26. The point is the difference between the Old Testament believers who were still under the *paidagogos*, immature, still waiting for the revelation of the faith about to come, and the New Testament believers, God's sons, mature, free, not needing a mentor. This is the position "the faith" and our baptism give us: Christ is here at last, and we are joined to him. Verse 27 explains "in Christ Jesus" as it is used in v. 26. As the latter is a real, saving connection, so v. 27 is not mere symbolism, not an act of ours such as swearing fealty.

28) The new statement is without a connective and simply parallels the previous one. In baptism all the Galatians are alike clothed with the garment of Christ's perfect righteousness. In God's eyes they are all alike. During the time the Mosaic law was in force, this law itself recognized and maintained differences. It had provisions for Jews over against Gentiles — many of them; for free men over against slaves; for men over against women. When the faith and Christ came, these distinctions were abolished. **There is no Jew nor Greek, there is no slave nor free, there is no male and female; for you**

all are as one person in union with Christ Jesus. Ἔνι = ἔνεστι and is an old idiom (R. 313). Yet ἔνι (the preposition ἐνί [= ἐν] turned into an adverb) implies, not ἐστίν the copula, but ἔστιν, denoting existence: *es gibt*, "there exists."

The old distinction between Jew and Gentile is placed first; it extends to nations. Next is that between slave and free, and we must remember that this extended through the whole Roman world at that time. These two pairs are placed chiastically: for Jew was greater than pagan Greek, and free, of course, greater than slave. The last difference is a coordinate pair (note καί), two neuter terms: "no male and female," i. e., no male and no female sex. Paul stops with this; any other distinction can readily be added. He says: Since you Galatians are all sons of God by faith, clothed with Christ's righteousness in baptism, all these and similar distinctions and differences are wiped out as to your spiritual standing.

This does not involve a physical mutation. Christians of Jewish or of Greek descent retained their descent, free men and slaves kept their social positions, men and women kept their sex. The gospel changes nothing in the domain of this world and this natural life. In a way the gospel effects changes also in this domain. It has driven out slavery and has elevated the status of woman. But Paul is here speaking of the spiritual domain, of God's household in which all believers are equally sons of God.

Paul states this in a striking way: "For you are all one person in union with Christ Jesus." There are still many individuals, πάντες ὑμεῖς, and these remain "many." But in their union with Christ they are all εἷς, masculine, not ἕν, neuter, "one person," not just "one thing or body." The idea to be expressed is not that of the *Una Sancta*, namely Christ as the head and all of us one great organism or body of many members, each with his special gifts as pictured in Eph. 4:11-16. What union with Christ signifies for Jew, Greek, etc., is this that they are all alike in their spiritual standing, everyone has been baptized, declared righteous, etc., none are higher, none lower, none richer, none poorer, none better, none worse, none with more, none with less, in every respect they are exactly as "one person in Christ Jesus." All the Galatians are not a lot of sons of God with many differences in their sonship but a unit person. Whichever you take, the sonship is identical. Paul loves to end with a focal unit idea beyond which thought cannot go.

29) Now he even completes the circle by combining the end with the beginning. **And if you belong to Christ, then you are Abraham's seed, heirs according to promise.** The condition of reality assumes the fact which is indeed the fact, that the Galatians belong to Christ. "To be of Christ" is a Greek idiom: to be his, to belong to him. This defines what "being in Christ Jesus" means. Yet belonging to Christ fits exactly being heirs with him.

Ἄρα introduces the self-evident deduction: "then you are Abraham's seed," his true spiritual descendants (see v. 7). But this is only the intermediate thought; the final one is the apposition. With the word "promise" Paul reaches back to v. 8 where the promise is quoted, to v. 16-18 where the promise is connected with the testament, the inheritance, and the Supreme Heir. With "heirs" Paul recalls what he says of the testament in v. 15, 17, 18. God granted the inheritance to Abraham by promise (v. 17). So, then, as Abraham's seed we are heirs with Abraham, Abraham and we belong to Christ by faith alone. Or recalling that Christ is "the Seed" (v. 16) of Abraham, the Heir of the testament of promise, we who belong to Christ as Abraham's spiritual seed are heirs with Christ according to promise.

A silent contrast runs through all these blessed statements: the Mosaic law does *not* make sons of God, does *not* make us Abraham's seed, does *not* constitute us heirs. It is the promise alone which was fulfilled in Christ; it is faith and baptism and not works of law. Here is the answer to the Judaizers. Could the Galatians fail to feel its convincing power?

CHAPTER IV

2. (Continued): The Galatians Must Know the Limitations of the Law, 3:15-4:11

The law marked the heir as a minor; Christ brought him to majority.

1) When Paul says in 3:29 that by belonging to Christ the Galatians are Abraham's seed and thus heirs according to promise, one may well ask, "Were the Old Testament believers not also Abraham's seed and heirs according to promise?" In their capacity as heirs those Old Testament believers had the law of Moses; should the New Testament believers not also have it? This question is now answered in the most adequate and the most lucid way.

Now I say, for such a time as the heir is a minor he differs in nothing from a slave although he is lord of everything but is under guardians and stewards until the time fixed in advance by the father.

This is an illustration that is similar to the one employed in 3:15 regarding a human testament. This deals with an heir who is still a child, still a minor. Paul takes as his illustration a lad whose wealthy father has died and has left the boy a great estate. In this figure everything has to do with this orphaned lad and not with his dead father, hence the father is introduced only incidentally. We should not turn this illustration into an allegory. "Now I say" intends to emphasize what is said; it lays the finger on the point now stated about minors who fall heir to an estate. "The heir" has the generic article. Paul is not offering a fine legal point; so he writes merely νήπιος, infant, child, and thus a minor.

During the time that the heir is a minor he differs in nothing (adverbial accusative) from a slave although he is lord of everything (concessive participle) and really owns the entire estate. He is fed, nourished, and sheltered in the house, which is true also of a slave in the house. He has no control of the great property, which is likewise true of the slave.

2) Paul himself states what he has in mind. Just as a slave has his superiors who control him and his affairs, so this young heir. Paul thinks of a large inheritance as befits the great spiritual inheritance which he is illustrating. Hence he names two classes of superiors, ἐπίτροποι and οἰκονόμοι, which some regard as identical. But the former are those who are placed in charge of the young heir himself, call them guardians; the latter are those who manage his estates, stewards. The latter were often slaves yet were competent men, one being placed over this, the other over that estate of the owner. In our estimation the "guardians" were those who, among other things, attended to the boy's education.

Since Paul is writing to Galatians who are not merely Roman citizens, it is doubtful whether he refers to Roman law. This provided for a *tutor* (or several) until the age of puberty, the fourteenth year, was reached, after that for a *curator* until majority was attained, which occurred at the age of twenty-five years. The "guardians" of whom Paul speaks do not seem to be the *tutor* and the *curator* but those whose duty it was to provide the necessary teachers for the young heir. The point is that the minor heir is *under* others and that of necessity because he is still a minor.

The other point is the length of time he is under others, which is thus again mentioned, but now more specifically: "until the time set in advance by the father." Supply ἡμέρας with προθεσμίας, the genitive "of the father" is subjective. We need not puzzle about the legal date when majority was attained. Wherever the law specified the age, the will would naturally comply with this specification; wherever law and custom allowed latitude, the father's will would set a date that was agreeable to the father.

Much more important for Paul's illustration is this mention of the father. It is he who made the testament, he who designated the heir, he from whom the inheritance comes. Thus it is he who in one way or in another fixes the time when his heir is to enter upon control of the inheritance. The heir is no more of an heir after this date than he was before it as the participle used in v. 1 indicates; but after this date the heir is, indeed, no longer under anybody as he was before. This is the *tertium,* the essential point: once *under,* then *no longer under* according to the testamentary provision of the heir's own father.

3) So also we, when we were minors, had been put in slavery under the elementary things of the world; but when the fulness of the time came, God commissioned his Son, come to be from a woman, come to be under the law, that he should buy free those under law, that we should receive the sonship.

With "so" Paul introduces the great reality he has just illustrated by the standing of a minor heir. By "we were minors" he means "we Jews" just as he does in 3:23-25. Before Christ came, we were nothing but minor heirs. The distinction between believing and unbelieving Jews during the period before Christ is not stressed in this "we"; if we desire to stress it, we shall, of course, have to say that only believing Jews could be included. Yet "we" refers also to Paul himself as well as to all the Jews who came to faith after Christ came. So it is best to take "we" in this broader sense. God intended the inheritance for all Jews, treated all of them as minor heirs before Christ came, intended that all of them should enter upon the freedom from guardians and stewards after Christ came. The fact that so many frustrated all this for themselves by their unbelief is not considered here in order to make the main facts stand out the more.

During that entire period before Christ, while we were minors, "we had been put in slavery under the elementary things of this world." These στοιχεῖα were our "guardians and stewards." Paul has said that the minor heir does not differ from a slave in respect to being under superiors; hence he now says, "we had been put in slavery." The passive verb is causative. God is the agent in the passive. This condition of slavery had been imposed by means of the Mosaic law. The periphrastic past perfect reaches back to Sinai when this enslavement began and extends forward to Christ when it ended. A present perfect would imply that the enslavement is still in force; the past perfect reaches only to the time when God commissioned his Son.

What are these στοιχεῖα? This word has quite a range of meanings, M.-M. 591; C.-K. 1021: etymologically it means anything placed in a row, thus the letters of the alphabet; since Plato's time is was used to refer to the basic elements of which the world is composed, metaphorically it designates the elements or rudiments of knowledge. Of late the effort has been made to refer it to "the great angel powers which were said to preside over natural happenings and to rule over stars, wind, rain, hail, thunder, and lightning," "the spirits of the elements," "astral spirits." The usual discussion is limited to the meanings "elementary instruction" and "actual physical elements": we were under the *abc* instruction, in the primer department; or, we were under physical, material elements, were bound by law to all types of regulations regarding them. The point is not one that is difficult to decide.

Paul himself helps us. The genitive "of the cosmos" points to the physical. In v. 9, 10 he calls these elements "weak and beggarly," observing days, months, times, and years; in Col. 2:20 he adds regarding these elements the ordinances: "Handle not, nor taste, nor touch!" things which perish with the using, which are after the precepts and doctrines of men. These *stoicheia* need not be persons so as to match the guardians and the stewards of the illustration who are persons; for the point of the illustration is the fact that the young heir is really under those who are far beneath him. So the Old Testament believers were placed under material, earthly things that were beggarly, indeed, all of them far beneath these believers. They had to submit to regulations about food and drink, washings and purifications, sacrifices of all kinds, rules about places, times, bodily actions of all kinds.

These *stoicheia* were not the law itself but the earthly things with which the law had to do. In dealing with these perishable elements the law descended to the plane of human precepts and doctrines, Col. 2:20; for in all the pagan religions these likewise dealt extensively with material things. In the case of the Jews they were not self-chosen as they were in the case of the pagans but prescribed by God. Yet they constituted an enslavement, a burdensome one, indeed, and they became worse when the Jews laid all the stress on these beggarly things and lost sight of the purposes of God, of the promise, the spiritual inheritance, and faith in these. This divine purpose was the essential thing. Like a father, God so placed his young heirs under guardians and stewards and regulated all these earthly things only in order to safeguard them during their minority.

We thus do not accept the interpretation *Buchstaben* (Luther), elementary or rudimentary parts of religious knowledge; likewise the idea of "stars" and of heavenly bodies, and certainly not that of astral spirits or spirits that govern natural manifestations. "Under the elementary things of the world" contains a strong implication: God's sons ought to be *above* and not *under* these things. Since God placed his heirs under them, this could be only a temporary arrangement. What folly for the Judaizers to claim that this subjection to things beneath us is intended to be permanent!

4) This temporary period passed. In the illustration Paul has already said that in the case of the heir it was to last only until the date fixed by the father. We should keep to that and not suppose that the heir grows up and thus attains his majority. Let us stay with the *tertium* and thus with the reality itself. The idea that the Jewish Old Testament believers finally grew up is beside the mark. Think of how few such there were when Christ came.

"The fulness of the time" is the condition of being full as regards the time ($\pi\lambda\eta\rho o\tilde{\upsilon}\nu$ with the accusative), i. e., the full time. This fulness of the time should not be explained by means of philosophizing: "Until generations of mankind had learnt through years of social training to control some of the animal instincts of their lower nature, to rebel against its brutal passions, and desire to live in obedience to their higher nature," etc. (*Expositor's Greek New Testament*). Some think only of the Jews and find the fulness of the time in a certain ripeness and maturity that were finally reached by the Jews. But if Judaism was ever at a low spiritual ebb, it was so when this fulness of the time arrived.

All we are able to say is that God knew when the proper time had arrived. Judaism was bankrupt, and paganism had always been so. We can enumerate some of the providences which helped to open the way for the gospel such as the vast extent of the Roman

Empire, the spread of the Greek language, the facility of travel throughout the empire, the extensive diaspora of the Jews, its many proselytes from Gentilism, etc. All of these aided the spread of the gospel. What God saw and regarded as the fulness of the time in the spiritual condition of men, barbarian as well as Greek, is too difficult for us to predicate because his thoughts and judgments are too unsearchable for us. Paul, too, refrains from stating details.

Then God "commissioned forth his Son." This verb is the more vivid because it is not the usual compound with only ἀπό but has an added ἐκ. This means that the Son went out on his commission not only "from" God but "out from" God. John says that he was "with" (πρός) God (John 1:1) and was God and that he became flesh (v. 14). Not as an angel might be commissioned but as one of the three Persons of the Godhead. It is usually stated that the pre-existence of Jesus is indicated here, but that would apply also to an angel; no less than the deity is expressed here. When we translate "sent forth" we should note that the verb means more. While πέμπω is also used with reference to the Son even as he calls the Father "my Sender" (John's Gospel), ἀποστέλλω and ἐξαποστέλλω mean to be sent or sent out on a commission, to execute a great mission, the one here briefly described.

The action of the two aorist participles is, of course, contemporaneous with the aorist "commissioned," but what is their relation to the verb? The Greek and our two versions leave the answer to the reader. The relation is that of mode, hence participles are used which indicate subsidiary action. The son's commission involved his getting to be (derived) from a woman and thus also getting to be under law. The second participle states what the first involves; both are alike historical: the Son "got to be" ἐκ and ὑπό or "became" the one and the other. Our English has no word that can adequately render these two participles which mean neither the passive "was made" (A. V.) nor the intransitive "was born" (R. V.), the Greek for which latter is γεννηθέντα. Either will do as a translation if the English is not stressed.

In this connection we take note of the effort of some to eliminate the virgin birth from this passage. These can be divided into two groups: those who determine *a priori* the absolute impossibility of such a birth and cancel Matthew's and Luke's accounts; secondly, those who are more or less affected by the argumentation of the former. Over against all of them stands the church of the ages with its faith in the statements of the Word. The one aim of the church is to read what the Word says and then to believe that. "The Son of God" is the second person of the Godhead; he "became out of a woman" in executing his mission. This is the Incarnation, the miraculous conception, the virgin birth. God's Son became man, the God-man.

The phrase that begins with ἐκ denotes more than the separation from the womb, it includes the entire human nature of the Son as this was derived from his human mother. The word γενόμενον is exactly the proper word to express this thought, even the tense is very accurate. The Son's going out from God on his mission is seen in his becoming man. He did not cease to be the Son of God when he became man. He did not drop his deity, which is an impossible thought. He remained what he was and added what he had not had, namely a human nature, derived out of a woman, a human mother. He became the God-man.

Thereby he became, got to be, under law. The one getting to be involves the other, and both had as the object of his mission "that he buy free those under law," etc. The Son could do this and did it by having become man, by having come to be under law. The

God-man is our Redeemer from the curse of the law, "having become a curse in our stead" (3:13). Look at it from either side, from his going forth from God for his mission or from the accomplishment of that mission, and we see what the participial statements declare, namely the Incarnation of the Son and his subjection to law. By means of these two God's Son accomplished our purchase and our liberation. Cancel his deity, consider God's Son a mere human "son," and both are eliminated, his going forth from God and his purchase of condemned mankind.

It is true, the Galatians know that "out of a woman" refers to the Virgin Mary, and that Paul does not need to mention her name or her virginity in this connection. But these specifications are side thoughts. The two thoughts needed here are general: out of a human mother — hence "woman"; and under law — hence not "the law." The facts that this was a specific woman, and that this was a specific law are self-evident. The idea that ἐκ predicates only the birth and not also the conception is untenable. Does birth or does it not involve conception?

"His Son — out of a woman" pointedly omit mention of a human father. Why? Because this is God's Son who is co-eternal with the Father. He became man by way of "a woman" alone. Incomprehensible? Absolutely so! A miracle in the highest degree? Beyond question! Yet, if we were asked to state how God's Son could become man, should we say that it could not be done in this way as God says that it was but would have to be brought about by way of a human father? Would that remove the miracle?

The Christian mind rebels against speculations of this kind. It turns the pages of Holy Writ; it reads Matt. 1, Luke 1 and 2; Gen. 3:15, the woman's seed; Isa. 7:14; Micah 5:3; and all the others in this line, John 1:13, 14; Luke 3:22, 23, Mary's descent; Matt.

1:16 (see the author on the interpretation of these three passages). All of these present the *fact* of which Paul writes tersely, which is back of all his other references (Rom. 1:3 and many another); why *speculate* about how the fact might have been other than it was? *"Come to be* out of a woman" is not like Job 14:1: "man *born* of woman," which designates the frailty and the mortality of all men (hear the funeral bells ringing!). The participle is "became" and not "born"; it is predicated of God's Son and not of man in general or in particular. The God-man could die but did not need to die. He laid down his life voluntarily (John 10:18) as the ransom or purchase price for us (Matt. 20:28).

The point to be brought out in "come to be out of a woman" is expressed by the second participle which is appositional and specifying: "come to be under law." He who was greater than all law placed himself under law just as he who was greater than his mother became her child. Only this point is here brought forward, that by coming to be of a woman the Son of God came to be under law. This is due to the fact that Paul is speaking of the latter, of the Jews being under the elements of the world by virtue of the Mosaic law until the time set by God. Paul is speaking of the arrival of this time. It is when the Son of God became man, when he, too, came to be under law once for all to end this domination of law. The figure of heirs, of testamentary provisions concerning minority and majority merge into the reality as the Son's mission is described, which is too great for that figure; only the echoes of it remain, cf., v. 5-7.

We must note the anarthrous "under law" here and in v. 5. When "law" refers to the Mosaic law it often deals with it as belonging to the general category of law. It does so here. This point is important because of v. 5. How many did the incarnate Son buy free?

Only the Jews? No; all men. How many were "under law"? We have the answer in 3:10. In Rom. 3:19 we have more: when the Mosaic law spoke to the Jews who had this specific law, it stopped every mouth and made the whole world guilty before God as Paul shows at length in Rom. 3:10-18 from the Scriptures themselves, as he has shown it from the fact of the universality of sin in Rom. 1:18-32. Not only does such law as the pagans have condemn them in view of the final day of judgment (Rom. 2:12-16), the Mosaic law, as the pure revelation of God's opposition to sin, by condemning the Jews, stopped every mouth and made the whole world guilty before God.

The Son "came to be under law" in general and not only under the pure code of Moses, but by virtue of this code under all that mankind had left of God's law as written in their hearts. That is why Paul connects the Son's Incarnation with his coming to be under law and does not say that by his circumcision he came to be under the Jewish code. But why bring in the Roman law, Christ's dying because of a verdict pronounced by a Roman governor? That verdict was a travesty on Roman law as the Sanhedrin's verdict was a travesty on Jewish law. Paul says "law" and not all manner of civil and criminal codes.

"Under law" implies that the incarnate Son was to fulfill law and thereby purchase our Christian freedom. Paul is nullifying the contention of the Judaizers regarding the permanent validity of the Mosaic ceremonial laws for all Christians. That is why the sacrificial death of the Son, i. e., the passive obedience, is not treated here. It is the active obedience that nullifies all Judaistic ideas. By this, Paul says, the Son bought us free.

This answers the mistaken idea that the Son fulfilled the law *for himself* so that he might remain spotless in order to offer himself as a lamb without blemish to die for our sins. This at best conceives the Son's active obedience only as pertaining indirectly to us. But Paul says that the Son bought us by this active obedience. It was thus just as much substitutionary as his passive obedience. In fact, the two cannot be separated. Even in death the Son gave himself (active) and so was slain (passive). The two were indissolubly united during all of his life. We should never stress the one against the other because the passive obedience is more frequently mentioned in Scripture than the active.

This answers Meyer's attack upon the statements: "because of the sole merit, *complete obedience*, bitter suffering, death, and resurrection of our Lord Christ alone, whose obedience is reckoned to us for righteousness," *C. Tr.* 919, 9; "before God's tribunal only the righteousness of the *obedience*, suffering and death of Christ, which is imputed to faith, can stand," etc., 927, 32. We mention Meyer only because others agree with him.

5) God's purpose in his Son's coming to be under law was "that he should buy free those under law." In 3:13 Paul has said: "Christ bought us free from the curse of the law by having become a curse in our stead." Here he uses the same verb ἐξαγοράζειν (see 3:13). The fact that God's purpose was achieved is intimated by the aorist of the subjunctive. This first purpose clause is objective, for those bought free are "those under law"; the second clause is subjective, for those who are to receive its benefits are "we." We have already stated why "those under law" (no article with "law") describes men in general and not merely the Jews under their Mosaic law. But "we" in the second clause is the same as the "we" occurring in v. 3 and does denote Jews. By the purchase of all men who were under law the Jews in particular were to

be set free from the Mosaic law, this sentry (3:23), this *paidagogos* (v. 25), the subjection to guardians and stewards (4:2).

We cannot see that with "those under law" Paul refers only to the Jews and with "we" to the believers (either himself or Jewish Christians or the Jewish and the Gentile Christians combined). In Rom. 3:19 Paul himself states how what was done for Jews affected every mouth, the whole world; here he does not state anything that is similar, namely that what the Son did for the Jews also affected certain Gentiles.

The whole thought is a refutation of the Judaizers. God's Son set free all those who were under law; this purpose, being objective, was achieved. Furthermore, it was achieved in order that we Jews should receive the sonship. This was a subjective purpose that was also achieved, but only in the believing Jews, the unbelieving were hardened and cast away (Rom. 11:7). "The sonship" is modified by the context (v. 1-3) and thus signifies the status of sons who have advanced from their minority to their majority, to the status of full-grown sons who are no longer under guardians and stewards. "Adoption" is not the proper word, for it may apply to a babe, a minor son and heir.

This eliminates the question as to whether regeneration as well as justification is included in this "sonship." In their minority, before Christ came all the heirs were both regenerated and justified although they were still under the guardianship and the stewardship of the Mosaic law (v. 2). When Christ came, when their majority was attained, this involved the end of the guardianship and stewardship of law for them. Ever after that time they were entirely free of it.

6) Jewish believers were formerly minors, now that God's Son has bought free all those under law. Jewish believers have received the standing of sons who are in their majority. This fact pertains to all

Christian believers whether they are former Jews or former Gentiles and thus to the Galatians, most of whom were such Gentiles. It helps us to understand Paul's thought if we remember that during the period before Christ the many believing Gentile proselytes to Judaism also did not get beyond the status of minors. But now Paul is able to say to all the Galatian believers: **And because you are sons, God commissioned the Spirit of his Son for our hearts as crying: Abba Father! Wherefore no longer art thou a slave but a son. And if a son also an heir through God.**

Some think that ὅτι = "that," and that the whole clause is an adverbial accusative: "Regarding this that you are sons" the evidence is that God, etc. This translation assumes that the sonship of the Galatians is now to be proved, and that the possession of the Spirit is the proof. But the sonship is proved in v. 4, 5, and what is now added is the result of this sonship, the corroboration of it, exactly as is done in Rom. 8:14, 15, which treats the possession of the Spirit as one of the great results of justification. A result may, of course, be used to prove its cause; but here Paul does not reverse matters in this way, he states the cause and then its result. In 3:2 he inquires for the source of the effect and thus does reverse the two.

The moment we note that "sons" means sons who are no longer in their minority but in their full majority, we see how Paul has, indeed, proved the Galatians to be such sons: God's Son has abolished all minority, no minor heirs now exist, all guardians and stewards over minors are now and forever abolished. It is in this sense that the Galatian believers are "sons" also with the evident result of such mature sonship and freedom from superiors, namely that God commissioned the Spirit of the Son with the cry of sons, "Abba Father."

Note the close parallel: "God commissioned forth his Son" (v. 4) — "God commissioned forth the Spirit of his Son." These are the two great historic acts. All the promises of Jesus regarding the sending of the Spirit apply, John 14:16, etc.; 15:26; 16:13, etc.; Acts 1:8. The fulfillment came on Pentecost and remained for all believers of all time. The things to be noted are not the outward miraculous signs which occurred at the time of Pentecost, which are like the angels singing at the time of the nativity; but all the statements of Jesus that the Spirit could not come to the disciples until Jesus had gone to the Father. When redemption was entirely complete, the Spirit came, "commissioned forth" as Jesus had been. Then all the guardians and the stewards were dismissed, the Spirit took their place, for the heirs' minority was ended, the Galatian believers were "sons" in this full sense.

We need scarcely say that the Spirit wrought in the Old Testament, that the faith of the Old Testament believers was produced by the Spirit. To think that the Old Testament believers were devoid of the Spirit is to imagine an impossibility. Pentecost ushered in a new era, the era when the Spirit is able to glorify Jesus as one having come, to take all that Jesus has achieved, to declare it unto us, John 16:14; this is his world-wide mission. And this means: no longer minor heirs waiting for this era. "You are sons."

For such "sons" the Spirit of God's *Son* is intended. When Paul says that he is in *"our"* hearts and changes from the second person plural to the first, we must go on to v. 7 where he changes to "thou," the singular, every individual. These different pronouns are not stressed over against each other; they merely turn the thought in every direction. "Our" hearts thus include Paul and the Galatian believers. Paul himself and the great mass of Jewish believers in the Christian

Church had come to faith *after* the Son brought redemption. This includes the 3,000 who came to faith after the Spirit was poured out at Pentecost. Like the Gentile believers, all of them at once became "sons." Do not forget that among the 3,000 there were not a few proselytes (Acts 2:10), former Gentiles. All of them were not minors but sons in their majority. There was no further waiting for the testamentary promises to be fulfilled, no further supervision for minor heirs.

Κράζω may, perhaps, be rendered "exclaim." *Sermo vehemens, cum desiderio, fiducia, jure, constantia*, Bengel. We do not see how this can refer to congregational praying. Nor does "Abba Father" recall the Lord's Prayer which begins, "Our Father who art in heaven"; it brings to mind Christ's prayers in Gethsemane (Mark 14:16) together with Heb. 5:7, "strong crying" (κραυγή which is allied to κράζω). While the crying of the name is predicated of the Spirit, this is evidently to be understood mediately as in Rom. 8:15: "in whom we cry." The Spirit is said to utter this cry when he moves us to utter it. The fact that he is in our hearts is the result of our sonship, and his presence makes this cry possible.

The nominative form ὁ Πατήρ is quite regular after the vocative Ἀββᾶ; it is the repetition of the Aramaic and the Greek terms for Father that is so exceptional. Various Hebrew and Aramaic expressions were taken over by the early Greek Church, but this one is a combination of Aramaic and Greek. Jesus himself certainly spoke Aramaic in Gethsemane and thus would not add the Greek "Father" to the Aramaic "Abba." It seems that Mark, who loved to report original Aramaic expressions and who alone tells us that Jesus cried "Abba," added ὁ Πατήρ to it for the sake of his Greek readers. This had probably been done before when the Gethsemane story was told. Thus, we may assume, "Abba Father" entered the language of the church and became an established liturgical expression which combined the word that was dear to the Jewish ear and tongue with its Greek equivalent. The thought of the apostle is that we sons who are now in full possession of all that we have in the Son and in the Spirit of the Son direct our "Abba Father" to God in our fulness of sonship.

7) Paul makes this most personal and individual by harking back to v. 1 and the thought that the minor heir differs from a slave in no respect. "Wherefore no longer art thou a slave (in the sense of v. 1) but a son" who has attained his majority; and that means "an heir through God," one who possesses and enjoys the spiritual fulness of the inheritance accorded by the testament (3:15, etc.). The inheritance involved is not yet the heavenly glory but the salvation that has been fully wrought out by the Son. He is the Heir Supreme, we are his joint heirs (Rom. 8:17).

There is no reason for raising a question in regard to the υἰοθεσία (v. 5) when this is taken in the sense of "adoption" and asking whether Paul has in mind the Jewish law regarding adoption or the Roman law. In this section Paul does not discuss the question as to how we become "sons" (by adoption) but discusses what the position of minor and of major sons is irrespective of the point as to how they become sons and heirs. Therefore it is better to translate this word "sonship" rather than "adoption." We thus consider irrelevant to the present connection the evidence of adoption adduced from the Old Testament: that of Esther by Mordecai, of Eliezer by Abraham, of the sons of concubines as legal sons, of Joseph's sons by Jacob to share equally with uncles, etc.

The phrase "through God" is, however, vital. Our present standing as heirs in possession and not merely in anticipation is due entirely to God. Διά views God as the medium by whom this our high standing has been effected; the explanation appears in v. 4 and 6: God commissioned his Son and the Spirit of his Son. Thus we are what we are today and have what we have as heirs.

Do the Gentile Christians in Galatia want to go back into the old bondage?

8) In contrasting the condition under the law with that when one is freed from the law Paul used a comparison (v. 1) which applied directly to the Jewish Christians and indirectly (v. 3, "the elements of the world") to the Gentile Christians. He now completes this by doing the reverse, by speaking directly about the Gentile and indirectly about the Jewish Christians.

Paul has said of the former that they, too, are "sons" who are not minors (v. 6), that everyone is an "heir" in possession of the inheritance and not a slave (v. 7), i. e., a minor who does not differ from a slave (v. 1). Just what had the position of the Gentile Christians been before they became Christians? **Now at the time, not knowing God, you slaved for those who by nature are not gods.**

'Αλλά is merely copulative and adds the further fact (R. 1185, etc.); it is *not* adversative, does not mean "but." Τότε μέν, "then" or "at that time," is in contrast with νῦν δέ (v. 9), "but now." The condition of the Gentile Christians before their conversion and during the whole time when the Jews were still in the position of minors is described by the constative participle, "not knowing God." Οὐκ instead of μή makes the participial negation more clear-cut, R. 1137. It is a simple fact, the Gentiles did not even know the true God; they lived in utter pagan darkness and blindness. The Galatians will not question that fact.

In correspondence with that ignorance "you slaved for those who by nature are not gods." In this way these Gentiles were most miserable slaves; they slaved for idols. Note the likeness: under the Mosaic regulations even the Old Testament believers were in a position that was no better than that of a slave (v. 1); the Gentiles, who were ignorant of God, were outright slaves under idols. There was, indeed, a difference: the Mosaic law was divinely given while the false gods were human inventions; Jewish believers had sonship as minors, pagans had nothing. Yet a certain likeness existed regarding the point of slavery. The frightful condition of the slavery of the Gentiles was the fact that "they slaved (constative aorist, expressing the entire action as a unit) for those who by nature are not gods." They were imaginary beings, fictitious gods. The negative with the participle is the common μή, which, however, does not express only Paul's judgment; it negates the fact in the ordinary way.

All of the paganism found in the world today presents the same picture of the vilest and the most pitiful slavery. The pagan gods are not gods in any true sense of the word. The thought that Paul expresses a certain measure of excuse for the Gentiles because they did not know God contradicts Rom. 1:19-32, especially v. 19-21. The context is against the idea of an excuse, for the idea to be expressed is that of a most wretched and base condition.

9) But now, having come to know God, rather having come to be known by God, how are you turning back to the weak and beggarly elements for which you are wanting to slave over again?

The two participles are good examples of the ingressive aorist. We have trouble in conveying by translation what these two participles mean in distinction from the one used in v. 8. C.-K. 388 distinguishes: εἰδέναι = the knowing of an object which enters the per-

Galatians 4:9   211

ception of a subject; γινώσκειν = the attitude or relation of self to the object that is known. The latter is not exact enough. The Lutheran fathers defined the latter as *nosse cum affectu et effectu.* They also gave the same meaning to the Hebrew *yada'*, "to know with affect and effect," a knowing with approval and love, with full acceptance, John 10:27; II Tim. 2:19. In Matt. 7:23: "I never knew you," means I never knew you in love as my own. God, of course, knew them intellectually or mentally.

Note that both οὐκ εἰδότες and γνόντες have the identical object, and these are direct objects. This is one of the evidences for the view that in the case of the latter the basic idea of knowing remains and is never altered to signify an act only of the will: to choose or elect, a synonym of ἐκλέγεσθαι. R., *W. P.*, expresses this predestinarian idea when he comments on the passive participle "known by God": "God's elective grace." Does Paul say that we *elected* God, and that we *were* elected by God? The question answers itself.

"Rather having come to be known by God" is not intended to cancel "having come to know God" nor to correct the active by means of the passive. The addition is a fuller statement as to how the great change with regard to the Gentiles came about. They got to know God as their own in faith and in love but not by their own ability and effort. God wrought upon them so that he could know them as his own in love, and so these Gentiles got to know God of whom they had been totally ignorant before. The change of voice in the two expressions is most effective. Luther states it in a fine way: non *ideo cognoscuntur quia* cognoscunt, sed contra, *quia cogniti* sunt, *ideo* cognoscunt.

The ingressive aorist participles speak of the start the Galatians have made and thus leave room for the question, "What about the present and the future until the end?" "How are you turning back" = how is it that you are turning back? The first meaning of πάλιν is "back" (place), the second "again" (time); both are used here. Observe the two present tenses "are you turning — you are wanting": the defection was not yet accomplished, it had just recently begun. Are the Galatians turning back "to the weak and beggarly elements"? Here we have the same term that was used in v. 3 (which see), and the relative clause, "for which you are wanting to slave anew," attaches the same thought of slavery. These elements make slaves (passive in v. 3), and men are willing to slave for them (active here in v. 9). The Mosaic law formerly held the Jews to "the elements of the world," regulations about food, drink, and all kinds of material things and outward actions. They were no better than slaves. The Galatians were formerly in a similar state, the Gentiles among them being tied in slavery to their pagan religion with all its material, cheap earthly elements of sacrifices, temples, ceremonies, etc. God's Son bought them all free (v. 4), and the Galatian Christians, Jewish and Gentile, had, by faith in the Son, entered on this freedom, the great and complete sonship. Paul asks how they can possibly now turn back and become slaves again, actually willing slaves in a slavery they had so happily left.

By accepting the works of law of the Judaistic teaching these Gentile Galatians would only exchange their old pagan *stoicheia* for the abrogated Mosaic and and Jewish *stoicheia*. Paul places these *stoicheia* on the same plane and even calls them "weak," unable to bring man into the blessed relation with God, most certainly not when they are used as works of law after the manner of the Judaizers; in addition he calls them "beggarly" (poor in this sense), having no wealth to give such as the Son gives, keeping those who cling to these "elements" in servitude as slaves. Both adjectives have the strongest persuasive force, both state undeniable facts.

As in v. 8, "you slaved for those who are not gods," so here Paul again has the dative "for which you are wanting to slave." We need not identify the *stoicheia* with the pagan god although the idols were material, carved images and thus could be called "elements." It seems better to think of all that was connected with pagan worship, temples, sacrifices, ceremonies employing material objects just as "elements" of this kind were used in the Mosaic regulations. The difference that the elements in the Jewish regulations had been appointed by God while those in paganism were merely of human choice, is disregarded as being immaterial. John 4:21-24 helps us in the interpretation. Worship in spirit and in truth is devoid of all elements of the world in the sense in which Paul uses the term.

10) Paul's intensity of feeling is reflected in the lack of connectives for introducing v. 10 and 11. "The intense pulse beat of the agitated mind expresses itself in the short hammer blows of speech." Zahn. These are declarations and scarcely questions. **Days you are carefully observing and months and seasons and years! I am afraid about you; perhaps I have labored for you in vain!**

Here we see what success the Judaizers had had with the Galatians, which agrees with the present tenses used in v. 9; also in how far they had failed, for the Galatians had not yet accepted circumcision otherwise Paul would have mentioned this and most likely have named it first.

The terms used refer to Mosaic regulations. While all of them refer to time, the terms expressing time are not themselves the *stoicheia* but refer to the elements involved in these terms. Thus all labor with earthly things was forbidden on the Sabbath, the Jewish fasts forbade eating food, etc. Material, earthly things are always involved. "Days" are singled out by being placed before the verb; the compound verb is perfective: "you are carefully observing" (R. 613), and is an indirect middle: "for yourselves," R. 810. These are the days fixed by the Mosaic law, the Sabbaths, the fast and the feast days such as the Passover, the new moons, etc.

"Months" are often referred to new moons, but these are "days." Months signify entire months such as the seventh month Tisri, called Sabbath month since its first day was treated like a Sabbath; also Nisan, the first month which introduced the Jewish church year and was distinguished by the Passover.

The καιροί or "seasons," as distinct from "days" and "months" on the one hand and from "years" on the other, are the seasons of prayer and fasting prescribed by the law. The "years" refer to the sabbatical year and to the interval of years. It would be speculative to conclude that a sabbatical year was in progress at the time when Paul wrote. His meaning is that the Galatians had accepted the Jewish system as far as it was marked by these terms referring to time. The Galatians had been under Judaistic influence for only a brief period yet had begun the observance of time; how many Sabbaths, etc., they had already kept is immaterial. The tense of the verb means that the Galatians were launched upon this Jewish legalism.

11) "I am afraid about you; perhaps I have labored for you in vain!" J. M. Moulton, *Einleitung in die Sprache des Neuen Testaments*, 303, etc., offers the best explanation of μή as it is here used. Φοβοῦμαι has its direct object; the μή clause is paratactic, and μή = "perhaps," to which πῶς or ποτέ is commonly added. This is not a verb of fearing with μή meaning "lest" (our versions and the usual explanation); B.-D. 370, 1; R. 1169. The perfect indicative of the verb

"to labor" is used which fits the actual work done during the extent of time in the past. Note the emphasis on "in vain" which is placed before the verb, also on the phrase "for you" which is placed at the end and pointedly repeats the pronoun, "I am afraid about *you*." Can it be that *for the Galatians* Paul has done all the hard work he has done entirely in vain? The verb denotes trying labor. Luther comments: *Lacrymas Pauli haec verba spirant.* The simple accusative in the sense of "I fear *for* or *about* you" (not "I fear you") is unusual.

Paul's work would certainly be in vain if all that it eventually accomplished would be to make the Gentile Galatians exchange their old pagan elements and observances for the old abrogated Jewish elements and observances. Neither brought justification and salvation. Worse than never having had salvation with its liberation from these "elements" is to have had it and then to give it up and to turn back to such "elements."

3. *Paul Admonishes the Galatians to Drop Their Legalism, 4:12-5:12*

From this point onward the epistle is admonitory yet with a difference: 4:12-5:12 deals with dropping legalism itself, while 5:13 to the end deals with the evidence that it has been dropped, the Christian life exhibiting this fact.

Personal appeal: the Galatians and Paul once and now

12) The break in thought is marked by the turn to admonition and thus also by the warm address "brethren" (see 1:11). The transition from the previous section is made in a natural manner by v. 8-11. **Be (ever) like me; for myself also (became) like you, brethren — (this) I beg of you!**

This is admonition in the form of direct, most personal petition: "I beg of you!" Note the durative present imperative which we express by adding "ever." The Greek uses γίνεσθαι, not as differing from εἶναι, but as expressing movement. It is generally recognized that in the ὅτι clause we must supply the aorist and not the present which loses the thought; hence not: "for I *am* as you *are*" (our versions), which contradicts the facts, but: "for I, too, *became* like you," i. e., I became as you yourselves once were. The view that we should construe together: "for I myself beg you as (once) you yourselves (begged me)," is peculiar; the Galatians never begged Paul.

The thought is striking, paradoxical, involving a chiasm. The Galatians were formerly Gentiles without the Jewish legal system. Paul was formerly a Jew under this Jewish legal system. Then he became a believer in Christ, dropped this legal system, and thus became like the Gentiles who never had it. But the Galatians, who were originally without the Jewish system (insofar as they were of Gentile descent) and, on becoming Christians, were still without this system, were at this late date beginning to adopt at least large parts of it (v. 10). Paul begs them not to do so but ever to be as he is who had dropped all of it. Once he became as they had been while they were pagan — without the Mosaic law. Now the Galatians are to reciprocate — after having taken up a part of that law under the influence of the Judaizers, they are to drop it entirely just as Paul had done.

But note that there is a plus on Paul's side. It was a revolutionary act for a bigoted Jew such as Paul once was to relinquish the Jewish regulations; it was a far slighter thing for the Gentile believers in Galatia to relinquish these regulations which had been only recently foisted upon them. Paul is begging them to do a thing that is far easier and much smaller than the one he had done.

Paul's appeal involves still more. He was the one who had converted the Galatians, who had brought them full Christian liberty, freedom from all material and earthly *stoicheia*, pagan as well as Jewish. He did that and could do it only as one who was himself wholly free. Think of the blessed fruits of Paul's arduous labors on the Galatians! Are they now to be lost (v. 11)? Will the Galatians now become unlike Paul to whom they owe everything? Do they intend to turn to the abrogated Judaism from which Paul had turned when salvation came to him? This personal relation of the Galatians to Paul is here touched upon in "like me — like you — I beg of you" and in the affectionate "brethren." Paul intends to make it prominent in what follows. He will contrast the love with which the Galatians first received him with the way in which the Judaizers try to gain the Galatians for themselves.

Without a connective Paul adds: **No wrong did you do me.** From his present petition Paul turns to the past, to the time when he first came to the Galatians. Note the aorist which accords with those that follow so that we must regard all of them in the same way. Paul has no complaint to make concerning the treatment he had received during his past relation with the Galatians. The negative statement to the effect that the Galatians had done Paul no wrong is in fact a litotes: they had treated him properly, how very properly he describes in the following. Because of the way in which the Galatians had hitherto treated Paul he feels that they will now heed his request (v. 12); they will surely not wrong him now.

Because of the constative aorist and its connection with what follows it seems unwarranted to interpret: by their defection the Galatians had in a way done Paul wrong, had shown themselves ungrateful (although, unlike the Corinthians, they had not turned against Paul personally), but that he did not want the Galatians to think that personal feeling and resentment moved him to take his readers to task, that he is jealous of his own honor. This would place the force of the aorist into the immediate past. It would also not be true. If Paul had anything approaching this in mind he would have said so and have done so with more than three words.

13) Paul refers to his previous connection with the Galatians in which they had done him no wrong: **but you know that because of illness of the flesh I preached the gospel to you at the first; and the temptation to you in my flesh you did not despise nor loathe; on the contrary, as an angel of God you received me, as Christ Jesus.**

This is the lovely treatment the Galatians accorded Paul when he first came among them. Instead of stating merely the facts Paul adds "you know," a touch of intimacy, friend speaking to friend about an experience shared together.

"Because" Paul was ill he preached to the Galatians on that first visit to them. All of the texts have the phrase with the accusative: "because of my bodily illness"; the proposal to change this to the genitive: "despite my bodily illness" ($διά$ as in Rom. 2:27; 4:11), is unwarranted. This proposal is due to the supposition that when Paul came from Paphos and landed at Perga and then continued on to Pisidian Antioch in Galatia, he had not intended to stop here but purposed to go on past this country.

But whither did he intend to go? We are told, "To Ephesus." A glance at the map shows that this conjecture is unconvincing; for if that had been his intention, he would have landed at Attalia and taken the road westward or would have sailed on to the harbor of Ephesus. Acts 13:13, 14 says that he landed at Perga and, instead of preaching here, went forthwith to Antioch and to the other Galatian cities. The wrong supposition is that sickness prevented Paul from going beyond Antioch; the right conclusion is that his sickness forced him to leave Perga at once and to hurry to Antioch. He could not remain and work in Perga which lay in the lowlands, he had to seek the higher elevations; Antioch and the Galatian region lay over 3,000 feet above sea level. Here Paul could hope to work even while he was sick, could gradually shake off his illness and then later on evangelize Perga — the very thing he did.

Thus, *because* of illness he preached in Galatia. This fact lends great support to Ramsay's conclusion that Paul's illness was malaria combined with severe headaches. He simply had to hurry to higher altitudes. In Perga he would have been completely prostrated; in the uplands of Galatia he would gradually recover. We have no reason to think of the thorn in the flesh, for this affliction, whatever it was, was permanent; the ailment that drove Paul from Perga to Galatia was not permanent.

Τὸ πρότερον is more definite because it has the article. It is comparative and thus implies at least one additional visit for the purpose of missionary work, and we do know of a second visit made by Paul (Acts 16:1-4). The idea that this epistle is the second evangelization cannot be entertained because it is addressed only to those who are already "brethren," already evangelized.

14) The translation *"my* temptation" (A. V.) follows a very inferior reading. The genitive is objective: "the temptation of (to) *you*" — "of you," the objective genitive. When this sick man appeared in Galatia with the gospel, the Galatians were tempted to

despise him. A sick man is never impressive and assuring. A sick man who claims miraculous powers and heals others while he himself remains sick would certainly raise serious doubts regarding any message he might bring. Yet the Galatians received Paul as if he were an angel of God, yea, as if he were Christ Jesus himself. Luke corroborates this regarding Antioch in Acts 13:43-48, when Paul's ailment must have been at its worst.

Paul uses a concentrated expression when he writes: "The temptation to you in my flesh you did not despise nor loathe." To do this with a temptation is to get rid of it, not by resisting and overcoming it, but by being overcome by it, by yielding to the loathing. The Galatians did the opposite. We thus do not make this accusative adverbial: "with respect to the temptation you did not despise nor loathe me." B.-P. 431 offers a mixture of two ideas: that the Galatians did not despise Paul in his illness, and that they did not yield to the temptation to despise him on account of his illness; but the construction is rather simple.

Does Paul intend that the aorist of ἐκπτύω, "to spit," is to be taken literally? This word occurs only here in the New Testament. Some prefer the literal meaning (B.-P. 380) and say that spitting was a sign of disgust or was a prophylactic to ward off evil spirits. Yet Homer uses the word in the sense of loathing, and Plutarch in the sense of rejecting. Since the metaphorical usage of the word is assured, we are satisfied; the more so when some say that spitting was an evidence that Paul's ailment was epilepsy, for the ancients expectorate at the sight of a person who is in an epileptic fit. On the question of epilepsy see II Cor. 12:7.

The Galatians received Paul "as an angel of God." Because of the genitive "of God" the term certainly means "angel," a supernatural being and not merely "messenger"; but "as" reduces the phrase to a comparison. How little is gained by reducing it to the meaning "messenger" we see from the addition "as Christ Jesus," which plainly recalls Matt. 10:40: "He that receiveth you receiveth me." Paul states it strongly because of the contrast: once the Galatians listened to the gospel that was coming from Paul's lips as if they heard the voice of an angel from heaven or the voice of Christ Jesus himself, but now they had started to drink in the false words of the Judaizers as if these were a divine message. The Galatians have had many followers.

15) **Where, then, is the felicitation of yourselves?** What has become of this counting yourselves blessed for having received the gospel from my lips? The genitive is objective. It was not possible that the Galatians deemed Paul blessed (subjective genitive); nor would such a question be fitting, nor could "me" be omitted.

So great was their feeling of being blessed by the gospel that Paul is able to add: **For I testify to you that, if possible, your very eyes you, having dug them out, would have given to me.**

This is the testimony Paul gives the Galatians when he thinks back of those early days he spent with them. These *carissima membra corporis* (Pelagius) they would have sacrificed for Paul to show their gratitude. The condition is one of past unreality, ἄν being omitted as is sometimes done in the Koine. "If possible" shows that Paul is speaking hypothetically only. The expression about digging out the eyes and giving them to another is surely proverbial for making a sacrifice of something that is really priceless. So greatly blessed the Galatians counted themselves that nothing that they had could be too great a price to offer in return.

From this statement some conclude that Paul's ailment was ophthalmia, a bad disease of the eyes, which made him look so loathsome that people would spit in disgust or in superstition at sight of him. But how would Paul be able to use the plucked out good eyes of others in place of his own diseased eyes? Are we to carry the idea to this absurd length? A man who had disgustingly diseased eyes would never have obtained permission from the elders of the synagogue to address the meeting, but in Antioch the elders even asked Paul to do so (Acts 13:15, 16).

This supposed eye disease is also connected with 6:11, as though Paul wrote with large script because he could not see well. See 6:11. But in Acts 13:9 Paul's eyes were certainly effectively used on Elymas. All is quite clear if Paul suffered from malarial attacks in Galatia which still left him periods of respite. Ἐξορύσσω is the verb commonly used to express blinding by piercing the eyeballs, thus "digging out."

16) Paul's emotion betrays itself in the ellipsis of his thought. At one time the Galatians counted themselves blessed for having Paul in their midst, but this is passed. Is the opposite now the case? **And so have I become your enemy by telling you the truth?**

Read this as a question; ὥστε means, "and so," R. 999. "An enemy of yours" is active, one who hates you, and not passive, one who is hated by you (C.-K. 459). The perfect tense "have I become" is used in the Greek fashion from the standpoint of the readers and refers to the time when they read this letter in which Paul tells them the truth. Will they then say: "Paul has become hostile to us"? Ah, but it is the best and the truest friend who honestly tells us the truth about ourselves even when he knows we shall not like it. False friends are the ones who hide such truth from us and do so in order to remain in our favor.

Some regard this statement as a declaration: "Wherefore I have become your enemy by telling you the truth." But that is not true (v. 19). If he intends to imply that the Galatians now consider him as being hostile to them, this thought is expressed far better by a question. The declarative idea is made more confusing when the inferior reading in v. 15 is adopted: τίς οὖν ἦν; *"What,* then, was your felicitation of yourselves?" and supplying in thought: "Nothing but superficiality," and then attaching: "Wherefore I have become your enemy." Paul regards the self-felicitation of the Galatians as being genuine; he even states the strongest reason for his so doing: that they were willing to sacrifice their eyes for him.

Again, Paul is not their enemy. Finally, the ὥστε clause cannot be construed across the intervening γάρ statement and attached to the question asked in v. 15. The reason: "I testify," etc., would be contradicted by any declaration that Paul is an enemy of the Galatians. Regard the sentence as a question, and all is readily understood.

17) Paul is the truest friend the Galatians have even as he is telling them the truth. But, in contrast, what about the Judaizers? **They are zealously seeking you in a way not honorable but want to lock you up in order that you may zealously seek them.**

Paul has characterized the Judaizers in a brief and succinct way in 1:7. Here he refers to them only by the plural verb ending, the indefinite "they." The slight is both marked and intentional. They more than deserve this treatment. Here the slight comports with the characterization that their whole action is "not honorable"; it is not done καλῶς, "honorably." The adjective means "good" only in a general way; specifically, especially when it is referred to persons and their actions, it signifies excellent, noble, admirable. To the Greek one is *kalos* who bears the character of a gentleman in our nobler use of that term.

Ζηλόω, when used with the accusative of persons = *sich um eine Person beeifern*, to busy oneself about somebody, "they zealously affect you" (A. V.), one might say, "they court you." Paul had done the same thing in a noble way, in a noble and an honorable cause (the gospel, preached to the Galatians in Christian love). Not so the Judaizers — their whole courtship of the Galatians is decidedly "not honorable." To state it in this negative way is really an understatement which is the more damning because it is expressed only in this way. Paul might have used a positive adverb; if he had done so, any adequate adverb would have been much harsher. Yet we should not think that Paul intends to deal mildly with these people who ruin the church. Quite otherwise. By using a positive adverb Paul would invite the Galatians to challenge it by any possible denial that might occur to their minds. This he prevents by using the negative "not honorably" which makes the Galatians think of what would be honorable, of what the Judaizers should at least have done.

Paul's psychological handling of the Galatians is most masterly. We often make serious mistakes in estimating the effect of our words upon the people we seek to win from error; however excellent our intention may be, by our mistakes we cause them to cling only the more firmly to their wrong ideas. Paul is a good master to teach us. One might write a wonderful book on the way in which Paul handled the people and the situations of his ministry.

With ἀλλά he does mention the positive. This is in opposition to the entire clause and not merely to the adverb "not honorably." The entire zealous concern of the Judaizers is that "they want to lock up the Galatians in order that the Galatians zealously seek (only) the Judaizers." The present tenses say no more than that the action is in progress. The Judaizers have not as yet accomplished their will. We have noted similar tenses in the preceding; all of them are significant as to this vital point. The object of these men is dishonorable because of its pronounced selfishness. They want the Galatians completely for themselves.

Whether we translate "lock up" or "shut out" we see from the purpose clause, which names persons ("them"), that the infinitive indicates separation (aorist: complete) from other persons: to lock up and keep away from Paul and his assistants, thus, of course, also from their influence and their teaching. The Galatians had hitherto zealously sought Paul, had listened only to him (see an example in Acts 13:43); the Judaizers worked hard to substitute themselves for Paul and his assistants. Since Paul was far away, they hoped to succeed quite easily. While ζηλοῦτε might be subjunctive by contracting οη like οε (R. 325, 342, 984), the Koine allows the indicative after ἵνα so that the question of mode is here an unessential problem.

18) The whole subject of zealously cultivating people is now clarified by being expressed abstractly. This is always the proper thing to do: brush all personal considerations aside and look at the principle by itself. Clarity of thought is thus achieved. Otherwise personal considerations becloud the issue. When he does this Paul uses the passive since, as he has just said, the Judaizers wanted to be sought zealously by the Galatians to the exclusion of all others, of Paul in particular. This passive not only turns the thought so as to take in being sought besides seeking (being sought involves someone who is seeking); it enables Paul to make an application to the Galatians and to himself in the simplest and the briefest way. Principle and immediate application are thus joined in a

few telling words, the quintessence of thought that penetrates fully.

Now it is honorable to be zealously sought in an honorable thing at all times.

The matter is stated abstractly. We see that it is true beyond question. But note the implication in the passive. When somebody seeks us zealously in a dishonorable way, this being so sought is a reflection on us who permit ourselves to be sought thus. The dishonorableness of the seekers casts dishonor upon those sought. They must not imagine that they remain honorable. It is honorable for them only when they are being zealously sought in an honorable thing, which will naturally include an honorable way.

The Galatians may apply this to Paul: he had sought them in an honorable thing, i. e., in the gospel which is ever supremely honorable. The fact that the Galatians have been sought thus by Paul and are still so sought by him is, indeed, blessed and honorable. Turn it around: The fact that Paul is sought by the Galatians in the gospel is honorable for him. We may also think of the delegation the Galatians had sent to Paul, which caused the writing of this epistle. But add the reverse, what this means to the Judaizers and the Galatians. All these applications become almost automatic once the principle itself is clearly stated.

It is most unexpected and thus of arresting force when Paul adds: in an honorable thing — "at all times." Certainly, "at all times"! At one time to be sought in an honorable thing, at another time in one that is not honorable — need we say what this means? It is as yet stated in general terms but is food for serious applicatory thought for the Galatians and for us today.

But this matter of being sought applies not only to the Galatians whom Paul seeks and whom the

Judaizers seek; it applies also to Paul and to the Judaizers. The latter, Paul himself has said, wanted to be zealously sought by the Galatians. Paul makes the application only to himself. He does it in a startling way by suddenly introducing himself and the Galatians into this point of constancy, "always." Yes, always **and not only when I am present with you.**

In a flash Paul makes the Galatians see themselves. He was the one who was once so zealously sought by them when he labored in their midst. He was the one whom they should ever seek because of the honorable thing he honorably brought them. But now that he had left them to pursue his honorable work elsewhere, what had they done? They had begun to listen to men who dishonorably wanted the Galatians to seek them to the exclusion of Paul. Is Paul no longer to be honorably sought by the Galatians? Is his mere absence to end their honorable course?

One must feel what καλός means to the Greek in order to appreciate the turns Paul gives to this word as adverb, adjective, noun. It is typically Pauline. He balances all on the point of moral excellence, nobility, and honor. Will this fade the moment Paul turns his back? Is this so shallow in the Galatians that constancy is so soon at an end? Ἐν with the substantivized infinitive is one of the common ways of expressing "when," and πρός with persons is the face-to-face preposition.

The Judaizers were proselyters; they merely invaded the young churches that had already been founded in order to appropriate them for themselves. Instead of being καλόν, this was meanly, despicably κακόν ("base"). They zealously sought and affected their victims, courted them in every way, clung to them like leeches. The proselyters of today continue this type. Ζηλοῦσθαι is not a middle that is equal to little more than the active; the New Testament affords no support for such a middle. The form is passive. The true preachers of the gospel and all true believers are also filled with a fervent missionary spirit that earnestly seeks to save the lost. This differs from all proselyting by its unselfishness, by its purity of motive, by its spirit which truly reflects the love of Christ. We see this difference in this epistle and also in Second Corinthians.

19) Zealously seeking the Galatians is not the half of it. Paul's concern is like that of a mother, as if he were giving birth to the Galatians anew, suffering all the pains a second time. Although the Galatians have begun to turn to the Judaizers, Paul's heart remains constant and true. Yea, their defection causes him to suffer these pains anew, to suffer them for the life of the Galatians. This is the acme of love and constancy. Few more touching passages have been written.

My little children of whom I am again in travail until Christ be formed in you, I would even be present with you now and change my voice because I am perplexed in regard to you!

The figure of the mother in travail advances the thought of zeal for the Galatians; by making this a second travailing Paul illustrates his unchanged heart: he would do over again all that he had once done for the Galatians. Yet the figure does not remain with the thought that has already been expressed, it extends to the new thought of pain, for the verb means to undergo birth pains. This also is included, that the Galatians are making the maternal heart of Paul suffer all the birth pains a second time, something which no offspring ever does in nature. When a babe is born, it does not know what pain its birth causes, but these Galatians have already been born, and they should, indeed, know that unnecessarily, unnaturally they are causing Paul to suffer all these pains over again in even a more severe way. But he is ready to suffer so if only Christ be formed in the Galatians by this new ordeal he is undergoing.

The claim is unwarranted that, because Paul ordinarily uses τέκνα, "children," he cannot use the diminutive τεκνία here, where not only the best texts have it, but where also the context so plainly requires this tender "little children." Yet Paul does not use "babes" as though the Galatians were coming to birth for the first time. They have had that birth; what is now happening is something that should not be necessary, a second ordeal of this kind for Paul in connection with the Galatians. But what true mother would not undergo a second ordeal for her "little children" if it were required of her? The relative is masculine and is construed *ad sensum* with the neuter antecedent.

This is one of the rather numerous instances in which a figure is used for something that never happens in nature. Such figures are misinterpreted when they are interpreted as though they were to be understood in the common way. Their very force lies in what may be called their unnaturalness, here the fact that Paul has to suffer birth pains all over again for the Galatians. Why did they compel Paul to do this? Another, moved by thought for himself, might merely abandon them and refuse such second suffering, but not Paul. The Galatians were "my little children" to him. He had brought them forth as a mother in travail. Children can have only one mother. Behold how Paul reaches out to the Galatians in order to draw them to his heart with the most tender love! All the connotations of the figure grip and hold one.

Paul is not dominated by the figure but dominates it and says, not that he is giving birth to the Galatians a second time as though their spiritual life had ceased, and they were to receive it a second time, but that he is in birth pains "until Christ be formed in you." Keep the reality which the figure merely serves to illustrate. This clause is no longer figurative, it is simple reality and is placed beside the figure in order to prevent our turning the figure in a wrong direction. By inculcating trust in ceremonial works of law the Judaistic error was taking Christ out of the hearts of the Galatians, and Paul's strong efforts in this epistle, which wrench his heart like travail pains, sought to put Christ back into the hearts of his little children.

The tense is important, it is an aorist: "be completely formed in you," i. e., so that no Judaistic ceremonialism will ever affect them, that they will ever be immune. The verb itself is expressive, for μορφή is always the form which expresses the essence, the inner reality; it is never a mask or an assumed form which one may lay aside. All that Christ really is Paul is at great labor and pains to have formed in the hearts of the Galatians. The unnamed agent in the passive need not be Paul, for this is really the Spirit, yet he ever uses the gospel for this and thus the true preachers of the gospel; these may thus be considered as means or as agents.

We see what this verb means when we compare paspages such as Rom. 8:29: we are finally to be σύμμορφοι with Christ in glory, "to be conformed with him"; even our vile body is to be σύμμορφον, formed like the glorious body of Christ, Phil. 3:21. There is no need to extend the force of this verb. Paul is not speaking of our conduct which is, of course, also to be comfortable to Christ in holy living and abundance of good works. This subject is considered later in the epistle (5:13-6:10). Here Paul deals with faith as embracing Christ, him fully, him alone.

20) No dash or hiatus is needed, (R.V., American Committee, and others). Omit the relative clause for a moment, and the close connection appears: "My little children, I would be present with you," etc. It is anomalous to suffer birth pangs when children are far away. Paul also labors to have Christ brought to full form in the Galatians and is at a disadvantage by being so far away from them, unable to hurry to them. If he were with them he could change his voice so as to meet their need in the most perfect way; as it is, he labors under a handicap, he must secure his information about the Galatians at secondhand, cannot be perfectly sure of meeting all their inmost thoughts, and must resort to writing, which is never as effective as the voice. What prompts Paul to say this is his intense love which has already been so tenderly expressed.

The imperfect is the tense of politeness (R. 919, a good discussion) like our English "I would" and refers to a strong present desire. Just what the force of δέ is puzzles everybody. It is probably no more than a slight intensification: *ich moechte doch jetzt bei euch sein*. An adversative idea seems too strong although Paul's desire to be with the Galatians is possibly to be placed in contrast with the zealous seeking of Paul on the part of the Galatians only when he was present with them (v. 18). Regarding Paul's changing his voice R. 1199 remarks: "There never was a more nimble mind than that of Paul, as he knew how to adapt himself to every mood of his readers or hearers without any sacrifice of principle. It was no declaimer's tricks, but love for the souls of men that made him become all things to all men (I Cor. 9:22). He could change his tone because he loved the Galatians even when they had been led astray."

Ishmael — Isaac: bondage — freedom

21) It has been well said that, although he is at a loss because he is so far away from the Galatians, the fertile mind of Paul, in his attempt to separate them from all legalism, finds another effective mode of approach. From personal appeal he turns to a clear case that is recorded in Scripture, which is illustrative of both bondage and freedom, the account of Hagar and Ishmael and of Sarah and Isaac. To the subjective and personal Paul thus adds the Scriptural and objective.

The use of this Scriptural account has been termed a rabbinical argumentation by which Paul seeks to turn the arguments of the rabbinical Judaizers against themselves. But this is not an *argumentum ad hominem*, not a turning of the Judaizers' guns against themselves. The argument is not merely negative, it is powerfully positive. Nor does Paul convert the history into an allegory. He uses the history, for only as historical fact has it the power of conviction that Paul needs. But this Paul does: he brings out God's own thoughts that are embedded in this history as they teach and instruct us Christians for all time. This is far beyond the old or the new rabbis. It is divine reality. How the Old Testament histories ought to be read, not superficially for their mere externals, but for their real content, Paul shows us in many places, notably in Rom. 4 (Abraham), Rom. 5:12, etc. (Adam and the patriarchs before Moses), also Gal. 3:16 (Abraham having the covenant hundreds of years before Moses and the law came into existence).

The substance as well as the absence of a connective indicate the beginning of a new section. **Tell me, you who want to be under the law, do you not hear the Law?**

The question at the head of this exposition is arresting. The Galatians and certainly those who were becoming enamored of law as a means of salvation had heard the Law. But that is exactly to what Paul refers: hearing the Law and yet wanting to be under law. "Tell me," Paul says, "how this can possibly be." Whatever one may say about the old Jews (II Cor. 3:14, 15), the Galatians had at least learned to read the Torah without such a darkening, blinding veil. Distinguish between "under law" without an article and "the Law" with the article, here in the sense of the Torah, the Pentateuch, "Moses" (II Cor. 3:15; John 5:46). "Under law" is under law in general, a state which these Galatians were trying to achieve by getting to be under the Mosaic ceremonial system. One gets under law by means of some legal system or other.

The fact that "the Law" refers to the Pentateuch we see from what follows, namely the story of Hagar who lived long before the ceremonial law was given (3:17). Paul is citing one of the histories of the Pentateuch. The Books of Moses were constantly read in the synagogues; they were divided into *paraschas* or regular lections, the other Old Testament books were likewise divided into sections, their lections being called *haphtharas*. The early Christian congregations continued this practice of reading the Old Testament until the New Testament canon was gradually formed when lections were selected from these New Testament writings. We see no reason for excluding reference to these readings in the Christian assemblies, nor for intensifying "do you not hear" as meaning, "do you not understand?"

22) With γάρ Paul introduces the section he has in mind. **For it has been written** (see 3:10), **Abraham got two sons, one from the slave woman, and one from the free.**

Paul sketches briefly what is on record, all of it is well known. The aorist is punctiliar: "got two sons," not "had," which would require the imperfect. In the New Testament a παιδίσκη (John 18:17; Acts 12:13) is always a slave girl or woman; this must have been the position of Hagar (Deissmann, *Light*, etc., 186, and others). She is here contrasted with "the free woman" (the feminine adjective needing no noun). The fact that Hagar was not a wife, and that Sarah was, is not the point; but that one was a slave and the other free is. Thus the one son was a slave, the other free as was always the fact in such a case. The mother and not the father determined the status of the sons.

23) Continuative ἀλλά carries the sketch forward and is not adversative. **Now the one from the slave woman has been born in (mere) flesh fashion, but the one from the free by way of promise.**

First the status of the two mothers, then — still more important — the difference between the two births themselves. The one son was born in the ordinary, natural way, the other by a gracious, miraculous intervention of God. Κατά names the norm, the one norm we observe in all human births, ordinary copulation and its resultant conception and birth. Διά denotes means, in this case that special divine means which is God's promise. At the time of this birth both Abraham and Sarah were beyond the age of procreation, he was one hundred years old, she ninety and permanently sterile. Yet God promised them a son despite their age, and so "by way of promise" Isaac was born. Yet, instead of employing a simple aorist which would state the past, historical fact and seem to be sufficient, Paul uses the perfect "has been born," which is neither "was born" (A. V.), nor "is born" (R. V.). B.-D. 342, 5 notes that these two births still have their peculiar significance for us and that this is the reason for the tense; compare the perfect tense occurring in 3:18; Heb. 11:17; 12:3.

24) Matching this perfect is the periphrastic passive perfect: **Things of this character have been spoken as conveying** (also) **another meaning.** Ἅτινα is more than ἅ since it refers to a characteristic of the things mentioned (B.-D. 293,4) and hence does not mean "which things" (our versions) but "things of this nature or character," implying that the ones just mentioned belong to an entire class, that more of them are found in Scripture. This does not refer to the mere words penned by Moses but to the things themselves which are narrated by the words. All such things, thus also the ones here indicated, "have been spoken as conveying (also) something else," something that does not lie on the surface. The perfect tense (here periphrastic) means that all things of this nature permanently carry this additional meaning and convey it even to us when we contemplate properly the things thus spoken. Paul does not say that he gives such things their additional meaning, nor even that God does this. He says that because of their very nature such things have another thing involved in them, and whenever they are told they always have also this other meaning.

The verb contains ἄλλο, "something other," we need not say, "something different." For this "other" agrees, corresponds; it is not diverse, heterogeneous. The historical facts are like a shell that has its natural kernel and is not stuffed with a foreign substance. This "other" has always been, will always be included in the original historical facts. They are not an illustration for this "other," an illustration that Paul's mind has found. There is nothing adventitious about the whole matter. This "other" is also not an abstraction, for it, too, is as historical as the facts with which it agrees. The only difference is that the original events happened first and may thus be viewed by themselves. But when this "other" came to be, one can see that it is of the very same nature.

It does not seem adequate to call this "allegory" and to use the verb "allegorize" although this is quite generally done. Luther translates: *Die Worte bedeuten etwas,* which is nearer the truth. The rabbis were great allegorizers, namely inventors along this line. Rabbi Akiba found a mystical sense in every hook and crook of the Hebrew letters; but these were mere fancies. Philo, the past master of allegory, called what he found the spiritual sense. Wherever it suited him, he made free with the original historical data. One should know that only traces of Messianic ideas are retained by Philo, and among them are neither the person nor the name of the Messiah. The Alexandrines copied his method and carried it still farther. We have it even today.

We thus see at once that when Paul uses this verb he has in mind something that is far different from the method of interpretation devised by those ancient Jews and any of their followers. Their allegories dissipate the original sense of Scripture. The simplest and the plainest things no longer mean what is said about them but something the allegorizer's fancy distils from them. The ordinary reader is completely disconcerted; he finds that he cannot understand a thing in Scripture until the allegorizer offers him his distillation. There is an air of mystery, of profound learning, of deep spirituality about such allegorizing; but the most of it is mere fancy which is often unwholesome. The worst feature about it is the fact that the solid Scripture facts are turned into curling vapor.

An illustration is selected, a parable constructed in order to aid in presenting some fact. Both are legitimate and may be more or less successful. Allegory does the reverse; it takes a fact (a Bible statement or an account) and turns it into a picture of something else which is often no more than a fancy. This is really not legitimate and must be condemned in most cases. A type is different from all of these, for both type and antitype are firmly based on Scripture, the type being a miniature that is furnished in advance, the antitype the great major that follows. They are equally divine.

What Paul presents is akin to type and antitype, but only akin. Hence also he does not speak of a type. All types are prophetic; Paul is not presenting prophecy and fulfillment. Paul does not go a step beyond the Scriptural facts; what he does is to point out *the same nature* in both: mere flesh in Hagar's birth and thus slavery — the same slavery in all those whose birth is no better; divine promise in Sarah's birth and thus liberty — the same liberty in all whose birth is connected with promise. Thus in v. 24-28 Paul identifies: Hagar = Sinai = the mother of all who do works of law; Sarah = Jerusalem from above = the mother of all believing the promise. Yet in v. 29 Paul only likens: "even as then — thus also now." In the case of things of the same nature one may do either, identify them: this is that; or liken them: as this, so that. Paul does both in this paragraph.

The word γάρ begins to explain how the Scriptures have spoken with another, an added meaning in their account about the two sons of Abraham. The two mothers, the one the slave woman who has given birth only in fleshly fashion, the other the free woman who has given birth by way of promise alone, present this *allo* or "something other." **For these are two covenants.** Paul at once characterizes the first and then identifies it with the one mother, the slave woman Hagar: **the one from Mount Sinai, giving birth into slavery, which as such is Hagar.**

The feminine "these" is not due to attraction to the feminine predicate, for the women themselves are referred to, of course, in so far as they have given such diverse births, i. e., the two women as mothers. "These *are*," Paul says, "two διαθῆκαι," expressing the thought intensively because slavery *is* in the nature of the birth of the one, being only a fleshly birth, and liberty *is* in the nature of the birth of the other, being wholly by way of promise. The copula should not be stressed beyond Paul's meaning which he makes plain in what follows.

Paul describes only the one woman and does not follow "the one" by formally adding a coordinate statement regarding "the other"; he lets his readers do this. In v. 26 he at once advances to "the Jerusalem above" without first identifying this with Sarah. This is not a grammatical diversity as though the intervening statements have thrown Paul off the track; this is the advance of the great thought itself.

The translation "covenants" says too much. The Sinaitic legal system was a divine "disposition," something that God placed or appointed for the Jewish nation, and is thus paired with the divine promise; the German *Verfuegung* is a good rendering. Paul describes the one with a phrase, a participial modifier, and a relative clause. "From Mount Sinai" = from this place where Israel received its whole system of law. To name the place is also to indicate the late date (3:17) and the character of this "disposition" as law. This brings to mind all that Paul has already said on the inability, the inferiority, the temporal nature of this law in contrast with promise (3:17, etc.). Here all of this is concentrated in the participial addition: "giving birth into slavery."

The idea of motherhood continues. The law produces children, but ever only slaves "for slavery," and in this sense the law "is Hagar," who, as a slave woman, could do no more. Note that ἥτις is like ἅτινα and adds the note of character: "which (disposition or covenant) as such." Not Mount Sinai in general or even the Sinaitic law as law is Hagar but this system which brings forth only "for slavery." In regard to this point and to this alone the identification is made. As we have said, they are of the same or of an identical nature and produce mere slaves.

25) Textual evidence as well as meaning support the reading τὸ γὰρ Σινᾶ ὄρος ἐστὶν ἐν τῇ Ἀραβίᾳ, **For the Sinai mountain is in Arabia.** This is not a trivial geographical remark but a significant statement. Arabia includes the Sinaitic peninsula. Hagar went south to Beersheba, and Ishmael dwelt in Paran, the territory near Sinai. Sinai is thus connected with Hagar's son and his descendants, and Arabia, in which Sinai is located is *not* connected with the promise as all Bible readers know. Not in the promised land but in the Arabian desert, which separated Israel from Canaan when it was at Sinai, was the law given. This law was thus not the fulfillment of the promise given to Abraham. The very place where the law was given, Arabia, Sinai, connected it with the slave woman Hagar and with her son Ishmael, born "to slavery." Paul's statement that Sinai lies in Arabia thus justifies the identification of Hagar with Sinai, with the law and slavery.

Our versions have unfortunately translated the reading τὸ Ἀγαρ, the R. V. even the one that has δέ instead of γάρ. But this means that the *word* Hagar = Mount Sinai. Yet the word Hagar means *se separavit, reliquit,* "flight," and Sinai means "connected with the coast strip *Sin*" and is used to designate the peak *Musa;* see Ed. Koenig, *Woerterbuch* (Hebrew). Thus neither in sense nor only in sound is there a play on the words. All the labor spent on establishing a connection of this kind has netted very little; nor is it clear how Paul could resort to anything that is so superficial. When Paul puts the name "Sinai" before "mountain" he may intend to emphasize the name "Sinai" in contrast with the other name and the other place, namely "Jerusalem."

For he continues: **and is in one row** (or line) **with the present Jerusalem, for she is in slavery together with her children.**

The original military meaning "to be in line with," to be in the same row with, is quite expressive (M.-M. 612) although some prefer the modified meaning "to correspond with" ("answers to," our versions). Sinai is in the same line with the present Jerusalem. The two march together step by step. This is not merely the Jerusalem of Paul's day but the Jerusalem of the legalistic Jews of all ages including the present. The idea of the mother is retained: she and her children, all whom she has brought forth in her legalism. "For" explains: she with all her children are "slaves," do nothing but slaving. We may say that she is a very Hagar in all the births she gives. Hagar — Sinai — the present Jerusalem are all just one on the score of giving birth to nothing but slaves.

But Hagar is not merely a slave like any other slave, she is a slave in Abraham's family. So also Sinai has Moses who wrote all that he wrote concerning Christ (John 5:46, 47) and who himself was a type of Christ (Deut. 18:15, 18). So also the present Jerusalem has this same Moses with his writings about Christ and eventually has come to have the whole Old Testament. In spite of all this connection with the gospel the story is one of slavery, is stamped entirely with Hagar and not with Sarah.

Paul speaks only historically. While no promise, while only flesh was connected with the birth of

Ishmael, it would be hasty, indeed, to conclude that both Hagar and Ishmael disbelieved, spurned the promise of the covenant made with Abraham, and, when they left for Arabia, were lost spiritually. Remember that Ishmael received the covenant sign, circumcision, from Abraham (Gen. 17:23). Not from Ishmael was the Christ to descend; the line of descent went through Isaac, Jacob, Juda, David, etc. But this is only the line of descent. All the other sons of Jacob, for instance, and so also the nations that descended from them were to have the Messianic blessings of that line by faith. Even as Abraham, the head of that line, had it only by faith, so Hagar and Ishmael were not excluded from this faith. The home of Abraham was filled with gospel promise that appealed for faith.

So it was with Sinai and its Moses, so it was with Jerusalem which even had its promise. There were always the Old Testament saints, the true believers. Theirs is the story of faith. The Messianic line ran through a succession of individuals, among them were the former pagan, Rahab, a Canaanite, and Ruth, a Moabitess. This line itself was heavily stained with sin. As the line advances in the individuals who formed it, thousands of believers and by no means only Jews held to the promise by faith. Distinguish this succession of hosts of believers from the Messianic line as such. Down to the time when Christ was born we see these believers. Forget not the Magi who followed the star and worshipped the newborn King of the Jews. And yet for even these there was Sinai with the effect described in v. 1-4; they were only minor heirs, no better, as Paul has said, than slaves.

That is why Sinai, located in Arabia, is here connected with the present Jerusalem. The promise to which all the believers held did not come from Sinai, only the law came from there, the law which made even the believers only minor heirs. Although the present Jerusalem was located in the promised land and should, therefore, with all her children have been marked by faith as minor heirs, this Jerusalem clung only to Sinai, only to the law, only to works of law as though it, too, were located in Arabia, the land that was devoid of promise.

The Ishmaelites eventually lost the promise and the faith, and the present Jerusalem with her children, i. e., all those Jews who bore her distinctive stamp of Sinai and law alone, were no better than the Arabian Ishmaelites: "She is in slavery together with her children." The great facts are plain once they are pointed out. The history is composed of the facts; there is no allegory about them. The *allo* presented is only the real inwardness of the facts. The superficial reader sees only the surface, but there is much more to see, the facts in their full reality.

26) **But the Jerusalem above is free, who as such is mother of us.** "The present Jerusalem" implies another that also deserves the name Jerusalem but in a higher sense; this is "the Jerusalem above." The name of no other city is mentioned as having a higher counterpart. "Jerusalem" = city of peace. The capital city of the Holy Land was to be the center and the source of heavenly grace and peace for the chosen nation, a type and symbol of heaven itself which is thus also called "the new Jerusalem" where all that the earthly Jerusalem was to be reaches its consummation and final realization. But the Jerusalem that is "now," as Paul sees it in its long history up to the very time of his writing, had failed of its spiritual purpose. Hear the cry of Jesus: "O Jerusalem, Jerusalem!" Matt. 23:37, 38. Soon it was to sink into ruin. Paul places it in the same

row with Sinai. It no longer knew the promise, it knew only the law. Its own significant name testifies against it.

But that significance abides in "the Jerusalem above." "Now" and "above" do not seem to form a perfect contrast. In order to obtain it we should not introduce the idea of a *future* Jerusalem. An ordinary contrast is not intended. For "now" points to the depth to which the earthly Jerusalem has sunken; the one "above" is ever the same, namely higher, spiritual. "The Jerusalem now" has descended to a Sinai, a Hagar, a slaving mother of slaving children.

Motherhood is the thought connected with both Jerusalems, the one mother slaving and bringing forth slaving children, the other mother being free, all her children being free like herself. This second mother is therefore not the *"new* Jerusalem" (Rev. 21:2) which is heaven with its blessed inhabitants. "Our mother" has her children here on earth and is thus herself on earth where she can be a true mother to them. Her name is "the Jerusalem *above.*" The other mother is identified with an earthly city which is in line with an earthly mountain; not so "our mother." The one is engrossed with the law, which Paul has said deals with "the weak and beggarly (earthly) elements" (see v. 3, 9); the other is "above" anything of this kind, works with promise and the gospel, all her children are spiritual. She is thus bound to no city or place (John 4:21-23). Call her the Christian Church on earth.

On ἥτις, "who is such," see the two relatives occurring in v. 24. In "mother of us" Paul includes himself plus the Galatians, whether they be former Jews or former Gentiles. Do not overlook the appeal that lies in "our mother." Will the Galatians desert their free, noble mother who has born also them as free men and will they adopt this Hagar-mother with her slavery? What folly especially for Gentiles who had been brought to the Christian Church apart from Judaism!

27) Paul corroborates what he has just said about "the Jerusalem above" being "our mother." In Isa. 54:1 the prophet addresses Israel after the Messiah, the great *Ebed Yahweh,* has died and risen again (chapter 53). Paul follows the LXX. **For it has been written (3:10):**

> **Rejoice, thou sterile that dost not bear!**
> **Break forth and shout, thou that dost not travail!**
> **For many more the children of the desolate than of her having the husband.**

The prophet is speaking of the Christian Church as it appears after Christ's redemption and exaltation. He bids her be happy and shout because of her many children. But he uses imagery that is taken from Sarah and Hagar, the very two who are here used by Paul, and the chief point of this imagery is motherhood. Paul's quotation is not merely apt; the Scriptures themselves are the source which provides him with the identification of Hagar with Sinai and Jerusalem and of Sarah with something higher.

"The deserted" and "she having the husband" are expressions that allude to Sarah and Hagar, but to these two at the time when Sarah gave Hagar to Abraham. We should not, however, translate *die Vermaehlte.* This ἀνήρ, "husband," was not Hagar's. She was not even a concubine. This was Sarah's husband, Hagar "had" him only for the purpose of copulation. Sarah thought she could get an heir by such proxy. Human scheming never fulfills the promise. The whole proceeding was useless. But it is highly interesting to find Jerusalem prefigured by Hagar. It is not some other city, it is the Jerusalem which should have been the holy city, should have been Sarah but made herself nothing but Hagar. The episode with regard to Hagar transpired in Abraham's household. It was Sarah who substituted Hagar for herself and secured no heir. Yet God's promise was carried out despite all this.

We thus see what the "sterile" one means. It is confusing to say that this does not mean that she had no children before this time. The idea back of this view is the thought that there were many saints in the Old Testament, many long before the Christian Church came into being. But all these Old Testament saints — and these include also Gentile believers, think of Rahab and of Ruth — were spiritual Isaacites, a part of Sarah's many children of promise *after* Sarah's sterility was turned into fertility.

"Thou sterile one" is even re-enforced by the appositions, the substantivized present participles: "thou that dost not bear," "thou that dost not travail." Present participles describe conditions that last a long time. The clause about Sarah's many children who were at last born to her through Isaac shows that the sterility ended. We know how it ended in Sarah's old age by a miracle of grace. Blass observes that the LXX regularly used οὐ with participles when it translated the Hebrew *lo*; B.-D. 430, 3 thus lists this negative as a Hebraism. Moulton notes that in the Greek individual concepts are negatived by οὐ (*Einleitung* 366; see also 205). R. 1138, etc. We may translate: "thou non-bearing one," "thou non-travailing one."

The contrast is only between Sarah and Hagar, the present Jerusalem and the Jerusalem above. But in the case of Sarah it includes all her spiritual children until the end of time, in the case of Hagar only those who slave with her in the present Jerusalem. We should keep to what Paul says and not lose ourselves in self-made expansion regarding Hagar. Thus

Sarah's children are, indeed, "many more." Μᾶλλον ἤ is used with the positive as a substitute for the comparative (R. 663).

28) **Now we on our part, brethren, are, in accord with Isaac, children of promise.** This is the complement to the statement that "the Jerusalem above is our mother." The address "brethren" is significant. All these children of the sterile Sarah are, indeed, brethren, all one family, thus also Paul and the Galatians are brethren. Paul reaches the climax of his instruction and thus draws the Galatians to himself in this great brotherhood of freedom. The silent contrast implied in the emphatic "we" are the Judaizers, children of the present Jerusalem.

But now Paul advances from Sarah to Isaac and does this with the κατά phrase. This means more than, "as Isaac was," more than, "as brothers of Isaac," we as he (our versions). Isaac, like Abraham and Sarah, is not only a product of, he is the channel of the promise. In accord with him we are "children of promise," its spiritual product. "In accord with Isaac" is the opposite of "in accord with Ishmael," i. e., "in accord with flesh" (v. 23), mere physical nature. It is "promise" full of divine grace, that is "above." "Children of promise" is a practical compound like "children of light" and similar combinations, the genitive being ethically qualitative. In Paul's time the promise was already fulfilled in Christ. Children of promise are those who hold to the promise and its heavenly contents by faith.

29) Paul completes his account by a reference to a further portion of Scripture in which the main point is the command to cast out Hagar and Ishmael because the latter is not to be a co-heir with Isaac. **But even as then the one born in accord with flesh kept persecuting the one** (born) **according to spirit, so** (it is) **also now.**

Galatians 4:29

Instead of continuing with the identification, Paul uses a simple comparison: "as then — so now." The idea of birth is retained, for both Ishmael and Isaac are indicated by the vital difference obtaining in their birth, "the one born in accord with flesh," "the one according to spirit." The two phrases are such direct opposites that we cannot follow our versions when they capitalize "Spirit." The idea that the Holy Spirit was especially involved in Isaac's birth does not appear in Scripture; all we know is that his birth was miraculous. Flesh and Holy Spirit are not proper contrasts, for in such a contrast flesh would be too highly elevated.

There is a reference to Gen. 21:9. When Isaac was weaned, Ishmael made sport of him, *lachte ihn aus* (Delitzsch), not in mere playfulness but in scorn of Isaac's being the heir. That this attitude was due to Hagar is easy to imagine; we also see why Sarah proceeded to be rid of both Ishmael and Hagar. When Paul calls Ishmael's action "persecuting" and even uses the durative imperfect, some think this is too strong a term for the word used in Gen. 21:9, that Paul must be following the late Jewish tradition which tells of Ishmael's shooting arrows at Isaac in apparent playfulness but with murderous intent. Paul is excused for doing this sort of thing because it is no more than *harmlose Ausspinnungen*.

Now tradition did report some facts that are not otherwise recorded; their use in New Testament Scripture is legitimate. But these late fancies about Ishmael are not true tradition. When Paul writes "kept persecuting" he gives full expression to what was involved in the action of Ishmael. Paul does this because of the parallel that the same thing is continuing now; he that is born in accord with the flesh still keeps persecuting him who is born in accord with spirit.

The debate as to whether Paul refers to the persecution instigated by the hostile Jews against the Christians, or whether he has in mind the Judaizers in Galatia, seems unnecessary. Why restrict the reference to the Judaizers? Why modify the verb "persecute" so as to mean only opposing the gospel? The great instigators of persecution during the apostolic time were undoubtedly the Jews. While we read nothing about outright bodily attacks on the part of the Judaizers, yet, as in Corinth, these certainly attacked Paul and his helpers by slander and vilification.

But any distinction between Jews and Judaizers is beside the mark; the real point is that those who, like Paul and the Galatians ought to be children of Sarah, born of promise, spiritual offspring of Isaac, by their very action showed themselves to be Hagarites, Ishmaelites by repeating in full and complete form the early act of Hagar's slave son. Yet Paul does not mention this in order to comfort the Galatians. This whole section is not written for comfort.

30) Paul writes in order to induce the Galatians to hold to their liberty since they were born spiritually to freedom and to reject the yoke of slavery the Judaizers were trying to impose on the Galatians. That is why he adds: **Yet what says the Scripture?** What does it say to this day, present tense? What does it say in its record that we may today apply to those Ishmaelitic actions from which we are made to suffer? This is more direct than if Paul had said, "has been written," the perfect tense with present implication which is so often used in quotation. **Cast out the slave woman and her son, for the son of the slave woman shall in no way inherit together with the son of the free woman.**

Paul quotes Gen. 21:10 with slight modification, which relates the demand that Sarah made on Abraham when she saw the action of Ishmael that had been inspired by Hagar. God himself endorsed Sarah's demand and bade Abraham act upon it. Hagar and Ishmael were cast out. This verdict stands in the case of all who have no higher birth than Ishmael's. It stands in the case of "the present Jerusalem." This present Ishmael shall not inherit in company with (μετά) the son of the free woman, the Isaac of promise, the believers in that promise. Οὐ μή is used with the subjunctive and with the future indicative. The aorist is decisive.

Von Hofmann and Zahn interpret this as an order that the Galatians are to throw out the Judaizers. But God alone decides who shall inherit. This Scripture passage means much more to the Galatians and to us today. If the Galatians and we forsake the gospel freedom for the slavery of the law and legalism we make ourselves one with Hagar and Ishmael so that: "Throw them out — they shall not inherit!" becomes God's verdict on us. "God forbid!" should be our answer to that. This is the real object of Paul's exposition.

31) **Wherefore, brethren, we are not children of a slave woman but of the free woman.**

Paul draws the conclusion from his entire discussion, the conclusion at which he and the Galatians ought to arrive: no slave mother for us (no article; no mother of this kind) but only the one free mother (the article specifying her). While the same thought is expressed in v. 26 and 28, we here have the negative and the positive side by side and in the simplest form. This befits the final statement. This is what we (Paul and the Galatians) are; now you Galatians stand firm as you are. The reading διό is textually well assured. A few other variants have about the same meaning except δέ which commends itself neither textually nor in meaning.

5:1) The variants are found also in this verse. The one which starts with a relative, and the one which inserts a relative pronoun lack manuscript attestation and stand discredited already on this score. The latter is translated by the A. V. In regard to inner evidence we might state that any wording that has relative clauses would be far weaker than a wording that has brief independent sentences, especially here where Paul concludes the whole subject. If this verse starts with a relative clause, the clause may belong to the preceding: " . . . but of the free woman by means of the freedom with which Christ did free us." If it is drawn to the following, we get the arrangement found in our A. V.

Associated with this is wavering regarding the point at which Paul closes the paragraph. Some begin the new paragraph with 4:31; some with 5:1; we with 5:2. The distinctive terms freedom and slavery continue through to 5:1 and stop there. A new line of thought begins with 5:2; all the characteristic terms used in 4:21-5:1 are absent in 5:2, etc.: slave, free, mother, birth, children, inheritance. This means that the great paragraph is not intended to be didactic but admonitory. All that is didactic is only to be the basis for the call: "Stand fast, therefore!"

Thus we have the ringing declaration: **For freedom Christ did set us free.** For nothing less. This is not a dative of means that is merely cognate to the verb: "With freedom Christ freed us," i. e., merely emphasizes the verb: "Christ *really* did free us." This is the *dativus commodi*: "for freedom" he freed us (R. V. margin) so that we should have, maintain, exercise, enjoy this freedom. Hence also the article is used. We are children of the free woman (4:31), and for the very freedom involved in this our birth Christ freed us.

Galatians 5:1 251

Christ is not mentioned until this point. The paragraph could not end without a mention of him. All that has been said about Abraham, Sarah, Isaac, freedom over against slavery, and its application to the Galatians and to us, has its consummation in Christ. As befits the conclusion, the terms are now literal. Christ is not presented as a parent, he is our great spiritual Liberator. The aorist "he freed us" is to indicate the historical fact. But the pronoun "us" (Paul and the Galatians) makes us think not only of Christ's redemption on the cross but of this together with its saving effect in the hearts of the Galatians.

For freedom Christ *freed* us! Shall this blessed act be annulled, this freedom be lost? Never! **Keep standing fast accordingly!** Ever and always as the durative present tense implies. None can set themselves free; this is the work of the Liberator alone. But after we are once set free and endowed with the spiritual power of that freedom, our Liberator moves us to exercise that power. He is now doing that for the Galatians in these words of power through his apostle.

How this positive command is to be understood the accompanying negative states: **and stop enduring again a yoke of slavery.** The verb is middle, "to hold up for oneself," "to endure," and is here construed with the dative (Moulton, *Einleitung* 93; it is often construed with the genitive). R., *W.P.*, translates, "ensnare by trap" and speaks of "trying to lasso," but that is scarcely the meaning of this word. Perhaps it was suggested to Robertson by our versions which translate, "be entangled." A yoke galls, and thus one endures it. The present imperative is conative according to Moulton 203, etc., "do not try to endure"; R. 851, etc., is better, "stop enduring." The present imperative is often used when an action has been begun and is to cease. That is the case here. The Galatians had begun their Judaizing and were to stop enduring such a yoke.

Note the absence of the articles: the Galatians are to tolerate no yoke of any kind of slavery. They are to keep clear of anything of this nature. The genitive is appositional, "yoke" is figurative, but "slavery" is literal. Paul has in mind the Judaistic legal slavery but broadens his expression so as to include this in slavery in general; he also includes the yoke of paganism which the Gentile Galatians once bore.

Paul's admonition and urging are most effective because they are based on the strongest grounds, which reach back even to Abraham and to Isaac, and also operate with the noblest motive, that of the desire for freedom from slavery. All this is enriched by what is said of the promise and the inheritance. The positive is placed beside its negative throughout the paragraph.

CHAPTER V

The sharp warning against accepting circumcision

2) Language as well as substance indicate the beginning of a new paragraph. The Judaistic yoke which Paul wants the Galatians to avoid is assumed by accepting circumcision. This, of course, refers to the former Gentile Galatians. The former Jewish Galatians had been circumcised while they were still Jews; what their circumcision amounted to Paul tells them in v. 6, compare Rom. 2:28. Such Christians were to disregard their circumcision entirely.

See, I myself, Paul, declare to you that, if you let yourselves be circumcised, Christ will profit you nothing! The new subject is circumcision. Ἴδε has become stereotyped since it is used also with plurals (B.-D. 144). It helps to make the statement dramatic. With the words "I myself, Paul," the apostle puts forward all the authority at his command. There are times when this must be done. Apostolic and ministerial authority is to be used at the proper time.

In 4:10 Paul has stated what the Galatians were accepting from the Judaizers. But he did not mention circumcision; so we are forced to the conclusion that the Galatians had not yet advanced that far. Circumcision was the crucial requirement of the entire Judaistic system. It was that already in the case of all proselytes who united with the Jewish synagogues. The reason the proselytes of the gate were considered outsiders was that they had not accepted circumcision. The Judaizers had not yet gained that victory in Galatia. The observing of Jewish holy times (4:10) could never satisfy them. Their goal was to persuade the

Galatians to accept circumcision. A man placed himself under the entire Mosaic system by submitting to circumcision. Circumcision would make the defection and fall of the Galatians complete. The Judaizers knew this although we may be sure that they were very careful in working toward this goal. Paul exposes the whole issue in the most open, direct, and decisive way.

With ἐάν he vividly supposes the future case that the Galatians let themselves be circumcised. This form of condition is used, not because Paul expects this to happen, but in order to confront the Galatians with the actual results in case it does occur. Due to the common ground occupied by the middle and the passive, the latter may be used to express the idea of "subjecting oneself," "allowing oneself or letting oneself," for which use we have a good example here (Moulton, *Einleitung* 225). It is the causative (R. 816) or permissive passive: "cause yourselves or permit yourselves to be circumcised." Paul says: "If you are going to accept that, you will inevitably lose Christ, he will profit you nothing." R. 482, 484 explain "nothing" as a second or cognate accusative. Why not make it adverbial: "in no respect"?

But is Paul's statement true? The Judaizers did not give up Christ and did not ask the Galatians to do so. They merely mixed the gospel with their Mosaic legalism and asked the Galatians to do the same. Yet Christ cannot be halved. Remove a fraction of Christ, and the entire profit or benefit of Christ is lost. One may mean ever so well when doing this, the result is fatal nonetheless.

This does not seem to be obvious to all Christians. Stand on Christ with both feet, and you are safe. Place one foot on something else, that something else gives way, and you fall. Christ is the entire bridge; on him you may cross safely. But if only one foot of that bridge is made something else, the whole bridge collapses. This is a case of either all or none; ninety-nine per cent Christ plus one per cent anything else is just as fatal as no per cent of Christ. *All* the saving power lies in him alone, and no less than all of it saves. "Christ" = all that he is in his person and his work. In 4:11 Paul says that he has perhaps labored in vain among the Galatians. He now advances the thought — Christ would be in vain.

3) Paul adds with full solemnity: **Moreover, I testify once more to every man letting himself be circumcised that he is debtor to do the whole law.** The preceding, "I, Paul, say to you" is now varied to "I testify." A witness is to tell the truth, and this Paul does in the most simple and direct way. With δέ Paul adds another, a clearly corroborating fact. "Once more" or "again" states that Paul has testified to the Galatians at a previous time. We have no difficulty in determining the time when this had been done; it certainly happened during Paul's second tour through Galatia when he brought with him the resolution adopted by the Jerusalem conference which asked the Gentile Christians to abstain from certain things for their own sakes and for the sake of their Jewish fellow Christians (Acts 16:4, 5). All the Gentile Christians received this conference resolution with joy. Paul certainly told the Galatians how the resolution had been passed, how it disavowed the Judaistic demand for circumcision and submission to the Mosaic regulations (Acts 15:1, 5). Then Paul also had the call to testify fully to the Galatians what submission to circumcision involved.

It is Paul's way of writing to change from the plural of v. 2 to the singular and at the same time from the specific "you" to the general "every man." The latter brings out the fact that what Paul testifies to the Galatians is true for every Christian no matter when or where he may be living. The passive participle is again causative or permissive. Its tense is properly present, not because the act is extended, but because of "every man," no matter *when* a man subjects himself to circumcision in obedience to the Judaizers.

Every man of this kind "is debtor to the whole law." It was ever thus: circumcision made one an out-and-out Jew. Circumcision was not only a part of the Jewish ceremonial law like observance of the Jewish holy days and seasons (4:10), it ever involved the observance of the whole system just as Paul states. The aorist "to do" involves completeness. Even a Jew who did not do the whole law was a recreant, spurious Jew because of the fact that he was circumcised and did not discharge his resultant obligation. That is why the pivotal point of the Jerusalem conference was the Judaistic demand for circumcision (Acts 15:1, 5), it involved all else. That is why circumcision was so incompatible with Christ and the gospel. R. 1062 explains the infinitive as a complement to the noun: "debtor for doing." It is often so used with substantives (R. 1076). To accept the Judaistic circumcision meant to abandon the liberty for which Christ liberated us and to go back under the yoke of slavery (v. 1), to exchange Isaac for Ishmael.

4) Paul once more states his warning in a direct personal way. **You get severed from Christ, such of you as try to be declared righteous in connection with law; you get to fall from grace.** Paul now broadens his thought. In v. 3 he states that it is Judaistic circumcision which subjects to the Mosaic legal system, "the law." But anything that is "law" (no article) is useless for obtaining justification ("without works of law," Rom. 3:28), yea, worse than useless, it is actually fatal. It is difficult to translate κατηργήθητε

ἀπό so as to conserve the force of the verb, the tense, and the preposition. Paul uses the verb in all manner of connections (again in v. 12) which necessitates various translations, all of which are more or less inexact. The basic idea is, "to make idle, inactive" so that nothing results; the preposition adds the idea that this action removes "away from Christ," separates from him.

Both aorists are timeless (Moulton, *Einleitung* 218) but still punctiliar and thus different from timeless presents. Our versions render them quite well. The A. V. translates the sense of the first verb well, the R. V. the sense also of the preposition, and both versions reproduce the timelessness of both aorists by means of the English present. The punctiliar idea is, however, not conserved; we try to convey it: "you get severed — get to fall," such of you as try to be declared righteous in connection with law. The moment one even tries to be justified in connection with anything in the nature of law, this is what happens, then and there the terrible damage is done. It all happens in an instant: completely out with Christ and fallen from grace.

These are clashing opposites: anything in the nature of law — Christ and his grace ("law," 3:12; "grace," 1:3). They are as exclusive as the two aorists indicate. It is impossible to combine them. Although it is worded in the second person, the statement is general, and thus, of course, applies to the Galatians. The sense is: if there are any such among you Galatians. Paul neither asserts nor denies that there are such.

The present tense is conative (R. 880): "try to be declared righteous," try to obtain a favorable verdict from God. The R. V.'s "would be justified" comes much closer to this conative present than the A. V.'s "are justified." The thing is impossible, any attempt to do it not only fails but causes defection from Christ and fall from grace. The trying is both hopeless and itself fatal. Ἐν = "in connection with," and the connection is the fact that we drop Christ and grace by starting to do works of law (v. 3), whether these be Jewish or some other kind.

Paul states the straight facts as they always are and always will be. The result is ever the same. The Galatians are put face to face with it by an effective warning.

5) Over against all such who seek justification in connection with law Paul places the emphatic ἡμεῖς with an elucidating "for." **For we on our part by means of the spirit out of faith wait for the hope of righteousness.** This is what *we* are doing, the direct opposite of what such as those mentioned in v. 4 are trying to do. By changing to "we" Paul includes himself and the Galatians as being people like himself. Nor does he divide the Galatians into two classes, those who are one with him and those who have fallen from grace. He gives up none of them. What he says with "if" and "such as" in v. 2 and 4 is a warning and not a statement of a sad actuality regarding the Galatians.

We hesitate to render the simple dative as do our versions, "through the Spirit," or as do many commentators, "in the Spirit." True, the Greek does not need the article with "Spirit" when it names this divine Person. The thought is also attractive: Spirit, the *causa efficiens salutis*, the objective means; faith, the *causa apprehendens*, the subjective means. One may then expand the thought and say much about us who have the Spirit and about all that our having him means. But note that none of the four nouns has the article, that the four are consequently to be understood in their general qualitative sense. Can the one noun then refer to a person?

Again, this is an unmodified dative without a preposition such as "through" or "in"; it is to be construed with the verb "await" and denotes means. Now the analogy of Scripture never makes the Holy Spirit a means that *we* use just as Christ is not a means or medium used by *us*. Is this analogy set aside here?

Then consider the thought itself: "we await with or by means of the Holy Spirit," which is so incongruous a combination that we decline to make it. This is simply "spirit." "Law" deals with outward works; all our waiting is inward, spiritual. It is done "by means of spirit," by means of that in us which has spirit quality. Nor do we thus lose the Holy Spirit, for he alone produces in us what can be truly called "spirit," the opposite of flesh.

Our waiting grows "out of faith," which is again qualitative, again opposed to "law" in v. 4, coordinate with "spirit" but not to be construed: "with a spirit (derived) from faith" although we admit that this construction, too, has its attraction. Faith is the source of our ardent waiting, which is done entirely by means of spirit in a truly spiritual way.

What arrests attention most of all is the fact that Paul speaks of the "hope of righteousness" and of our awaiting this hope. To wait for a hope is, of course, to await its fulfillment. Hope and waiting go together (Rom 8:25). One also sees that "hope of righteousness" contains either the objective or the appositional genitive: hope for righteousness or hope (objective) which consists of righteousness, with little to choose between the two. The genitive also makes the anarthrous "hope" definite. But does faith not *now* possess righteousness, i. e., the quality produced by the divine verdict of acquittal? How can we still be waiting for and hoping for righteousness? The answer is not difficult. Now our righteousness is due to the secret verdict pronounced by God in heaven the moment we believe. Our assurance of that secret verdict is the Word of Scripture which we must believe. We await the great hope when, on judgment day, the heavenly Judge will pronounce that verdict face to face with us before the whole universe. Then our great hope of righteousness will be consummated.

This is what Paul opposes to "such as try to be declared righteous in connection with law." Vain is their trying. Neither now nor on that day can they possibly attain it. Faith produces the sure hope, the glad waiting which can never make ashamed. "We are saved by hope" (Rom. 8:24), a hope that does not make ashamed (Rom. 5:5) at the last day.

6) Paul returns to circumcision as such with another γάρ. For us Christians circumcision amounts to nothing; the one thing that is everything for us is faith. **For in connection with Christ Jesus neither circumcision amounts to anything nor foreskin, but faith working by means of love.** Paul does not say, "for the Christian" but, "in connection with Christ Jesus." Apart from him, outside of the circle which he forms, men may value either foreskin or circumcision as they please; but in the saving sphere or the connection with Christ Jesus (office and person) neither has strength, i. e., neither is effective in any way. To imagine that circumcision is effective is to hug a delusion.

At one time this was a great issue, namely when the gospel advanced from the Jews to the Gentiles; it is now dead save as it involves the great principle set forth by Paul that all legalism is abolished root and branch by gospel liberty. The church is still troubled on this score and men like Paul and Luther are needed to keep it free. The present-day Jews, of course, still circumcise, but they in no way affect the church.

One thing and one alone is effective. It is already stated in the phrase "in Christ Jesus," which is placed forward for the sake of emphasis, and that is faith. But why does Paul add "working or showing itself operative and effective by means of love"? Because he has in v. 5 referred to the final judgment and our hope for that day. The whole Scriptures testify that in the great judgment the Judge will refer to the works of faith. As such evidence the works will substantiate the public verdict of the Judge, and all the universe will declare that verdict just.

There is a sharp contention with the Roman Catholic Church regarding the voice of this participle. This church insists that it is the passive and stakes its doctrine of the *fides caritate formata* on this voice and calls faith that is not so formed by love a *fides informata*. Love and works thus give form and substance to faith; to the Romanist, faith without these is *informata*, without form and void. The R. V. margin supports this claim with its Romanizing translation: "wrought through love." But this verb is never passive in the New Testament; it appears only in the active and in the middle voice, and when it is used in the middle it never has an object or a personal subject (C.-K. 441; B.-P. 412). This is the linguistic side of the matter. The middle is always = *vim suam exserere*.

Then, too, to the Romanist "faith" is not faith in the Biblical sense of the term. The Romanist doctrine is not understood until one understands what Romanist faith is. Rome hurls its anathema against the teaching that faith consists of knowledge, assent, and *fiducia*, confidence or trust. It cancels the first and the third factors, especially the third. It leaves only assent, namely blanket assent to whatever Rome teaches, whatever that may be. Such assent is indeed *informata* and needs something to make it *formata*, to give it form and substance. Rome declares that this substance is love and good works. When assent has enough of these it is fully formed. Since we seldom know when we have enough we cannot be certain of salvation. Hence also justification is not forensic, not instantaneous and complete but medicinal, gradual, for the most part completed in purgatory; any certainty is doubtful in this life according to Rome's own teaching.

Luther uses strong language when he writes on this subject: "Therefore faith is not such an *otiosa qualitas*, that is, a thing so entirely useless, lazy, dead, that it may lie hidden in the heart of a mortal sinner like light, useless chaff or like a fly in wintertime sticking in a crack so long until the dear sun comes to it and wakes and makes it alive."

There is logic in the Roman Catholic doctrine. *If* faith is, indeed, only assent, then it certainly needs a good deal to fill out its form. Rome says that what it needs are love and works. Many others besides Rome have conceived faith to be only an opinion, something in the intellect, and thus also preach love and works as the real essentials. Many opponents of Rome live on Roman contraband although they deny the source of their goods. In any dispute about what faith does it is essential to lay bare with exactness what "faith" is conceived to be. A Romish, a Pelagian, a Semi-Pelagian, a synergistic, a rationalistic or modernistic "faith" is not the faith of Scripture. It is a waste of effort to dispute about the predications made about such a "faith." Get back to faith itself, define that from the Scriptures; then true agreement is reached, and the predications will fall in line.

Paul here makes "love" (see 2:20, the verb) the means (διά) with which faith works. The means is certainly not the faith, still less its real *forma*, contents, or substance. Faith is ever complete in itself. No *fiducia* or trust is without the person or the object which it trusts. It is a cup that is never empty but is always filled with Christ Jesus. It may be a small or a large cup, it is never an empty one. The entire value and the power of faith lie in this its divine content. And since this is Christ who loved us and died for us, faith ever brings forth its fruit of love. How can a heart embrace him who is supreme love without glowing with love and love's energy? Circumcision and foreskin, any legalistic outward observances? They fade away automatically.

Paul's final warnings and his confidence in the Galatians

7) The subject of circumcision has been concluded. Paul begins dramatically with a rhetorical question. In v. 2 it is *he*, Paul himself, who makes a declaration to the Galatians; now he asks *them* a searching question. He has had to correct them regarding circumcision and regarding faith. Should this be necessary for people such as they are? **You were running well. Who cut in on you for you to start not to obey the truth?**

The course of Christian faith is often likened to a race for a prize. The Greeks had their great games, and, as is the case in our athletic era, everybody knew all about them. Thus Paul's figure is natural although the running of races is vastly older than the Greek contests. The imperfect pictures the Galatians as running well with every prospect of reaching the goal.

Now the question of shocked surprise which is similar to 3:1. The tenses are important here, an aorist in the main verb, a present in the infinitive. Somebody did cut in on the Galatians, but thus far only to induce them to begin not to obey the truth. The present infinitive is inchoative. The Judaizers had not as yet succeeded. The usual translation is, "who did hinder you"; R., W. P., has the more expressive, "who cut in on you." The picture is not one of halting the runners but one of throwing them off their course. One may run with all his might, but if he gets off the course he is automatically disqualified and might as well never have run at all. The course is narrow and never broad so as to allow running over to works of law. The runners do not lay out the course, nor can they change it while they are running.

Thus far Paul has employed a figure; now he turns to the reality. This is constantly done, thereby he makes the figure self-interpretative. This method of Paul's writing is often not appreciated, is perhaps even criticized; yet it is both beautiful and certainly most valuable. We must get clear in regard to the use of μή with the infinitive. Zahn finds it so incompatible, so contrary to Rom. 15:22 which has no negative that he resorts to a very inferior reading and makes a new and a separate sentence with the help of this reading: *Solchem, was Wahrheit is, nicht zu gehorchen, (darin) gehorchet niemandem*. But while this μή is not necessary and thus is at times not used it is frequently found with verbs of hindering and denying; it is pleonastic (R. 1177; B.-D. 429), "a redundant negative repeating the negative notion of the verb just as double negatives carried on the force of the first negative" (R. 1094). Why let this common negative move us to a change of reading? B.-D. 488, 1b also alters the reading without a convincing reason.

Paul purposely states the matter mildly by using this negative. "For you to start not to obey the truth" is really a litotes which is milder because it states only what was being omitted instead of what was being committed. "The truth" is also far better than the reading "truth" without the article, for this is the truth of the gospel, which is decidedly definite as it should be in this closing admonition. This truth marks out the narrow track for the runners; it is run by faith that is active by means of love. Obedience to this truth is the essential, even the elementary requirement.

8) The mild negative form of expression continues. **This persuasion** (is not derived) **from him who calls you.** It has a far different source which is sinister, indeed, if Paul should name it. Our English loses the *paronomasia* in πείθεσθαι and ἡ πεισμονή, "to be persuaded (i. e., and thus to obey) — the persuasion." The agents in the passive infinitive are the Judaizers, and "the persuasion" is their activity which is not "from him who is calling you," not from God. These Judaizers are not God's agents. That ought to be enough for the Galatians. Theirs is an alien voice; read John 10:4, 5 for a fine commentary. The article is plainly demonstrative: "this persuading or persuasion," that indicated by the preceding infinitive.

So rare is this hapaxlegomenon that it affords opportunity for those who, like Zahn and B.-D., alter the reading to dispute its meaning and to make the word passive: *Folgsamkeit* instead of persuasion, i. e., obedience on the part of the Galatians instead of persuading coming from the Judaizers. B.-P. 1025 rightly rejects a passive sense for this word since this supposed passive sense is based on an altered reading.

9) There is a close connection when Paul adds: **A little leaven leavens the entire lump.** The object is placed before the verb in the Greek for the sake of emphasis. Only the beginning of wrong obedience had been made in Galatia. It was like introducing a little yeast into a mass of dough. Let the Galatians not close their eyes to the danger. Give a little yeast time and it will penetrate the entire dough. The expression may be a proverb or common saying. Paul's use of it here and in I Cor. 5:6 has led to its being quoted frequently.

Here the little leaven refers to doctrine and not to persons. In I Cor. 5:6 the application is made to a different matter (see that passage). Those who refer it to persons point to the singular "who" in v. 7 and to ἐγώ and to ὁ ταράσσων in v. 10 which designate persons. But they disregard "not to obey the truth" in v. 7 and "this persuasion" in v. 8, both of which refer to doctrine which is insidious like spreading yeast and seeks to penetrate all that the Galatians had hitherto believed. The whole lump = the Galatians and all of the doctrine they had hitherto believed.

To say that the Judaistic doctrine was not a small bit of yeast but a great mass of doctrine, the whole of which opposed the whole gospel, and that, therefore, doctrine cannot be referred to, overlooks what Paul is saying. He is not placing the one doctrinal system over against the other but is issuing the warning: *Principiis obsta,* resist the beginnings. The Judaizers were not so foolish as to unload their entire doctrine upon the Galatians at one time; they injected it little by little. Paul refers to the little leaven that had already been injected, the fact that the Galatians had begun to observe times (4:10) although they had not as yet yielded to circumcision. If it be not stopped, that little would eventually leaven and alter everything.

To speak of persons is beside the mark, i. e., that a few false teachers are enough to pervert the entire church. We know nothing about the number of the Judaizers in Galatia, in fact, the number is irrelevant. These teachers, whatever their number, could corrupt the entire church only by their doctrine and in no other way. Instead of this reference to persons it would be rather profitable to note the aptness of likening yeast to evil persuasion. Both work silently, insidiously. The figure of yeast is used in a good sense only once (Matt. 13:33), otherwise it is used in an evil sense (Matt. 16:6-12; I Cor. 5:6; here).

It is only too true: the admission of a little false doctrine into the true is highly dangerous. One infected apple infects many others; the many sound ones never make the infected one sound. A little yeast alters the entire dough; and the entire dough never turns the yeast into dough. In our day especially, when so much is known about spores, ferments, and bacteriology, Paul's homely warning should be most effective. This proverb should be death to doctrinal indifference. But many still imagine that a little deviation from the truth of the gospel will do no harm to them and to those who hear them. They even pride themselves on harboring at least some deviation and, while they want their food and their drink pure, cast their flings at the *reine Lehre*.

10) Not until this point has been reached does Paul contrast the persons, and now he does it plainly. Here, too, is a warning that is plain and direct. **I on my part am confident regarding you in the Lord that you will mind nothing else; but he that disturbs you shall bear his judgment, whoever he is.**

The opposition, "I on my part — he who disturbs you," is marked. The second perfect is used with present force: "I am confident," and this confidence of Paul's regarding the Galatians is not merely light optimism that exists in his own mind but is connected with the Lord who will give power and efficacy to Paul's words.

Paul is confident "that you will mind nothing else." This "nothing else" does not refer to the contents of the entire epistle but to what has just been said in v. 9. The Galatians will see that a little Judaistic leaven will eventually leaven the whole lump, that they must fear the very beginnings they have already made and end them forthwith.

Paul has his confidence in the Lord. But what Paul says about his own sure confidence implies that "he who disturbs you" is also to have *his* confidence, one that is also connected with the Lord, namely, that "he shall bear his judgment," no matter who he may be, of what quality or in what class (R. 727). The idea that Paul has in mind a single individual, the leader among the Judaizers, cannot be upheld. In 1:7 we have the identical designation in the plural; compare 4:17; 5:12; 6:12, etc.

The indefinite relative clause "whosoever he is" is intended for any disturber. Every disturber of the Galatians shall bear his judgment for his nefarious work. Excuses, pleas of good intention, etc., shall not avail. The future tense is prophetic. Paul uses the indeterminate κρῖμα, "judgment," and does not say outright κατάκριμα, "condemnation." He does not mean that this will not be an adverse judgment. Paul leaves this in God's hands. It may come in part already in this life, but will come surely and fully at death.

This is a passage which the disturbers of the church might well take to heart. It is no light thing to scatter the leaven of false doctrine, it never was. Paul, however, writes this to the Galatians in order to warn them. Will they continue to listen to men whose doom is awaiting them? If they do so, will they not come to share that doom?

11) The thought of the judgment awaiting these Judaizers brings to Paul's mind the foul and even fatuous means to which they resort when they are spreading their leaven. Recently, while he was in Lystra, Paul had taken Timothy as his assistant and, in order to enable him to work among Jews, had circumcised Timothy, Acts 16:3. Paul had also very likely not objected when Jewish Christians chose to circumcise their male children and had not made an issue of it as long as no legalistic and Judaistic ideas were connected with such circumcisions. Thus Jewish Christians also continued to eat

kosher as James himself did. This was a matter of liberty. But, it seems, the Judaizers sought to make capital of this liberty in support of their legalistic demand for circumcision. Did Paul thus not preach circumcision by his own acts? These Judaizers were blind to the common fact that, when two do the same thing, it may not be the same thing. Paul blasts them with the most withering irony. **But I on my part, brethren, if I still preach circumcision, why am I still persecuted? Has the deathtrap of the cross been abolished? Would that they who unsettle you would even have themselves castrated!**

The condition of unreality deals with an assumed reality. Paul did *not* preach circumcision. What he preached on that score, v. 6 restates. The Judaizers asserted, on the grounds indicated, that Paul *did* still preach circumcision. This alleged fact Paul picks up and for a moment speaks of it as being a fact. He places the pronoun forward for the sake of strong emphasis: "I on my part, if I," etc. The address "brethren" likewise lends weight.

The statement is so silly that Paul is still preaching circumcision. Paul tears it to pieces with two questions, "Why am I still persecuted?" Why, then, are the Jews still after me? It is not necessary to assume that the Judaizers were persecuting Paul. This persecution is also actual persecution and not mere vilification such as these Judaizers launched against the absent Paul whom they had never met. The unthinkable thing is the fact that the Jews would still persecute a man who preached the central demand of Jewdom, namely circumcision. The worst persecution Paul had suffered so far was experienced at the hands of Jewish fanatics — because he preached *against* circumcision.

One may make the following statement a deduction with the reading ἄρα (our versions) or another question with the reading ἄρα; either is good. We regard it as a question because a question precedes. Paul is above thinking of himself alone, of his still undergoing persecution; his thought automatically reverts to Christ. The second question also rests on the assumption of fact "if": "Has the deathtrap of the cross been abolished?"

Σκάνδαλον is the trigger stick of a trap, to which the bait is affixed, which springs the trap when the bait is touched. It has nothing to do with "stumbling block" despite our versions (on the verb see M.-M. 576). The difference is not one of the figure only but of the sense. A *skandalon* is a fatal, deadly thing, it kills and is intended to kill; a stumbling block (for which the Greek has a different word: πρόσκομμα) at most causes a fall from which one arises and generally designates a lesser hurt. In Rom. 9:33 the two are found together so that our versions could not repeat their usual translation. To be sure, *skandalon* is used metaphorically, but if we translate it "offense," it must always be mortal, fatal offense, no less.

If I am still preaching circumcision as the Jews have always preached it, has this astounding thing then been done, has the deathtrap of the cross been abolished? Why, then these Judaizers would have all they want! "The *skandalon* of the cross" = I Cor. 1:23, "Christ crucified for the Jews a *skandalon*." The cross, the crucified Messiah, is deadly to the Jew to this day. Although it is the very power of God to save (I Cor. 1:24) by freeing us from the curse of the law in that Christ on the cross became a curse in our stead (3:13), by clinging to their law the Jews are still struck by this curse, by scorning Christ crucified have him as an odor of death unto death. At the heart of their fatal legalism is circumcision. If they could keep their legalism, if they could put into the cross something that is not atonement but only example, a great model, a so-called inspiration, the Jews would adopt the cross. Many modern Jews, as also all deniers of Christ's deity, do this very thing. But the *skandalon* cannot be abolished. The cross can be perverted, it cannot be changed. It means atonement, justification by faith, abolition of law and works of law, complete Christian liberty. No, brethren, Paul would say, the *skandalon* of the cross is not abolished by such a silly allegation as that I still preach circumcision.

12) Paul's hot indignation against these Judaizers who stoop to anything they think may further their cause is expressed in the ironic wish that they might have themselves even castrated. This still rests on the condition stated in v. 11. But the sense is not that, by having themselves castrated, they might become even holier than by being merely circumcised. The idea of holiness does not lie in the context. With their circumcision these Judaizers want to outdo Paul and take the Galatians away from him. But if they have no more to offer than Paul offers, if, as they claim, he, too, still preaches circumcision, how will they be able to outdo him? Well, there is a way — would that they might try it! Let them have themselves castrated! Then they would, indeed, leave Paul behind who, as they say, still preaches only circumcision. But this is said with an eye to the Galatians, a fact which we should not overlook. These Judaizers, who are unsettling the Galatians in order to get them away from Paul, who boast that they have something better than he has, can outdo him only by going to the full length of their claim: if they can say that Paul still advocates circumcision they should adopt castration. How the Galatians would then admire and follow these eunuchs!

Ὄφελον is a mere particle for expressing a wish, it is developed from the imperfect ὤφελον with the infinitive by dropping the augment. Here alone it is followed by the future in order to express a wish regarding the future; elsewhere it is followed by the aorist in order to indicate a wish regarding the past, or by the imperfect in order to designate a wish regarding the present. R. 923. B.-D. 384 calls Paul's wish fulfillable; R. 923 non-fulfillable. It all depends on how the wish is regarded.

The verb itself is the regular term for "to castrate" whether it is used alone or with a term that names the parts cut off. There is no gain in thinking of a figurative modification: cutting the Judaizers off from the congregation, from sin and error, or from the truth and the mercy of God. The form is middle and not passive, R. 809 makes it the causative middle, B.-D. 317, "let themselves be," etc. They would, of course, castrate themselves by having the operation performed by a competent person — no issue regarding that.

The point of castration was highly effective in the case of the Galatians, who had among them the castrated priests of Cybele, a Phrygian goddess, who was by the Greeks identified more or less with Rhea, the mother of their gods. Castration appears in various other pagan cults. So these Judaizers, who had advanced to castration, would be out and out pagans! On the status of eunuchs among the Jews compare Deut. 23:1; Isa. 56:3.

The gospel of Christian liberty has thus been unfolded anew for the Galatians (3:1-5:12). In the last part of this section Paul admonishes the Galatians to drop their legalism (4:12-5:12). This brings us to the third main part of the epistle.

PART III

How the Galatians Should Use their Christian Liberty, 5:13-6:16

After the liberty itself has been unfolded for the Galatians so as to remove them from the slavery the Judaizers were seeking to impose on them, it remains necessary that Paul show how this liberty manifests and exercises itself in the Christian life. To be liberated, to be free is to act with freedom. Action is freedom's very domain. Christian liberty, however, is always controlled; its controlling power is love. It remains liberty only when it is under this control, otherwise it becomes license which runs wild. Thus an anomaly results which Luther has put into a striking paradox (Erlangen ed. 27, 176):

"A Christian man is a free Lord over all things and subject to no one.

"A Christian man is a subservient slave of all things and subject to everyone."

Luther learned this from Paul whose best pupil he is. The key to the paradox is love. Love makes liberty both the safest and the most valuable possession. It fills this liberty with both beauty and happiness.

Liberty exercised by means of love

13) **For you on your part, brethren, were called unto freedom; only (use) not this freedom as a starting point for the flesh, but by means of love slave for each other.** "For" at the head of a paragraph = "in order to elucidate still further." The elucidation now offered concerns the use of Christian freedom. Paul places "you" emphatically over against the Judaizers, those making it a business to unsettle you (v. 12).

Whatever Paul may wish for these men, the great fact remains, and the Galatians must ever keep it before them: for their part they were called unto liberty.

The aorist states the past fact, and throughout the epistles the calling is always to be understood in the effective sense, i. e., including acceptance of the call. When the gracious gospel call won the Galatians to faith, it was entirely for freedom. The call itself was a liberation and ushered into the fullest liberty. Ἐπί with the dative is used to indicate an aim or a goal as in I Thess. 4:7 (B.-P. 447). The address, "brethren," is placed after the sentence as in 4:12 and is thus less emphatic although it still marks a new section, acknowledges the Galatians, and expects them to heed.

But this fact, that they were called to freedom, is only the basic statement, the summary of the entire second part of the epistle. On this basis rests the new part regarding the use of this freedom. Paul also states this in a summary fashion, both negatively and positively. In the negative statement the verb is absent. It is not necessary that we supply a verb, yet the negative μή conveys an imperative tone. The thought is complete: for freedom, "only not this freedom as a starting point, an impetus for the flesh," i. e., in favor of the flesh still left in us.

Here lies the danger for all the called. They are ushered into a wonderful land of freedom. Yet freedom is like a great fortune of money, it may be a great blessing if it is used aright, a curse if it is abused. It is like being a great king who must be kingly and not a tyrant. As the freedom mounts, so does the responsibility for its use. Otherwise the freedom itself disappears. The danger lies not on the side of the reborn spirit in the Christian but on the side of his flesh, the power of sin still left in him. In a war an ἀφορμή is a basis of operation, and in the metaphorical use of the word this idea is retained. Our sinful flesh may appropriate this freedom as if it were intended for itself and may thus start turning it into license. "Only not this!" Paul writes. The flesh must be checked at the very beginning.

The positive statement is paradoxical: "but by means of love slave for each other." Our freedom means that we must slave. It seems contradictory yet is perfect harmony. Freedom is the free exercise of love. This is the love born of faith, the love of real intelligence and understanding coupled with corresponding aim and purpose. The Greek article is quite in place although it is not needed in English. Love itself is free. Love goes out toward its object with intelligent and purposeful devotion. Here the object is expressed by "each other," and the devotion by the strong verb "to slave." Compare I John 4:20, 21. Paul does not write that we are to be "slaves of each other" (genitive); we are God's and Christ's slaves. The slave *of* another is bound to make the other's will his own. To slave *"for* each other" (dative) is to do our work for each other according to our Lord's will.

Here we have the whole exercise of our Christian freedom. Its great medium is the love that fills us, its great activity, voluntary slaving for each other. When we exercise ourselves in this work we have freedom indeed. The reading of a few texts which have the dative: "with the love of the spirit (or Spirit)" has nothing to commend it either textually or as far as the thought is concerned. Such a dative still leaves love as the means, and the combination "the love of the spirit (Spirit)" would occur only in this variant.

14) Luther writes on this verse: *Theologia brevissima et longissima; brevissima quod ad verba et sententias attinet, sed usu et re ipsa latior, longior, profundior et sublimior toto mundo.* What impressed Luther so deeply is the fact that Paul sees that the law itself establishes the gospel freedom since the free love

brought forth by gospel faith freely fulfills the very heart of the law, its demand for the love the law could never achieve. That is what Paul states in words so brief, that involve amplifications so long, wide, profound, sublime as to comprise the whole law and the gospel. **For the whole law stands as having been fulfilled in the one word, namely, Thou shalt love thy neighbor as thyself!**

"For" substantiates, and the marvel is the fact that the very law from which the Christian believer is free should substantiate this very freedom. Yet this becomes simple and clear the moment we stop looking at the many individual requirements of the Mosaic legal system, especially those of a temporary ceremonial nature, and see what really fulfills "the whole law," namely love. The moment the Christian freedom from law is exercised, its one means is love, it does what love prompts down to actual slaving for others. That is the very fulfillment of the whole law as this is voiced in its own one, summary command: "Thou shalt love thy neighbor as thyself!"

Real freedom from law is not license for the flesh but slaving for others by means of love, and the law itself proves that this is freedom from law. The law should certainly be able to demonstrate who is still held as a slave by it and who has been set free from it as at last being a free man. It does this by setting up the commandment of love. A slave of the law he must remain who, despite a thousand labors in complying outwardly with other commands, fails in regard to this one which asks love. He who clings to law ever remains only such a slave, for no law ever produced love no matter how strenuously it may make this demand. But he who accepts the gospel gift which frees from law, by his freedom, if that freedom become not license, without the law achieves the whole law, its very crown, namely love. The whole law says so since its fulfillment lies in love. This has often been put into the simple statement: "What the law demands the gospel gives."

From one viewpoint the law and the gospel are direct opposites; hence the only salvation is freedom from the law. Yet from another viewpoint these two correspond, the one dovetails into the other although they lose their identity; hence the very love produced by the gospel freedom stands as the fulfillment of the law's demand which is love. The law, once a tyrant, becomes the free man's servant. Theologically expressed, this is called the third use of the law.

Observe that this was true also in the time of the Old Testament. Paul cites Lev. 19:18. The Old Testament had the gospel just as we now have it; only the form differed: then it was in the form of promise, now that promise as fulfilled in Christ. That gospel promise which was older than the law of Moses (3:17) ever wrought faith and love just as it now does. Therein the whole law was fulfilled also for those Old Testament saints, therein alone. Yes, they had the ceremonies of Moses which are now abolished since Christ has come. They were the shadows, he the substance (Col. 2:17). But also in the Old Testament love and not in mere outward observances lay the fulfillment. Paul has elucidated this subject at length in 3:23, etc.; 4:1, etc.; also the freedom in Sarah, Isaac, etc., in 4:21, etc.

"The whole law" places this in contrast with single commandments such as those mentioned in 4:10, and especially the Judaistic demand for circumcision. Piecemeal dealings with the law lead to nothing (Matt. 23:23). The whole of it alone suffices. It is entirely "in the one word," $\dot{\epsilon}\nu\ \tau\ddot{\varphi}$, "namely," the definite article makes a substantive of the quotation. Paul cites only the love to our neighbor, but this is never without the love to God (I John 4:20, 21). In Mark 10:17 Jesus cites only the Second Table, and in Luke 10:30 he exemplifies the concept of neighbor by pointing to the good Samaritan. As regards "one another" in v. 13 and "thy neighbor" here in the commandment note Paul's own statement in 6:10.

The perfect tense "has been fulfilled" has its present connotation so that we translate: "stands as having been fulfilled." See Rom. 8:13; 13:10. The future indicative: "thou shalt or wilt love," is common in legal precepts (R. 874). It is the love itself in the Christian's heart, born of faith in the gospel, which stands as the whole law's fulfillment despite the fact that this love still lacks so much in its outward manifestation. Yet the law cannot object on this account, for Christ has freed us from all its condemnations (v. 1), and Christ's righteousness covers all our imperfections.

15) The negative side of the Christian's freedom in slaving for others by means of love is stated drastically: **But if you keep biting and devouring each other, take heed lest you be consumed by each other!** Freely to slave for each other is to *conserve* each other; to let the flesh (v. 13) have its way is to be *consumed* by each other. The figure is taken from the jungle and the forest where tooth and claw reign and the denizens are exterminated by each other. The first two verbs are durative: "if you go on biting and devouring"; the last is an aorist derived from ἀναλίσκω and states what the end will be: "you will be consumed."

We note that Paul does not use negative imperatives: "Be not biting, etc.," which, if they were expressed by present imperatives, would mean: "Stop biting," etc. This would imply that the Galatians had, indeed, begun to bite each other. Nor does Paul use ἐάν with a condition of expectancy. This would imply that he has reason to expect such biting, etc. He uses the ordinary condition of reality which may mean that Paul conceives an actual reality and speaks of it as being real; yet it may mean only that he assumes the acts as being real in order to speak of them more drastically although the acts are not real. In other words, no conclusion as to the occurrence of actual biting and devouring in Galatia can be drawn from the conditional clause here used. This is also true with regard to the apodosis, "see to it," which merely matches the protasis and adds nothing beyond it but means only: "then see to it."

In regard to admonitions that involve conduct we must observe that the extreme is mentioned because it includes and intends to include all that is less down to the least. The extreme must, of course, be mentioned, for sins sometimes go that far. So the commandments forbid murder and adultery, but in Matt. 5:21, etc.; 5:27, etc., Jesus expounds and shows how these extremes include all that is less and yet of the same nature. A tiny sprout is as poisonous as the full-grown plant. So Paul mentions the extreme in order to include all that is the opposite of Christian love which serves others even to the extent of slaving for them. It will not always be necessary to slave thus, often only a kind word, a little help will be necessary in the exercise of freedom in love.

The catalog of sins listed in v. 19-21 is objective, and one should not draw from it and say that "enmities, strife, jealousies, wraths, factions, divisions" were prevalent among the Galatians because biting and devouring are mentioned in v. 15. Paul did not include these sins in his catalog in v. 20 because they were prevalent among the Galatians, nor did he list the other sins in v. 19-21 because of their actual prevalence in Galatia. The admonitory form used in v. 15 warns against what lack of love causes. It emphasizes the admonition: "by means of love keep slaving for each other."

We thus decline to accept the conclusion that biting and devouring were actually in progress among the Galatians at this time. Those who think that this was the case admit that this one verse alone reflects the actual bad moral condition prevailing in Galatia and expresses surprise because of that fact. We think that if such conditions were actual in Galatia, Paul would undoubtedly have written more than one line regarding them. With this one line and this condition of reality Paul points out what the reality is bound to become where the freedom of Christian love is lost. At this very time the Jews, from whom the Judaizers sprang, were biting and devouring each other. Read their history during these years and note Acts 21:38 as an incident and Acts 23:12, 13 as another; in a few more years their whole nation was no more, they had consumed each other.

Love conserves, lack of love consumes. The fact that this consuming means destruction of the bond of Christian fellowship needs no further proof.

Following the spirit and not the flesh

16) Paul has mentioned "the flesh" in v. 13 in his preliminary admonition that our freedom must be exercised by means of love. Not to yield to the flesh means ever to follow the spirit. This is what Paul now presents. **Now I say** (my meaning is): **Keep walking with what is spirit, and you will not carry out any craving of what is flesh.** This is what Paul intends to convey to the Galatians as regards their daily life and conversation: that in thought, word, and deed they ever use what regeneration has brought to birth in them; then any stirring of what is still left in them of sinful flesh, their old depraved

nature, will not be carried out into action but will be crushed in its incipiency (v. 24). The translation seeks to conserve the anarthrous nouns, all three of which are qualitative.

Throughout the rest of the chapter "spirit" and "flesh" are contrasted, the new and the old nature. We see their antagonism, the freedom of the former, their fruits *in extenso*, finally the flesh crucified, the spirit living on in full activity. Rendall says that throughout this section Paul has in mind "spirit" and not "Spirit"; Lightfoot says it in regard to v. 17. Our versions plus the majority of the commentators prefer "Spirit."

All that we have already said in regard to v. 5 applies to this section. A comparison with Rom. 8:1-11 is decisive. In Romans we have "God's Spirit," "Christ's Spirit," etc., which leave no doubt as to the meaning; although the word is used seven times in Galatians, such a genitive does not appear in a single instance. Four times Paul has no article, and where he has it, the article denotes previous reference. All seven *pneuma* must be translated alike; our versions translate "Spirit" throughout. The commentators who follow them hurdle the difficulties that result and brush aside "spirit."

Here and in v. 25 the simple datives denote means and ought not to be translated "in the Spirit" (A. V.), for which thought Paul would use ἐν. The analogy of Scripture shows that *we* never use the Spirit as a means (see v. 5), but we do so use our own "spirit." So Paul here bids the Galatians to use in their walk and conversation what is spirit in its nature, i. e., the reborn, new man. Then when any craving, lust, evil desire of what is by nature flesh starts in them, they will not let it come to a head in action. "Flesh" and the "Holy Spirit" are not a contrast, but "flesh" and "spirit" are. Ἐπιθυμία is regularly used in an evil sense in the New Testament (C.-K. 501) although the classics use it as a *vox media*.

17) The reason for this admonition is: **For the flesh has cravings against the spirit, and the spirit against the flesh. For these lie opposed to each other so that you are not doing what you may want.**

The articles in "the flesh" and "the spirit" denote previous reference. Here ἐπιθυμεῖ is a *vox media* because it is used also with regard to the spirit; "lusteth" (our versions) is thus not a good translation because this word is too regularly used in only an evil sense. The old nature in us wants things that are contrary to the new, and vice versa. The two natures in us thus lie in constant conflict with each other. They are not opposites that as such live far apart, each following what it craves; they lie ἀντί, face to face, in constant clashing. Paul knows of no exceptions to this fact; he is not a perfectionist.

Lightfoot recognized that ἵνα is here consecutive, and Moulton, *Einleitung* 333, as well as R. 998 support him and free us from the labored interpretations that operate with purpose and even make this God's purpose. Paul says that *the result* of this clashing of flesh and spirit is that we do not go on doing (present, durative) what we may want to do. The indefinite relative clause means, "what we may want to do" in carrying out some craving of our flesh. The spirit in us succeeds in blocking this.

In v. 16 Paul urges the Galatians ever to walk with what is spirit and assures them that they will, indeed, not carry out any craving of what is still flesh in them. It is this context which makes v. 17 different from Rom. 7:15, etc., where the victories of the flesh are recorded. These are not denied here, but here the victories of the spirit are the subject. The fact that the flesh is also active is stated, but what it accomplishes beyond its cravings is not mentioned. This is also true in regard to v. 24. This makes plain that Paul does not here mean that what we may want according to our spirit is always blocked by our flesh (μὴ ποιῆτε, durative) even as this is not the fact. In the believer the spirit does, indeed, dominate; he has crucified the flesh (aorist, v. 24).

The verb ἀντίκειται cannot mean that God created the spirit and the flesh for the *purpose* that we should not do what we want. This view assumes the activity of three forces: we and our will, the flesh, and the spirit. God has then arranged it so that we never get to do our will but must do either what the flesh or the spirit (Spirit) dictates. A strange psychology! Regeneration renews, liberates, frees the will. The spirit = the liberated will. This liberated will is still hampered by the flesh which ever seeks to obtain control again in order once more to usurp the throne. The flesh does not succeed; we need but to keep on walking with what is spirit.

18) **Now if you are being led by what is spirit you are not under what is law,** in other words, you have the gospel freedom to which you have been called. This links back into the great idea of freedom (v. 13) by showing what this freedom involves in our daily experience. To be led by what is spirit (dative of the agent) is another way of saying that we are walking with what is spirit (v. 16) save that "spirit" is now pictured as our guide while in v. 16 it was our means. Under this blessed leadership you are free men; the opposite is equally true, without it you are slaves. Rom. 8:14 is a similar statement, but there "God's Spirit" is the leader, and the result is expressed accordingly, "sons of God." To be sure, where "spirit" leads, "God's Spirit" leads, for "spirit" is his creation in us. Nothing is lost by the qualitative term "spirit."

The freedom which Paul has described to the Galatians at such length is freedom from "law," which is equally as qualitative as "spirit." In Rom. 6:14: "not under law" = under grace which is spiritual freedom. Both the tyranny and the curse of anything in the nature of law are thus removed. This includes the Mosaic law but also every other law. The anarthrous noun allows no restriction. The Judaizers, of course, wanted slavery under the Mosaic code, especially under its ceremonial requirements. But Paul has passed beyond this Judaistic restriction and has carried the entire subject down to its basic principle, law as such, whatever in its nature is law. This makes slaves one way or another; to be completely free from law, wholly under grace, is alone freedom indeed. John 8:32-36.

19) Moreover, public are the works of the flesh, of which kind are fornication, uncleanness, unbridled conduct — idolatry, sorcery — enmities, strifes, jealousies, wraths — factions, splits, separate notions, envies — sprees, carousings, and the things like these, concerning which I tell you in advance even as I told you in advance that they who perpetrate such things shall not inherit God's kingdom.

Δέ adds this catalog of vices. Works betray and advertise their source. Paul lists the actual works after speaking of "flesh craving" in v. 16. The craving produces these wicked works and others like them. Again the full outgrowth is described, but again it includes everything from the first secret craving to these complete works. Where the flesh is in full control works like this result. They show publicly what the flesh is. One does not need to speculate in regard to the flesh; look at what is "public," open to the eyes of all. When a Christian gives way to his flesh he will head for some of these works.

In every one of Paul's catalogs the items are carefully chosen and carefully placed into proper groups,

Galatians 5:19, 20

the groups themselves are carefully arranged so that they form a whole. The entire list is always present to Paul's mind in its complete order before he sets down the first item. The most perfect arrangement appears in the list in II Cor. 6:4-10, which deserves the fullest study and appreciation. The world's godlessness and unrighteousness have never been described more adequately than in Rom. 1:18-32. As it was in 4:24, ἅτινα is qualitative, not merely "which" (our versions) but "of a kind which," thus already intimating that the list is not exhaustive.

We indicate the groups by means of dashes. Some make four groups: 3 — 2 — 8 — 2; we find five: 3 — 2 — 4 — 4 — 2. Eight would be unrhetorical, and a glance shows that it contains two fours. Five is the half of ten. Ten indicates greatest completeness (ten commandments, ten virgins, ten slaves in the parables, etc., i. e., in each case all); hence the broken ten = incompleteness which allows the reader to supply the remainder.

Some texts begin with "adulteries" and thus have four in the first group; this addition is probably due to Matt. 15:19, and Mark 7:21. This is the *sex* group, the nastiest, the most degrading, on which a special curse seems to rest, *Fleischessuenden* in a specific sense. "Fornication" = all illicit sexual intercourse. "Uncleanness" is broader and includes not only the other sexual aberrations but also all that leads to them — the whole mass of this filth. Ἀσέλγεια = *Zuegellosigkeit*, having restraint removed, plunging onward like a runaway horse; it is here associated with sex. As uncleanness spreads in all directions, so this third rushes on through to the limit and lets no consideration halt its course. These three and the next two are comprehensive singulars and thus again a significant five.

20) Now a closely associated pair that is probably placed next to the sex group because in the pagan

world they are so closely connected with sexual sins, call it the *godless* group. "Idolatry" was a constant danger to Gentile Christians. This was due not only to the fact that superstition drew them toward the old false gods; what often drew them still more were the festivities of the whole Roman world, celebrations and the mass of customs that centered in idol worship in one way or in another. Pagan skeptics scoffed at the gods but participated in the festivities and yielded to the customs.

All sorcery, witchcraft, charms, and the superstitions which furnish the soil and the atmosphere for their existence, are pagan throughout. In our times Christian words, names, and symbols have been introduced into witchcraft in Christian lands, but the basis is always pagan and idolatrous. So also is the notion that the devil operates in sorcery, etc. The writer here summarizes the results of an extensive study of this subject and of occultism in general. The sin is here named according to the drugs and medicaments so widely employed in secret pagan arts. But the word was used so as to include all magic and sorcery and is most properly paired with idolatry. All sorcery is idolatrous and thus pagan. Acts 19:18-20.

After five singulars we have ten plurals, yet not ten combined into one group but into three, hence not a unit ten (grand completeness) but a diverse ten (only hinting at completeness). There are two fours and a broken four: $4 + 4 + 2$. Four is the common, brief, rhetorical expression of completeness which is constantly and even intuitively used by writers and is thus distinct from the conscious ten. Paul breaks off in the middle of the third four; instead of completing it he adds: "and the things like these," thus in a double way ending his list as an incomplete catalog. *Addit "et iis similia," quia quis omnem lernam carnalis vitae recenseat?* Luther.

Who cares to review the entire hydra? When one of its many heads is cut off, two grow in its place. We accept the reading that has the nominative plural ἔρεις instead of the singular ἔρις (B.-D. 47, 3; R. 265); this plural occurs in a number of texts and could easily be made a singular since the more usual plural is ἔριδες. One singular amid a long list of plurals would be an odd usage in Paul's writings. Some texts also have the singular ζῆλος, but here the plural is textually well assured. Some texts insert φόνοι after φθόνοι as is done in Matt. 15:19; Mark 7:21; Rom. 1:29; I Cor. 6:9 (thus the A. V.). But already Jerome counted only fifteen items. The R. V. is textually correct.

Four types of *personal animosity* are listed. The first denotes personal hatreds or enmities; the second, the strifes and wranglings that result; the third, the motives so often involved, jealousies; the fourth, the outbursts of hot passion in anger; the first and the third point to motives, the second and the fourth to their product. Hateful animosities produce strifes; jealousies produce passionate outbursts of anger.

Four types of *partyism* follow properly. When persons clash, each so often has his following. People take sides. Relatives and friends rally to the support of the one as do those of the opponent to him. Thus the flesh produces "factions," this word indicates mercenary motives. Next there are outright "splits," divisions, sunderings. Third, αἱρέσεις from which our word "heresy" is derived. It denotes a choice of a special opinion for oneself. Thus the Pharisees had theirs and formed a *hairesis*, a sect with peculiar views and doctrines, and aligned itself especially against the Sadducees, another *hairesis;* see Acts 5:17; 15:5; 26:5. This word was applied to the Christians by the Jews, Acts 24:5, 14; 28:22. Its philosophic use came later, according to which it denoted a peculiar school of philosophy.

Here and in I Cor. 11:19 Paul uses the word in the plural with a severer meaning. These "heresies" are results of the flesh and are to be condemned. Paul also lists them after "splits" or divisions, for they are evidently their cause. The context in II Pet. 2:1 is the most damaging of all: false prophets, false teachers, *haireseis* of destruction brought in on the side by such as deny even the Master who bought them, bringing upon themselves swift destruction. It is easy to see the course the word has followed; it soon reached what we call "heresy," any false doctrine down to the very worst.

21) Paul has been criticized for adding "envies" which, we are told, should properly appear after "wraths." This criticism rests on the conception that Paul refers to cases of envy between individuals in common matters of life as when one envies what another has. Then "envies" might, indeed, appear in the group headed by "enmities." Paul places "envies" in the group headed by mercenary "factions" and intends to convey the idea that "envies" are one of the motives which help to create such doctrines and the parties and splits which they cause. Here we may note Matt. 27:18 and also Phil. 1:15.

The last pair: drunkennesses or "sprees" and carousings, *Gelage,* Luther translates: *Saufen, Fressen,* which is very much to the point. From the fact that Paul has four terms to denote hostilities and four to denote divisions the deduction has been made that such conditions prevailed among the Galatians at this time. Any deduction made would have to apply to the whole list, including even "the things like these." And Paul says that concerning all these things he has told the Galatians in advance as he now does again "that they who perpetrate such things shall not inherit the kingdom of God." This catalog evidently does not present a special selection of sins that had but recently developed among the Galatians. The present participle characterizes: "those whose mark is the practice of such things"; πράσσω is often used in the evil sense, "to perpetrate."

When Paul writes "shall not inherit" he calls to mind all that he has said regarding the testament (3:15, etc.), regarding the inheritance (3:18), regarding minor heirs (4:1, etc.), regarding full-grown sons (4:7), regarding inheriting like Isaac (4:22, etc., note v. 30). All this shows that Paul does not mean: shall not enter heaven, "God's kingdom" in that sense. His kingdom is inherited in this life.

"God's kingdom" is one of the grandest concepts of Scripture. See Matt. 3:2; Mark 1:15; Luke 1:33; John 3:3. The kingdom is the rule of God in grace and in glory. Wherever he so rules there is this blessed kingdom. Unlike earthly kingdoms, the divine King alone makes his kingdom. Those kingdoms exist apart from their kings, make and at times unmake their kings; not so this kingdom. The genitive is possessive: the kingdom belongs to God; but it is difficult to exclude authorship from this genitive: God makes the kingdom. It extends from Adam to eternity. On earth his rule is in grace, in heaven it is in glory. Jesus expounded this kingdom in his parables, each parable revealing one side of it. The new birth admits to this kingdom, John 3:3, 5. This is effected by repentance, Matt. 3:2.

We "inherit" the kingdom. Since we are sons of the King, it is ours. We are not subjects as are those of ordinary earthly kingdoms but royal princes (I Pet. 2:9) who bear themselves as such. Grand vistas open up here. "The kingdom *ours* remaineth," Luther. We own it as heirs. We already rule in this kingdom and shall rule. Since we are heirs of the kingdom, crowns await us. Only kings are crowned. This crowning takes place at the consummation of the kingdom. We shall sit with Christ on his throne. Superearthly is the kingdom, for all earthly kingdoms have only subjects, but this kingdom is composed of nothing but kings. It carries the idea of a kingdom to its *nth* degree. See the author's *Kings and Priests* for a full exposition. The future tense "shall not inherit" = shall never possess this inheritance, because they are doing these works of the flesh they cannot be reborn and become the King's sons.

22) **But the fruit of the spirit is love, joy, peace, longsuffering, benignity, goodness, faithfulness, meekness, self-control. Against such things there is no law.**

We have discussed the fact that Paul has in mind "spirit" in v. 16. He does not say, "the *works* of the spirit" (v. 20, "the *works* of the flesh") but uses the nobler word, "the *fruit* of the spirit." Compare the significant expression, "the unfruitful works of the darkness" (Eph. 5:11). "Fruit" is also singular although it is a collective. The flesh spreads out in many directions with its evil works; all its many activities are bad. The spirit follows one direction, produces unit fruit. The flesh has "works," deeds. In listing them Paul has used many plurals. As fruit of the spirit Paul lists nothing but virtues, the highest moral qualities, and thus also lifts this list above the other. The other list is heterogeneous: 3 — 2 — 4 — 4 — 2; this list is homogeneous: 3 — 3 — 3: each group has three members, and there are three groups. The other list is a jangle, this one a sweet harmony. While it may be only rhetorical and apparent only because we have the lists side by side, this appears intentional to the writer. Paul has the capacity for such perfect rhetoric.

First Corinthians 13 is Paul's own description of "love," the most essential product of faith, the mother of all other Christian virtues, hence the first in this list. Although it is little used in pagan Greek, this word has a fine history. In the LXX it still has lower meanings down to erotic love; but in the New Testament it rose to its fullest glory. God is love. It is not always adequately defined. As distinguished from φιλία, the love of mere liking and affection, ἀγάπη is the love of intelligent comprehension united with corresponding blessed purpose. So God loved the world, understood all its depravity and purposed to remove it. He could not embrace the foul, stinking world in *philia*, but he did love it with *agape* and sent his Son to cleanse it. We cannot offer affection to our enemies who would smite us in the face; Jesus did not love the Pharisees with *philia* and does not ask us so to love our enemies. It is *agape* that he asks, the love that understands the hatefulness of the enemy and purposes to remove it. This distinction comes to full view in John 21:15-17. Some of the lower uses still appear in the New Testament as when publican loves publican, but even here intelligence and purpose are involved. Warfield's idea that *agape* sees value in the loved object breaks down when the main passages are studied.

With this love goes "joy." This is a remarkable combination that was written by the man who composed II Cor. 6:4-10 on the basis of his own experience, yet note that "always rejoicing" appears even in this list (v. 10). Yes, joy is one of the cardinal Christian virtues; it deserves a place next to love. Pessimism is a grave fault. This is not fatuous joy such as the world accepts; it is the enduring joy that bubbles up from all the grace of God in our possession, from the blessedness that is ours (Matt. 5:3, etc.), that is undimmed by tribulation, that merges into the joy of heaven. This joy is the sunshine that ever beams for the believer. On "peace" see 1:3. As a Christian virtue it is subjective, the assured quietness of the soul, the opposite of dread and terror, the feeling of all who walk with what is spirit and indeed know that all is well between themselves and God. These virtues form the first trio as being the virtues which fill the spirit itself.

The second trio is composed of virtues which appear in our contact with men. "Longsuffering" — the mind holds out long before giving way to action. The Rheims Version has "longanimity" (Trench). This word is used also with reference to God. Men may provoke, the spirit holds out quietly.

Trench has written well regarding the synonyms χρηστότης and ἀγαθωσύνη. The former is exhibited by Jesus when he received the penitent sinner, Luke 7:37-50. It is always sweet, kind, mild, full of graciousness. The best English word for it seems to be "benignity." Close to it lies the other. "Goodness" seems to be a little pale; perhaps "beneficence" would be better since the derivation from ἀγαθός points to the bestowal upon others of what is good and beneficent. It is goodness, not as mere quiescent moral excellence, but as goodness doing good to others. Trench finds an exhibition of it also in the expulsion of the traffickers from the Temple by Jesus and in his invectives against the Pharisees in Matthew 23.

The division into verses places "faithfulness" into v. 22 and makes it a fourth member of this group. This division would be satisfactory if πίστις meant "trustworthiness," the fact that men could always trust us. But the sense is not passive, it is active, it is the German *Treue* and not *Glaube* (Luther), which latter the A. V. imitated with its translation "faith." It is a Christian virtue and not saving faith. We see that the term belongs to the third trio when we note that our being true and faithful refers to *God*, to his Word and his will; our being meek refers to *the world of men*; and our self-control refers to *our own selves*. Do not object that we are faithful also toward men, for this is only an exercise of faithfulness to God. The essential thing is ever to be faithful and true to God and to Christ.

23) So we shall also be full of "meekness" among men. When we are wronged or abused we shall show no resentment by threatening vengeance. The opposite is to be arrogant, vehement, bitter, wild, and violent. The greatest example of meekness is Jesus himself. Compare the author on Matt. 5:5, including the startling promise given to the meek. The last of this final trio is "self-control," κράτος, holding all our desires and passions in check. The "temperance" of our versions is inadequate, cf., Acts 24:25.

Some regard τῶν τοιούτων as a masculine since no antecedent is visible; some are undecided; some regard it as a neuter. We note the correspondence with τὰ τοιαῦτα in v. 21. When we are told that it is rather idle for Paul to say that law is not against "such things" (neuter), and that we therefore have the masculine, the question arises as to whether it is less idle to say that law is not against "such men." As far as grammar is concerned, since all of the antecedents are feminine, the neuter is preferable to the masculine. Of far more importance is the correspondence of this clause with the relative clause in v. 21. Still more important is the meaning that "law," of whatever kind it may be, is not opposed to these Christian virtues. That means freedom, the great gospel freedom which Paul has set forth. "Not against such things" means: as against the works of the flesh. "Such things" implies also that there are still more besides the nine here listed. This makes it unnecessary to add "things like these" as was done in v. 20.

24) Now Paul speaks of the persons. **And they who belong to Christ Jesus have crucified the flesh with the passions and the cravings.** The genitive denotes possession: "of Christ" = belonging to Christ. The Greek uses the aorist to express the past fact

whereas we prefer the perfect "have crucified." When we compare passages such as 2:20 and Rom. 6:6, it is well to note the fact that in these passages the expressions are passive and speak of a crucifixion we have undergone while here the active speaks of a crucifixion we have performed. Rom. 8:13 is active: we put to death (A. V. mortify) the deeds of the flesh; but it is durative, a mortification that ever continues, here one past act of crucifying the flesh is referred to. What Paul indicates is the fact that all who really belong to Christ have performed this act on their flesh, a decisive, effective act. It was not performed upon them, *they* themselves did it; it does not continue, it is done and over with. While it is expressed in the third person, v. 25 shows that the reference is pointedly to the Galatians. Once for all, at the time of their conversion, they killed the flesh. In Romans we died to the sin. This reverses the expression but has the same meaning.

The expression "they did crucify the flesh" is even more significant than "put to death" in Rom. 8:13. Yes, we murdered the flesh, it was a violent act to kill this old tyrant and thus to remove him from his throne in our hearts. But the verb "crucified" contains more, for is recalls the cross and the crucifixion of Christ. In conversion we accept the crucified Christ, "the cross" (5:11), in order ever after to glory only in this cross (6:14) as our deliverance. Then and there we nailed the flesh to this divine cross, to let it hang there.

Paul reminds the Galatians of this decisive act, and the third person states that all who are Christ's have done this. The act was radical, for with the flesh all its passions and all its cravings (singular in v. 16) were crucified. The fact that the flesh still troubles us changes nothing on this score. In conversion we did make a radical break, the one here put into strong figurative language.

Παθήματα, originally a *vox media*, is used fourteen times by Paul and always in an evil sense (M.-M. 473) to designate the affects and the stirrings forced upon us by the flesh in order to enslave us. They would literally carry us away (C.-K. 841); the ἐπιθυμίαι are the evil desires and cravings kindled in us. They are the flesh in its activity and were thus crucified with the flesh. Let them remain so crucified, let them never attain a resurrection so as again to control us!

25) The asyndeton states this in an effective way: **If we are living with what is spirit** (as we surely are), **let us also keep in line with what is spirit, brethren!** The two datives are abutted in a telling way in the Greek. Having crucified the flesh, let us be done with it! To crucify a man is to get rid of him as a shame and disgrace, as an utter abomination. So now we live "with what is spirit" (see v. 16). Our spiritual life lies in this spiritual means. In v. 16 the verb used is περιπατέω, the ordinary word for "to walk"; here it is στοιχέω, "to keep in line, to march in rank and file." Thus it is a little more precise than the other verb. The dative again indicates means: let us keep marching in rank and file by the aid of what is spirit, all of you, Paul included, he and the Galatians in one line. The picture is both beautiful in itself and full of effective appeal to the Galatians.

CHAPTER VI

Let each man look first to himself!

5:26) The absence of a connective helps to indicate the beginning of a new paragraph. The address ἀδελφοί belongs to 5:26 and not to 6:1; "brethren" is placed at the end as it is in 5:13; 6:18. **Let us not be vainglorious, challenging each other, envying each other, brethren.** How can "brethren" do such a thing! Paul comes to speak about direct personal admonitions in the use of our Christian liberty. This liberty is devoid of all selfishness. The hortative subjunctive is softened by the fact that Paul includes himself; this agrees with 6:4, 5. B.-P. 669: *Wir wollen keine Prahlhaense sein,* let us not be braggarts. The word "vainglorious," κενόδοξος, does not refer to empty (κενός), fictitious glory which the vainglorious person imagines to be real and genuine glory; the word denotes the praise which men seek without a genuine reason.

Persons who are covetous of all possible glorification on the part of men will thus challenge one another as though in combat, each wanting more credit and praise than the other receives. Back of this lies envy. Each will envy the other because of the praise he may obtain, especially if this is greater than his own. Phil. 2:3; Rom. 12:10b; I Pet. 5:5. The two participles are modal; they show how desire for honor among men manifests itself. "Brethren" indicates a new paragraph; more than that, "brethren" who are what the word means cannot and will not act in this manner, such actions are far beneath them.

1) Those who are filled with unholy ambition would be glad to see a brother blemished by some

transgression and do not see that they themselves are thereby already blemished in the worst manner. Paul applies the teaching of Jesus who bids one pull the beam out of his own eye before he attempts to extract the speck out of his brother's eye. Cleanse thyself first and then help cleanse also the brother who may need thy service.

If also a person gets to be overtaken in some transgression, you on your part, the spiritual ones, do you proceed to restore such a one in a spirit of meekness, watching thyself lest thou also get to be tempted.

Paul visualizes such a case as one that may well happen "also," i. e., besides the serious faults just mentioned. The idea that παράπτωμα means only a slight "fault" (A. V.), and that the word is chosen because of this mild meaning, cannot be upheld; this word is never used in the mild sense in the New Testament. Literally meaning, "something fallen by the side," i. e., as an auto that goes off the road into a ditch, in our idiom it denotes a "transgression," something that runs across or against what is right. The idea is something that is plainly wrong.

The aorist is punctiliar, "gets to be," etc. Luther's *von einem Fehl uebereilet wuerde,* which is followed by our versions, is quite correct and better than the proposed meaning, "gets to be caught or surprised in a transgression." The sense cannot be: if *you* catch a brother doing wrong; it could at best be only: if *the wrong* catches or surprises him into a fall. Paul cannot mean as the opposite: if *you* surprise him "before" (πρό) he can cover up his wrong.

Paul is excluding wilful, deliberate sin; he deals with sins into which one may be "tempted" (last verb) in some way. Include *Uebereilungssuenden* but also sins that are due to ignorance, weakness, the deceptive power of sin, the persuasion and the bad example of others. Deliberate sin is a fall from grace; the transgression here referred to is one that has not as yet reached such a fall. In every case of this kind brotherly love must come to the rescue and put the auto on the road again.

Paul says emphatically: "you on your part, the spiritual ones," i. e., who walk, are led, and keep in line with what is spirit (5:16, 18, 25), "do you proceed to restore such a one" (durative present). Only "the spiritual" can naturally do this restoring, but all of us ought to be spiritual. This is not a task for such as are not able to master their flesh. The present imperative is scarcely conative: "try to restore"; it may be iterative to include every case of this kind since "such a one" points to repeated cases that may now and again occur. Each case may also take time and patience.

We have "artisan" from this verb and its adjective, and κατά is perfective. The verb is used to designate framing a mechanism in an expert manner (Heb. 10:5; 11, 3) but more often to denote restoration, setting a broken limb, mending nets (Matt. 4:21), it is always an action that requires expert skill.

The task here mentioned requires spirituality in general and especially that feature of it listed in 5:23, "a spirit of meekness," the opposite of arrogance and harshness. Pour in oil and wine and with gentle fingers bind up the wounds. The addition: "watching thyself lest thou also get to be tempted," is not intended merely as a warning but as the motivation for meekness. We shall be meek in our treatment and show our expertness in this way when we remember that temptation may catch us also as it has caught this or that brother.

The aorist is effective, "be tempted into a fall." Let no one think he cannot be so tempted. Let everyone think what he would need in case he, too, should fall. Such a spirit will quickly mend a brother's case. It is, of course, remarked that Paul drops into the singular, which is not anacoluthic (R. 439) but intentional. Each must watch himself. "Watching yourselves" might be misunderstood as keeping an eye on each other — no, keep it on your own self.

2) This thought of correcting a brother who has fallen into some transgression leads Paul to broaden his admonition. There are many other burdens which we ought to help each other to bear. **The burdens of each other keep bearing and thus fulfill the law of Christ.** Support each other in every way. Weakness, ignorance, inexperience, difficult surroundings, grief, affliction, etc., are some of these burdens. This is the blessedness of Christian fellowship that each is not left to bear his load alone, others will help him to bear it. When many come to the support of one, he will be helped, indeed.

Paul might have said, "Thus you will fulfill the law of Christ." He retains the imperative but now uses the effective aorist: "and thus actually fulfill or fill up the law of Christ." This is the law of love, John 13:34, the law of true Christian liberty. No law is able to produce this love, only the gospel can do it. James 2:8 calls it "the royal law," it is devoid of all slavishness. This second imperative furnishes the motive for the first. Our one desire should ever be to fulfill the law of Christ to whom we belong (5:24), and bearing each other's burdens is the way to do this.

3) With "for" Paul substantiates his admonitions by pointing to the opposite. But not to the opposite action, refusal to bear the burdens of others; he at once goes deeper, namely to the delusion from which such refusal would spring. **For if**

one deems he is something while he is nothing, his mind deludes himself. Self-satisfied, such a man thinks that he is something and needs no help from his brethren in bearing any burdens he may have, he himself being capable enough. Thus also he will have no heart for his burdened brethren. For what makes us tender and helpful, meek and kindly toward others is the realization that we ourselves are nothing and that we, too, need our brethren. Satisfaction with self makes poor helpers for those in need of fraternal support.

The natural negative with the participle is μηδέν, and this belongs to the protasis although some would construe it with the apodosis: "being nothing, his mind deludes himself." But Paul does not claim that everyone is nothing. The fault he scores is that one who is nothing thinks himself something. It is no fault to be something and then to think accordingly in all honesty. Rom. 12:3 is plain regarding this. Grace made a good deal of Paul (I Cor. 15:10), and he says so. "To be something, while being nothing" naturally goes together as it is placed together, and as every ordinary reader would read it. The compound verb contains "mind" and "deceive" and is found in no earlier writing. The whole protasis warrants the conclusion: "his mind deludes himself," even his own mind which ought to know that nothing is never something.

4) Against such empty-headed self-estimation ("vainglory," 5:26) Paul advises: **But his own work let each one keep testing, and then in regard to himself alone he will have his cause for boasting and not in regard to the other person.** Instead of entertaining a vacuous opinion about himself, let him diligently test his own actual work. It is so easy to have a good opinion about oneself, but carefully weigh and test your actual accomplishment, that will tell

Galatians 6:4, 5 301

the story. The singular "work" with the durative "keep testing" is the sum of accomplishment and this submitted to constantly renewed and revised testing.

By no means does Paul say, "Then you will have no reason for boasting." The context is: "**in regard to himself alone** — and not in regard to the other person," and this context does not permit us to have ἕξει mean, "he will hold off his boasting" because he will find that his whole work amounts to nothing. Quite the contrary. The diligent tester — Paul was one — will find that he does amount to something, that he actually has a definite καύχημα, "ground for boasting." He will, of course, thank God for that. This constant tester may revise his estimate from time to time as he learns to make his tests more accurately by means of the Word. But, proceeding as he does, he will have his reason for boasting "as pertaining to himself alone (εἰς) and not as pertaining to the other person" (again εἰς). This does not mean that he will keep it to himself and will not, when occasion warrants or demands, tell anybody else. For then Paul disobeyed this rule in I Cor. 15:10, and still more in II Cor. 11:21-12:6. What Paul says is that this tester will get no wrong estimate by pitting himself against the other person and deciding that he is better than that other person (definite article). That is what happened to the Pharisee in Luke 18:9-12. *Wer sich an einem andern misst, vermisst sich.* Besser. He will stand on his own feet, "for himself alone."

5) **For each one will carry his own cargo** (Acts 27:10 has this noun) without reference to any other person. "Will carry" matches "will have" in v. 4, both refer to the final judgment. "Their works do follow them," Rev. 14:13. The opposite of vainglory (5:26) is not spurious self-abasement but genuine testing. Vainglory accompanies Judaistic and pharisaic

work-righteousness; love which tests itself, which restores others accompanies gospel freedom. Carry this and its work as a blessed cargo.

Receiving and imparting spiritual excellence

6) It would be a trivial thought so close to the end of the epistle to admonish the Galatians to be generous with their money. Yet this interpretation has been put upon this paragraph by not a few. The more the writer seeks to read Paul's words in this light, the more he feels that he cannot accept this interpretation. Δέ does turn to a different subject, yet to one that is allied. Verses 4, 5 emphasize, as does the participial clause in v. 1, that each must look well to himself even as each must carry his own load. The allied subject is fellowship, but certainly not merely in money and in earthly goods. The word "poor" does not occur in v. 9, 10. In v. 1 the spiritual life of an erring brother is at stake. In v. 3 we are to bear each other's burdens, which is already one kind of fellowship, the one that steps in to share the other's hardships. Paul now adds the rest of it: both our receiving and our imparting spiritual and moral good.

Moreover, let him who is being instructed in the Word be partaker with the one instructing him in all good things. The verb κοινωνέω is seemingly not properly understood. When this is regarded as meaning "communicate," "all good things" become material, and somehow or other it is thought that Paul says that pupils should reward or pay their teachers, congregations their pastors. This idea is also put into κοινωνία, the noun, which is thought to mean "contribution" in Rom. 15:26; II Cor. 8:4; 9:13; Heb. 13:16; this view has gotten into some of the dictionaries. The noun always = fellowship, and in the case of alms a fellowship that is exercised (*Teilnahme*, C.-K. 614) by means of alms. If the noun means "contribution" of alms in the four passages referred to, the verb would here practically make the teachers the recipients of alms, men who receive contributions as alms.

The verb means *participem esse* and then *participem facere*, to be or to make participant, the latter, however, in the sense "to share something with somebody, thereby not making him a fellow with oneself but *oneself* a fellow with *him*," C.-K. 612, on our passage. Consider in connection with this C.-K. 4 on "all good things," *im Sinne von heilbringend*, "good" as bringing salvation. The one who instructs has the good things; the one being instructed is to proceed to participate in them, in "all" of them. The riches are with the teacher of the Word, the poverty is with the pupil, and the pupil is to institute "fellowship" with the teacher so that he, the pupil, may be enriched.

Yes, there are not only burdens in which we must fellowship and aid those who bear them, there are also "good things," spiritually and morally beneficial things, in which we should delight to have fellowship with those who possess these good things. Who should have more of them than our teachers? The burdens are painful, the good things are conducive to salvation, delightful. With those who have the burdens and with those who have these good things we should keep fellowship, making *ourselves* fellow with *them*.

This is just about the opposite of the common view. In addition to the context and the meaning of the words themselves one must note that when Paul writes about the one instructing, the Galatians would at once think of their first and greatest instructor together with his assistant who had twice been in their midst. Could Paul tell the Galatians in this letter that they owed material contributions to him and to his helpers? Could he do such a thing with no further word of explanation? Paul never took money for his work. When he speaks of this subject in I Cor. 9 he does so with the fullest and the clearest explanation. See the same thought in II Cor. 11:7-12, which should be read in its connection with I Cor. 9.

We ought also not to forget the Judaizers who also came as teachers, on whose greediness II Cor. 11:20 enlightens us. When such greedy fellows were working in Galatia, Paul could scarcely write the Galatians to share "in all things" (material) with their teachers. Aside from the implication involving himself, such an admonition would reflect on the true teachers in Galatia and suggest that they were also men who were to be paid.

We need not discuss "the one instructing." Paul had not left the Galatian churches in an unorganized state; he had them elect elders and pastors who were qualified to teach. Apart from this office the gift of teaching was exercised as one of the most valuable gifts (Rom. 12:7); we constantly read of teaching in the Acts, note the teachers mentioned in Acts 13:1; I Cor. 12:28, 29. "In all good things" that were possessed by their instructors, Paul and his assistants among them, the Galatians should ever cultivate fellowship for their own enrichment. Then all would, indeed, be well with them. Pay for these teachers? There is no reason for mentioning it in this epistle.

7) The efforts to have what Paul now says support the idea that teachers are to be duly rewarded show that this conception is untenable. Paul and his assistants took no such reward. Sowing for the flesh and sowing for the spirit deal with a subject that is far greater, namely with the desire for all good spiritual things in which the Galatians should seek to share.

Be not deceived, God is not sneered at. The verb means, "to turn up the nose at someone" in disdain.

The implication is that God lets no one do that with impunity. Γάρ at once explains in what respect this warning is to be heeded. **For what a person keeps sowing, that very thing also he shall reap.** In II Cor. 9:6 the point to be stressed is the identity of what is sown and harvested. You cannot sow one thing and reap the opposite or even another thing. You will ever get the same thing, only very much more of it. Let nothing and nobody deceive you on that score. Turn up your nose to God on that if you will; inexorably you will be caught in the law of God.

The absence of the article with "God" seems to make the word qualitative: he who is no less than God. You may turn up your nose at men with impunity, but "God" is far different. The form σπείρῃ may be either present or aorist subjunctive, progressive sowing or just one act. Here it is the former, because ὁ σπείρων follows, the present participle: "he who keeps sowing" not the aorist: "he who finishes one sowing."

8) First the universal law or principle and God back of it. Now the application to the whole spiritual life in the form of the reason that we should never be deceived, and that God is never mocked with impunity. **Because the one sowing for his own flesh, from this flesh will reap corruption; but the one sowing for the spirit, from this spirit will reap life eternal.** The truth that what a person sows he will also reap is an axiom, it needs no proof, no "because." This clause proves what the "for" clause written in v. 7 elucidates, namely that we must not be deceived as to any possibility of God's being mocked.

We cannot understand those who refer "flesh" and "spirit" to two different kinds of *soil* and then say that the soil conditions the two harvests, and in addition to that state that Paul has not altered his figure from the *seed* to the *soil*. But it is not true that the *soil* decides the harvest. In Matt. 13:3, etc., we have four kinds of soil, but three kinds bring *no* harvest at all. These interpreters state that the seed is our material wealth: if we use that wealth by sowing it "into our own flesh," our harvest will be according to this soil, while if we use our wealth by sowing it "into the spirit," our harvest will be better. Supporting our teachers with our wealth is then thought to be sowing it "into the spirit."

This interpretation makes the second soil "the Spirit." But the idea that the Spirit is *soil*, and that this Spirit as soil is paired with flesh, flesh as also being *soil*, is untenable. We have already shown that Paul places "spirit" in opposition to "flesh"; see throughout 5:16-25 and the discussion under v. 16 and v. 25. Some direct attention to the fact that Paul writes "his own flesh" but not "his own spirit" since one cannot say "his own Spirit." But Paul means that the flesh is always our very own while the spirit is the new nature that is born in us by divine operation. To call both our own would be a mistake, for it would say that the spirit is our own in the same sense as the flesh, which would not be true.

The two sowers are contrasted. The one sows "for or unto his own flesh," the other "for or unto the spirit." Εἰς is not "into," one does not sow "into"; it is like the dative (R. 594). The one sows *for* his own flesh, to promote his flesh; the other for the spirit, to promote its interests. The sowing is figurative for what has already been stated literally in 5:16: walking by what is spirit; 5:18: being led by what is spirit; 5:25: living and keeping in line by what is spirit; thus the opposite is walking, being led, living, and keeping step with the flesh. Our life here is a sowing of the one kind or of the other.

The thought is the same as that expressed in Rom. 8:12, 13: debtors not to the flesh to live after the flesh and thus to die, but with the spirit (not Spirit) to kill the deeds of the flesh and thus to live (see this passage). The stress is on the two sowers and what their sowing promotes. Neither seed nor soil is mentioned, for no one sows without them. As to the seed, this is plainly implied. He who sows for his flesh will sow the seed his flesh furnishes and certainly not the seed furnished by the spirit; the same is true with regard to the other sower. We need no special statement on this point.

When Paul says, "from this flesh (of his) he will reap corruption," and, "from this spirit he will reap life eternal," the articles point back to the very flesh and the spirit for which each sower sows, so that we may translate: "from this flesh — from this spirit." The one sower does his sowing in order to promote his flesh, to get more and more of this flesh of his, for one always sows in order to get more of the same product. Paul has already said, "That very thing he will, indeed, get." Yea, in 5:19, etc., he has already listed the works of the flesh, the products which the flesh wants and brings forth. The other sower does his sowing in order to promote the spirit, to get augmentation of this product. He certainly gets it (v. 7), and 5:22, etc., states in detail what the spirit wants and produces. One should not overlook this connection with 5:19-25, for this passage shows the intermediate products of the flesh and of the spirit.

Paul does not go over this ground again, his readers are to remember what he has already said. Here he mentions the two final harvests. What one can grow *for* the flesh (the works of the flesh, 5:19, etc.) one reaps *out of* this flesh, *from* it, this very flesh furnishes the harvest. This is also true with regard to the spirit. Paul does not expand the thought so as to include seed and soil; he keeps what he says compact. The final harvest of the flesh-sower is "corruption." This has been explained already in 5:21, yet only negatively: he shall not inherit the kingdom of God. Here this is stated positively: "he shall reap corruption." The final harvest of the spirit-sower is the opposite: "he shall reap life eternal," i. e., shall inherit the kingdom. Thus each reaps what he sows.

Beyond question "corruption" and "life eternal" are extreme opposites. Rom. 8:13 is the parallel: "ye shall die — ye shall live." "Corruption" matches "the flesh," but not in a physical way. Yet R., *W. P.*, remarks: "Nature writes in one's body the penalty of sin as every doctor knows." True as this is, here Paul states far more. "Flesh" is not the body but our own sin-corrupted nature. Disease invades also the body of the godly person, his body, too, sees corruption in the grave (I Cor. 15:53). Paul is not speaking of this. Here φθορά has its first meaning, *Vernichtung* (C.-K. 1200), *Untergang* (B.-P. 1369 for our passage), ἀπώλεια, eternal death, the opposite of "life eternal." John uses the latter fourteen times.

The spirit itself is ζωή. It is the spiritual life principle itself; we get it by regeneration. It manifests itself as is indicated in 5:22, 23. Those who are without it are dead in trespasses and sins. This life may be lost, but it is to go on and on, is to pass unscathed through physical death, is to be "eternal," beyond death. It includes the body which only sleeps in physical death and is raised at last to have its full part in this everlasting life in heaven: "he shall reap life eternal."

All that Paul says goes beyond the proper use of our earthly wealth, being generous to spiritual instructors, and the like. Sowing for the spirit and reaping from the spirit include all our spiritual activity. The idea that Paul teaches the merit of good works with eternal life as their reward does not appreciate what "the spirit" is and what sowing "for the spirit" means. The kingdom of God is inherited (5:21) and not earned by works or human merit.

9) Sowing for the spirit is hard work, long-continued work, and, although the harvest is eternal blessedness, we may, while we are waiting for it, grow discouraged. Hence the admonition: **Moreover, in doing the excellent thing let us not be discouraged, for in proper season we shall reap if we do not relax.**

The connective δέ adds this as being something different. It certainly is very necessary. "The excellent or noble thing" = sowing for the spirit and comprises all that 5:22, 23 contains. The neuter is used in the Greek fashion as the equivalent of an abstract noun; it is all one noble unit with which our spiritual activity is concerned.

Paul employs this verb in II Cor. 4:1, 16 and uses it in the same sense: "let us not be growing tired, discouraged, faint, or fainthearted." The verb does not mean, "to give in to evil." It contains κακός in the sense of "inferior"; the "to be weary" of our versions is quite correct, as is also the "to faint" in II Cor. 4:1, 16. Many start well but tire sooner or later, especially when exertion becomes hard.

What is to keep our energy up to the mark, strengthen us ever anew, is the shining harvest which we shall reap in its own season. That season comes to each one as God arranges. The negative participle at the end: "we not relaxing, not being exhausted, not letting down," once more emphasizes the thought that we should not tire in our blessed task. The implication is a condition: "if we do not relax" (R. 1023).

Participle and subjunctive are present tenses denoting state or condition. To be doing "the (spiritually) excellent thing" is itself an inspiration, but in addition to this Paul points to the coming harvest. When the blessed harvest season arrives, we shall wonder why we ever thought of getting tired and of relaxing; to have waited a hundred times as long will then seem to us no reason at all for thinking of tiring.

10) This brings the concluding admonition which is based on the foregoing: **Accordingly then, while we have opportunity, let us work the thing that is good toward all and especially toward the housemembers of the faith.**

Verse 9 is negative: let us not grow tired, not be exhausted. So we now have the positive: do with energy. The emphasis is on "while we have opportunity" (the correct reading has the indicative and not the subjunctive as in Westcott and Hort). The idea is, however, not a reference to special opportunities which come now and again, "the good" then being some material help extended by us in charity. No; this is an ever-present *kairos*, "season" or opportunity; ὡς = *jetzt wo* (B.-D. 455, 2), "now while." In place of "the excellent thing" whose spiritual excellence is contained in itself we now have "the good thing," *heilbringend* (C.-K. 4), spiritually beneficial to others who are also named. This articulated neuter singular is classic and equal to an abstract noun; the article is generic (R. 763), all the good is a unit. In v. 6 we have the plural; it is characteristic of Paul to change from the plural to the singular.

It is true, v. 10 looks back to v. 6, but not in the way so commonly supposed, namely that in v. 6 we dispense material gifts to our teachers and now in v. 10 to all men in general and especially to our fellow believers. Quite otherwise: we are first to make ourselves participants with our teachers in all the spiritually good things they have to offer us. This is to be the *source* of our enrichment. Then we are to dispense our spiritual wealth to others with all tireless energy so that they may share it with us. This is to be the *outflow*. It is to go on "while, as long as, we have opportunity," as long as life lasts and without weariness. Jesus is the example, Paul is another.

We are told by some that moral good (spiritual would be correct) is our universal duty, in which no distinction can be made such as doing this good "especially" to our fellow believers; so, it is argued, Paul must here refer to material good. But dispensing Christian charity, no matter to whom, is ever as much a spiritual act as any other and is to be performed only in the same spiritual way. Dispensing charity especially to our brethren is required no more than doing other spiritual good especially to our brethren. They have *first* call upon us and our energy. It would be strange indeed if this were not true. Does Paul not call them the οἰκεῖοι of the faith, those who are in the same house with us, with whom we are in closest contact as "house-members"? All their spiritual needs are seen and felt by us in the most immediate way. They and we are of one divine family or household, we are joined together with them as we are with no others. This is the reason for Paul's "especially"; it applies to "the good" in every respect.

Paul might have said, "especially toward the brethren"; by saying "house-members" he justifies his special mention of these. In Eph. 2:19 he uses "house-members of God," those who belong to God's household, the church. The genitive is possessive, it is like "of the faith." The latter is thus another instance in which "the faith" (articulated) is objective faith, *quae creditur*, not subjective, *qua creditur*. It is interesting to compare ὑμῶν τὸ ἀγαθόν in Rom. 14:16 with τὸ ἀγαθόν used here and to ask ourselves whether the two have reference to the same thing.

Conclusion

All my glorying is in the Cross of our Lord Jesus Christ!

11) The final paragraph is no longer admonitory but thetical and summary and ends with a prayerful wish. It is marked as the conclusion by the first sentence. **See with what large letters I have written to you with my own hand!**

This simple sentence has caused much discussion. Paul is not exclaiming because of the size of his epistle. Yet Luther and others translate, "with how many words." The dative means "with how large letters." Others, like R. 846, regard the aorist as epistolary: Paul places himself at the time when his letter is read in Galatia, and his writing is then in the past. These assume that this letter was dictated, that, as in other dictated letters, Paul wrote only the concluding verses with his own hand, and that in this letter he wrote these last words in large, bold script. But Paul never uses the aorist ἔγραψα to designate the writing of only a few concluding words. He uses the aorist "I wrote" when he refers to an earlier letter, or to an entire letter that is reaching its close, or to a discussion he has just finished (I Cor. 9:15). He uses "I write" to indicate a statement just written, something he continues to write, even a letter that is almost finished. From this we conclude that Paul is here referring to this entire epistle and says that all of it came from his own hand, that none of it was dictated, that all of it was written in large script.

This raises two questions: "Why did Paul write with his own hand instead of dictating? Why was the script notably large?" The natural answers are: "Because no amanuensis was at hand; because Paul's hand had been badly hurt in one or the other of the severe beatings he had received when he was flayed by the lictors at Philippi or when he was stoned and left as dead at Lystra." The latter, namely a badly damaged hand, may be the reason that Paul dictated his other letters.

Writing at Corinth shortly after starting his work there, the delegation from Galatia found Paul alone, without a scribe, with nobody to send greetings to the Galatians. Thus Paul wrote this epistle with his own hand. The supposition that he did it in order the more to show his personal interest in the Galatians could be entertained only if Paul had had a scribe at hand and yet did not use him. Even then we think he would have used him.

The large script has been referred to as indicating eye trouble, this together with his practice of dictating, 4:15 is also introduced. Between this supposition and the one that Paul's right hand had been hurt we prefer the latter. The damage to his hand may well have been one of the stigmata to which he refers in v. 17. At least, we deem this the most tenable idea that has been offered on the subject.

12) The issue in Galatia centered on circumcision in a special way (5:2, etc.); hence Paul reverts to this in his conclusion. **As many as want to make a fair show in the flesh, these** (are the ones who) **are trying to compel you to have yourselves circumcised in order that they may not be persecuted because of the cross of Christ. For not even those who are circumcised themselves observe what is law, but they want you to have yourselves circumcised in order that they may get to boast for themselves in your very flesh.**

Paul exposes the Judaizers, these circumcisers, as to their base motive. They are not at all concerned about "spirit" but only about "flesh" (v. 8). In this domain they want to make a fair showing. This verb has finally been found in one of the papyri. This is a sample of what may occur in the case of other words that have hitherto been found only in the New Testament. B.-P. 506: "they want to play a role before men," which gives the sense but not the exact equivalent of the word. The German *gleissen* is better. They were good Jesuits.

These, Paul says, men of this type, are the ones who "are trying to compel you (conative present, B.-D. 319; R. 880) to have yourselves circumcised (permissive passive) only in order that they may not be persecuted because of the cross of Christ" (dative of cause, B.-D. 196; R. 532.) They want to make a fine showing with you Galatians by inducing all of you to get circumcised so that the Jews, who are otherwise so hostile to Christianity, may not persecute them, i. e., the Judaizers, although they confess the crucified Christ. The aim of the Judaizers is to win so much merit with the Jews that these will not attack them as they constantly attack Paul, having nearly killed him at Lystra.

Pause and note that, if Paul had yielded on the point of the necessity of circumcision, he, too, could have escaped this persecution, the instigators of which were uniformly Jews. It was his stand on circumcision that fired the dynamite of Jewish hate. See what it did to Paul in Acts 21:18, 19; he was nearly killed in the Temple on the suspicion of having brought an uncircumcised Gentile into the sacred precincts. What a temptation for Paul to advocate circumcision in order to curry favor with the Jews! Was circumcision not a matter that was merely ceremonial? Today many would compromise on a thing like that. The Judaizers also accepted Jesus and the cross; all they did was to soften the offensiveness of the cross to the Jews. Was that not wise? If many of our day had been in their place they would have agreed to this. Do they not today still make the cross palatable by removing its offense?

13) With "for" Paul explains how the Judaizers make only a fair showing in the flesh: although they demanded circumcision they themselves are not observing what is law. Note the absence of the article. We may also regard this present tense as conative: "do not attempt to observe law." Some think that the Judaizers failed to keep the moral parts of the law. But the unmodified word "law" does not allow such a restriction. It includes both the circumcision of the Judaizers and their demand upon the Galatians to be circumcised. For it is certainly not observing law in any true sense of the word to advocate circumcision only in order to escape Jewish persecution. To comply with the outward form of law with such a motive is anything but true compliance. Abraham did not do so when he accepted circumcision as a seal of God's covenant. What the Judaizers did with circumcision they did with law in general. Do the Galatians want to listen to and to follow such men?

The readings vary between the less well-attested perfect participle: "they that have been circumcised," and the present participle which is more adequately attested and which appears to be more difficult since it seems to mean, "those being circumcised" or, "those letting themselves be circumcised," which could then not refer to the Judaizers but only to Gentiles who allowed themselves to be persuaded to circumcision while here the former are undoubtedly referred to. Zahn regards the present as being timeless, as stating the custom which these people advocated, that of being circumcised. Paul wants to say more than that the Judaizers were once circumcised and then, of course, remained so (perfect participle). Paul and all Christian Jews were such men. These Judaizers were men who ever advocate being circumcised, *Beschneidungsleute* as they have been called, or rather *Leute des Beschnittenwerdens*. The term is intended to be derogatory.

So little are they concerned about actual observance of law that their purpose in having you Galatians subject yourselves to circumcision is only "that they may get to boast in their own interest (middle voice) in *your* flesh." That is why they want you circumcised so as to be able to point to *your* flesh, the amputation of your foreskin as their great accomplishment in order to win vast credit among the Jews. The possessive pronoun is used for the sake of emphasis; a simple genitive ὑμῶν would be without emphasis. "*Your* own" flesh like *their* own and like the *Jews'* own — to achieve that boast (aorist) in their own interest (middle) is their great purpose. This positive ἵνα supplements the negative one used in v. 12. These are the selfish, despicable Judaizers.

14) Throughout v. 12, 13 we have a description of men who are the direct opposite of Paul. This is made evident by the fervent wish: **But for me on my part let it never get to be** (that I) **try to boast save in the cross of our Lord Jesus Christ, by means of which for me the world has been crucified, and I for the world!**

The dative of relation is placed forward for the sake of strong emphasis and is thus set into opposition with all men such as have just been described. Paul uses this aorist optative of wish often, most frequently with only the negative particle: "Let it not be!" which in our versions is rendered, "God forbid!" The aorist is effective and has the infinitive as its subject, which is either a conative present: "that I try to boast," or durative in general: "that I go boasting" save in one thing only, namely in the cross, etc. The Judaizers wanted to escape the persecution that was connected

Galatians 6:14

with the cross by making their boast to the Jews that they were getting the Gentile Christians to submit to circumcision. Verse 15 shows that Paul has this in mind in his prayerful wish that the cross may ever be his one and only boast. Let what persecution will come, no other boast shall be his. The Judaizers are sincere only regarding themselves and not regarding the cross; Paul is the opposite.

His wish is made regarding himself but in such a way that every Galatian, every true Christian will repeat it with Paul. He adds the full, solemn genitive: in the cross "of our Lord Jesus Christ." The plural "our" includes all the Galatians and thus says much more than "my" would imply. He is "our Lord" in the full soteriological sense of gracious Lord who purchased and won us as his own, to whom we belong, under whom we live happy to be his and to serve him alone, whose name is "Jesus" or Savior, whose title is "Christ," which indicates his mighty office: the Messiah anointed of God.

"The cross of our Lord Jesus Christ" as Paul's one boast and glory is most comprehensive. We see this when he makes it exclude Judaistic circumcision and thus all legalism. When we today adopt Paul's great wish for ourselves we forget those old Judaizers. They have long ago faded from the life of the Christian Church. Oppositions to the cross bearing other names, using other legalistic tenets, dissolvents of newer kinds, have replaced the Judaizers. Against all of them we vow allegiance to the cross with Paul's words. Whatever side of the cross, whatever doctrine involved in the cross are attacked today, the cross, the whole cross and nothing but the cross is our one treasure.

Our poets have sung its praises in noblest strains, our congregations ring with these exalted strains, symbolic crosses decorate our altars, our pulpits, our spires, and our gravestones. It is the cross of "the blood theology," the cross on which the Son of God died for our advantage, the cross of expiation, substitution, ransom, and atonement, the cross which brought the resurrection of the crucified body and its exaltation at God's right hand of majesty and power and the future resurrection and exaltation of our mortal bodies. God help us ever to see it in the fulness with which it filled the eyes and the gospel of Paul!

The relative is to be connected with "the cross," on which also the genitive depends, even as the Lord cannot be dissociated from the cross which made him "our Lord." By means of this cross, Paul says, "to me the world has been crucified, and I to the world." Both pronouns are emphatic, both are in opposition to the Judaizers, both are to be uttered by every Galatian as they are by Paul. "The world" needs no article in the Greek as is the case with regard to other nouns that designate objects only one of which exists. "The world" as here used is all that among men is in opposition to God, to Christ, and to his cross (C.-K. 622), men who are themselves filled with this opposition or the opposition which fills them. The perfect tense "has been crucified" has its present connotation: once crucified and thus remaining so.

There is a causal sense in the double relative clause: Paul glories in the cross because by means of it a crucifixion has taken place for him and in him. When he came to faith in the cross, then the world was crucified and remained so for him, and he himself was crucified for the world and remains so. Both datives may be called ethical. The verb is figurative and not mystical. Crucifixion means death and more than death, a death of shame and abomination by which the dead one is cast out as one execrated. Here a double crucifixion, a double death of execration took place: in the one the world was nailed to the cross as far as Paul was concerned, in the other Paul was nailed to the cross as far as the world was concerned. Each was forever done with the other. This double thing was done entirely "by means of the cross of our Lord Jesus Christ."

So brief the expression, yet so tremendous. Perfection in wording to attain concentrated penetration of thought. The effect of the cross for and in the believer cannot be stated in a more adequate way. Even the two datives and the two nominatives are placed chiastically, and one verb is enough. Yet the two pronouns are placed first, for the change takes place entirely in Paul. The world is the same old wicked world of which Paul was once a part. Then the cross came into his heart and changed him completely. It was not he who then crucified the world in execration. This was done for him in his heart. So, too, it was the world which was crucified for him; this was done for him by another, again done in his heart. The passive leaves unsaid who did both. It was not the cross, for this was the great means. Was it not "our Lord Jesus Christ" who entered Paul's heart with his cross?

15) The cross has placed a great gulf between Paul and the world. It has liberated him from the wicked world. This liberation is the subject of the whole epistle. When Paul writes "world" he broadens to the greatest extent. So with "for" he now explains how the Judaizers are involved. **For neither circumcision is anything, nor foreskin, but a new creation.**

This recalls 5:6, and the substance is the same. The three abstract terms are often regarded as pure abstracts, yet the observation is correct that here, as is the case quite often, they are used as marking three concretes: all those who are circumcised — all those who have foreskin — all those who have been made new creatures by regeneration and faith in the cross. The two former are nothing at all, but the latter are something, the latter alone. Yet "neither — nor" is not parallel but diverse. For those who have been circumcised considered their circumcision as being something, yea, the great decisive advantage. Those with foreskin, of course, never boasted thus about their foreskin. The Judaizers and the Jews considered the uncircumcised as nothing. Thus Paul's meaning is: circumcision is nothing of advantage — foreskin is nothing of disadvantage; the one no gain — the other no loss. But to be a new creation is everthing.

This statement puts the whole matter into succinct and final form. It expounds the main clause of v. 14, Paul's glorying in the cross, and not merely the relative clause regarding what the cross effects. On the new creation compare II Cor. 5:17.

16) **And as many as shall keep in line with this canon, peace on them and mercy, even on the Israel of God!** Verse 15 states the objective canon; "and" in v. 16 adds the subjective use of this canon. "As many as" includes all of them whether living in Galatia or elsewhere. See 5:25 on the verb. From κανών we have our "canon" which eventually came to be applied to the Scriptures. The word refers to a measuring rod by which we take measure of something to verify whether it is of proper size or length. So we measure our doctrine and our life by the Scriptures, for these alone are the exactest measuring rod we possess. Paul speaks of those who will make their faith and their life tally with the blessed principle he has just stated.

On them "peace" shall rest, the peace of God, the condition in which all is well with them. See 1:3. We generally have "grace and peace," peace being named second as the result of having grace. We several times also have "mercy and peace" in the same manner. Paul reverses the order and places the phrase between the words, which leads some to think that he refers to "peace" in this life and "mercy" at the time of the final judgment. While one may mention the cause first (mercy) and the effect second (peace), it is also proper to name the effect before its cause. We so understand the order used here. We shall certainly enjoy mercy also in this life. To point to II Tim. 1:18 is of no help since it does not mention peace; neither do Matt. 5:7; James 2:13; Jude 21.

We need not be puzzled about καί and "the Israel of God." The future tense "shall keep in line" confines us to the future which is now beginning, and "as many as" omits none who could be added to this number. Is it possible to restrict "as many as" to the Galatians and then to add to them "the Israel of God" (believing Jews)? What about the other churches with their believing Gentiles? Gentiles and Jews in all the churches are together conceived as those who will keep in line with the canon.

This καί signifies "even" or "namely." "As many as will keep in line with the rule" constitute "the Israel of God." The objection that Paul should then say, "upon the whole Israel of God," is answered by the preceding future tense. The whole or all the Israel would include all the Old Testament saints; but Paul is not speaking of these. Paul has a special, telling reason for adding this explicative apposition. It is a last blow at the Judaizers, his final triumph over them and their contention. As many as shall keep in line with this rule, they and they alone constitute "the Israel of God" from henceforth, all Judaizers to the contrary notwithstanding.

17) Paul has reached the end of his epistle. **Henceforth let no one go on furnishing me troubles, for I on my part carry in my body the scarmarks of Jesus.** Paul is done with this trouble in Galatia. He considers the issue ended. So little does he expect any further danger from it that he will have no one extract further troubles from it for him. Paul was justified in this view. The Galatians must have taken a simi-

lar attitude, for we hear of no more Judaistic trouble for them or for Paul from them.

With "for" he assigns as the reason for thus calling the troubles from this quarter ended the fact that he is carrying in his body the scars that were inflicted by the Jews who hated him for successfully promulgating the great canon just stated in v. 15. He calls them the stigmata of Jesus, the marks the Jews inflicted on the body of Jesus. These scarmarks show the stand he has ever taken; they show to what extent he has already suffered for this canon. Let the Galatians think of these scars in Paul's body and then they will stand as firmly as he does.

It has been objected that the man who, as it were, was made for troubles and labor could not say he wanted no more of them. But this word is addressed to the Galatians in connection with one specific instance of trouble, and it is beside the mark to generalize. Κόποι enough awaited him, even further scars; but this Galatian matter he considered at an end. Let no one in Galatia prolong it.

This objection has led to a modification of Paul's meaning. The opinion of Marcion is revived that τοῦ λοιποῦ (supply χρόνου) is not adverbial: *fortan* (B.-D. 186, 2 and 160), but a partitive genitive: let no one "of the rest" of the Israel furnish me trouble, i. e., none of the Judaizers. This view is supported by the doubt as to whether Paul ever uses this genitive adverbially as do the classics; in Eph. 6:10 it is eliminated in preference to the other variant. But Marcion himself, as it seems, cancelled the reference to "the Israel of God" from v. 16, which eliminates this idea and any modern modification of it.

A good deal has been said regarding the stigmata and regarding what Paul means by referring to them. That they were the scars remaining from the scourgings, from the one stoning (II Cor. 11:25; Acts 14:19), and from other blows, is generally admitted. What is debated is whether Paul borrows the expression from paganism. Runaway and misbehaved slaves and criminals were branded on the brow or the hand; but this does not fit Paul although some think that by the mention of these stigmata Paul intends to designate himself a slave. M.-M. 590 adds: "Nor is there any evidence that the practice of soldiers tattooing themselves with their commanders' names, which others (i. e., commentators) prefer, was at all general." Devotees of a goddess or of a temple sometimes bore a brand; but this, too, seems out of place when speaking of Paul. The whole matter of branding and of tattooing as found in the pagan world is inapplicable to Paul.

The latest evidence is a papyrus found by Deissmann. It is thought to have a bearing on our passage because the find contains the words βαστάζειν and κόπους παρέχειν: carrying an amulet of the god Osiris in a godly act is to ward off getting trouble from any adversary. Paul's scars are made equivalent to the amulet. Deissmann lets Paul speak to the Galatians as to his "naughty little children," "smiling, with uplifted finger telling them: 'do be sensible; you cannot make me any trouble, for I am protected by a charm'" (*bin ja gefeit*), C.-K. 1021. Then Paul would end his great epistle in a jocular way! Zahn accepts this and excuses the pagan language!

Paul writes, "the stigmata of Jesus," the Jesus who suffered on the cross. There are no pagan implications of any kind; this is only a plain historical reference. Luke 24:39; John 20:25, 27. The scars on Paul's body belonged to Jesus, were like the wounds he himself suffered, for Paul's scars were truly suffered because of Christ. Compare II Cor. 1:5; 4:10; Col. 1:24. A far later age invented "stigmata of Jesus," a reproduction of the marks of the five wounds in the hands, the feet, and the side of Jesus. These "stigmata" are either violent pains in these parts of the body or marks that turn red and, in some cases, bleed. All of these peculiar phenomena are pathological and have nothing to do with Paul's scars.

18) The most probable reason as to why no greetings are added is noted in v. 11. Paul closes with a benediction. **The grace of our Lord Jesus Christ with your spirit, brethren. Amen.** His grace is to pardon and to bless (see 1:3). Paul writes the full title and name as he did in v. 14. But here he does not write, "with you," but "with your spirit," as he does in Phil. 4:23, and Philemon 25; the spirit is to triumph over the flesh. Note that the spirit has been mentioned repeatedly in 5:16, 18, 22, 25; 6:8. A heartfelt address "brethren" is placed at the end. It is placed at the end of a sentence in 5:13; 5:26; and nearly at the end in 4:12. Paul never uses this word without a due reason, see 1:11. "Amen" seals the closing wish as it does the opening greeting in 1:5. Paul parts from the Galatians as being his brethren. They remained that by the grace of the Lord.

Soli Deo Gloria

www.ingramcontent.com/pod-product-compliance
Lightning Source LLC
Chambersburg PA
CBHW071856290426
44110CB00013B/1170